TELEVISION COVERAGE OF THE 1980 PRESIDENTIAL CAMPAIGN

COMMUNICATION AND INFORMATION SCIENCE
A Series of Monographs, Treatises, and Texts
Edited by
MELVIN J. VOIGT
University of California, San Diego

TELEVISION COVERAGE OF THE 1980 PRESIDENTIAL CAMPAIGN

Edited by
William C. Adams
George Washington University

ABLEX Publishing Corporation
Norwood, New Jersey 07648

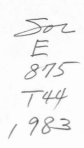

Copyright © 1983 by Ablex Publishing Corporation.

Printed in the United States of America.

Library of Congress Cataloging in Publication Data
Main entry under title:

Television coverage of the 1980 presidential campaign.

(Communication and information science)
Includes indexes.
1. Presidents—United States—Election—1980—Addresses, essays, lectures.   2. Television and politics—United States—Addresses, essays, lectures.   3. United States—Politics and government—1977-1981—Addresses, essays, lectures.   I. Adams, William C.   II. Series.
E875.T44   1983   324.973'0926   83-3768
ISBN 0-89391-104-6

ABLEX Publishing Corporation
355 Chestnut Street
Norwood, New Jersey 07648

CONTENTS

PREFACE

In November 1980, Americans gave over 51 percent of their votes for President to Ronald Reagan, and less than 37 percent to Jimmy Carter; 9 percent went to John Anderson. Reagan swept 45 of the 50 states.

For many more hours than Americans could have listened directly to Ronald Reagan, they listened to the broadcast journalists of ABC, CBS, and NBC explain, report, and interpret the campaign. How was the 1980 presidential campaign presented by the television networks?

The studies in this volume are intended to help answer this question. In the first chapter, the editor surveys some of the central issues in academic research on campaign coverage and reviews the 1980 change in popular media coverage of media coverage. The next eight chapters consider in detail how the networks treated the 1980 campaign.

In the second chapter, Michael Robinson shows the sharply divergent approaches CBS and UPI took in covering identical campaign news events. Four chapters analyze coverage of a few key campaign episodes: Thomas Marshall on the primaries (Chapter 4), Joe Foote and Tony Rimmer on the party conventions (Chapter 5), Robert Meadow on the debates (Chapter 6), and Paul Wilson on Election Night (Chapter 9). Two chapters evaluate coverage throughout the campaign of particular subjects: Anthony Broh examines network uses of opinion polls (Chapter 3), and Robert Sahr assesses the treatment of energy issues (Chapter 8). Some implicit assumptions of a typical campaign story are analyzed by Thomas Benson (Chapter 7). The editor's concluding chapter proposes seven factors with which to estimate the impact of TV content.

Eight of these chapters have not been published previously in any form. Two chapters are revised versions of material that has appeared elsewhere. Chapter 2 is an elaboration of a chapter in Michael J. Robinson and Margaret Sheehan's book *Over the Wire and On TV*, and is used here with the permission of Basic Books. Chapter 10 is used with the approval of the Institute for the Study of Human Issues, and is from a chapter in *The President and the Public*, edited by Doris A. Graber.

The contributors to this book have brought a wide range of backgrounds, techniques, and insights to the study of television coverage of presidential campaigns. Their chapters reflect many hours of careful content analysis and research. Their support for this volume and their cooperation in its assembly is deeply appreciated.

Colleagues at George Washington University have also encouraged and assisted this effort, especially David Brown, Rod French, Michael Harmon, Robert Lichter, and Burton Sapin. William Vantine, Mary Gillespie, Mark Duffy, Michelle Mrdeza, and Paula Fischman provided valuable research assistance, and thanks also go to Michael Robinson, Lyle C. Brown, Shirley Lithgow, Nancy Davis, Dee Hahn-Rollins, Victoria Thomas, Gwen Crider, Bellen Joyner, Lindsey Reed, Kelly Reed, Kathy Reed, and Charles Reed. The illustration on the book jacket is the work of Alexandria artist Linda Hendrick. This book is dedicated to my parents, Wilma Neeley Adams and the late Clayborne Bill Adams.

William Adams
July 1, 1982

CONTRIBUTORS

WILLIAM C. ADAMS, Associate Professor of Public Administration at George Washington University, is editor of *Television Coverage of the Middle East, Television Coverage of International Affairs*, and coedited, with Fay Schreibman, *Television Network News: Issues in Content Research*.

THOMAS W. BENSON is Professor of Speech Communication at Pennsylvania State University and has frequently contributed articles to such journals as *Central States Speech Journal, Public Telecommunications Review, Quarterly Journal of Speech, Southern Speech Journal*, and *Film Society Review*.

C. ANTHONY BROH is Assistant Professor of Political Science at Rutgers and a Faculty Associate of the Eagleton Institute of Politics. He is author of *Toward a Theory of Issue Voting, Voting Behavior: The 1980 Election*, and several articles on voting behavior, political psychology, and communications policy.

JOE S. FOOTE is administrative assistant to Representative David McCurdy of Oklahoma and former press secretary to Speaker of the House Carl Albert. Dr. Foote has taught at the University of Oklahoma and has worked as a broadcast journalist in Oklahoma and Washington, D.C.

THOMAS R. MARSHALL is Associate Professor of Political Science at the University of Texas at Arlington. His research on presidential campaigns has been published in such journals as *American Politics Quarterly, Western Political Quarterly, American Journal of Political Science*, and *Social Science*.

ROBERT G. MEADOW holds a joint appointment in the Political Science Department and the Communications Program at the University of California, San Diego. Dr. Meadow is author of *Politics as Communication*, coauthor of *Polls Apart*, coeditor of *The Presidential Debates*, and is a frequent contributor to professional journals.

TONY RIMMER teaches in the School of Journalism at Indiana University and did his doctoral work at the University of Texas, Austin. He worked for 10 years in news and public affairs television in New Zealand and has particular research interests in social aspects of new media technologies and TV news content.

MICHAEL J. ROBINSON, Associate Professor of Politics at Catholic University, directed the Media Analysis Project at George Washington University during 1980–81. Dr. Robinson and Margaret Sheehan are the authors of *Over the Wire and On TV* and other studies of coverage of the 1980 presidential campaign.

ROBERT SAHR is Assistant Professor of Political Science at Purdue University. He holds a Ph.D. from M.I.T. and a Master of Divinity from Yale University. A former Fulbright Fellow in Sweden, Professor Sahr's primary research interest is energy politics and policies.

MARGARET SHEEHAN received her Master's degree in politics from Catholic University and was assistant director of the Media Analysis Project at George Washington University during 1980–81. She coauthored with Michael Robinson *Over the Wire and On TV* and other studies of the media and the 1980 campaign.

PAUL O. WILSON is Vice President of Bailey, Deardourff and Associates of McLean, Virginia. He holds a B.S. in public administration and an M.A. in journalism from the University of Missouri, Columbia. At Bailey Deardourff, Wilson has helped direct over 20 statewide campaigns.

1

ANALYZING 1980 CAMPAIGN COVERAGE

WILLIAM C. ADAMS

Nineteen-eighty was a remarkable news year with American hostages in Iran; the Soviet occupation of Afghanistan; the creation of Solidarity in Poland; a mass exodus from Cuba; the boycott of the Moscow Olympics; an intense summer drought; riots in Miami; recognition of the 1970s' Soviet military build-up; the eruption of Mt. St. Helens; the deaths of Josip Tito, John Lennon, and the Shah of Iran; record interest rates of 22 percent and rampant inflation; the President's brother financially involved with Libya; the ABSCAM videotapes; widespread debate over the identity of J. R. Ewing's assailant; and upheaval in Central America. In the midst of such developments, Americans were "witnessing" a presidential campaign.

Few Americans actually saw or participated in the campaign first-hand; only a small fraction of the electorate ever saw the candidates in person. But, Americans did witness the campaign—on television and in the press. Television, in particular, brought to the voters a series of dramatic episodes, illustrated by the two summer nights in which Americans viewed Teddy Kennedy's electric address to the Democratic convention, Jimmy Carter's hapless acceptance speech, and the ensuing Kennedy snub of Carter during the concluding "unity" ritual. Television also broadcast campaign debates—the Iowa debates, the Reagan-Anderson debate, the Reagan-Carter debate—and news of the Nashua non-debate.

In addition to transmitting pictures of events, many of which were staged for television, broadcasters sometimes intervened more directly. For example, there was Roger Mudd's calm grilling of Kennedy, the early infatuation with John Anderson, decisions to downplay certain candidates (e.g., Jerry Brown, Robert Dole, Ed Clark), skeptical portrayals of Carter's Rose Garden pose, and critiques of Ronald Reagan's factual inaccuracies. In the process, there were some embarrassments like the coverage of Gerald Ford as Reagan's running mate, the premature dismissals of George Bush's campaign, some CBS graphics which crudely put "Xs" over pictures of Reagan, and the ABC post-debate telephone call-in "poll."

With the notable exceptions of the debates, small segments during the party conventions, Sunday interview shows, and some paid campaign broadcasts, most of the time the TV audience was watching network reporters and commentators—and not the candidates themselves—talk about the campaign. How did television news cover the 1980 presidential campaign? How was the contest for the White House presented to the American viewing public?

The collection of studies in this volume is intended to help answer these questions. Academic researchers have been especially interested in media coverage of campaigns since the early 1970s when scholarly concern with the subject was rekindled—stimulated in part by political attacks on media coverage, by the landmark research of several social scientists, by Edith Efron's book *The News Twisters* (1971), and by a renewed suspicion that media messages have a political impact. In varying degrees, the chapters that follow, like most media studies, weave between the two objectives of (1) a social science understanding of patterns in media content (and the resulting effects on the political system); and (2) a social criticism of the strengths and weaknesses of coverage.

Before examining further the central issues in academic research on television coverage of the 1980 presidential campaign, it is worth emphasizing that scholars were not the only ones writing on the subject. A breakthrough occurred in 1980 as national news media gave more attention than ever before to the question of media coverage of campaigns.

MEDIA COVERAGE OF MEDIA COVERAGE

In 1980, US news media significantly increased the amount of coverage of stories about media coverage of the campaign. Most of the stories were about television coverage. Many major newspapers featured numerous articles about TV's treatment of the campaign. The networks even broadcast a few programs involving evaluations of television campaign coverage. In all, the transformation showed a new willingness to recognize the tenor of TV campaign coverage as a newsworthy story in itself.

This change was a departure from one tenet of US journalism. During previous campaigns, most journalists espoused the "media-as-a-mere-mirror" theory and insisted their stories only reflected reality. As long as coverage was claimed to be passive and mirror-like, it could not have been newsworthy.

In contrast to the practices of past years, the 1980 approach constituted an acknowledgment that coverage was itself an important variable with potent and subjective elements. Thus, the character of coverage could be seen as genuinely newsworthy.

Several major newspapers assigned full-time reporters to "media-campaign beats" (in addition to their regular TV critics) and ran front-page stories on the topic. Appendix A cites some illustrative and some of the more noteworthy instances of print media articles. At ABC, CBS, and NBC, the modest introduction of some media criticism into a few special reports and Sunday morning television was a sharp turn from the network history of ignoring the subject altogether.

Although usually granting the fundamental "legitimacy" of other parts of the political-economic system, American media have—at least since the civil rights revolution, Vietnam, and Watergate—often taken an adversary and critical stance toward other institutions. While US newspapers and networks have subjected other institutions to public scrutiny, they have offered little in the way of serious analysis and criticism of their own performance. This is another reason the 1980 steps toward greater analysis of campaign news were important.

News personnel are undoubtedly under conflicting pressures to exclude and to include stories about the caliber and patterns in campaign coverage. On the one hand, why remind readers and viewers of the inherently subjective and fallible nature of news? Why damage the credibility and stature of prestigious news organizations, spur audience mistrust and cynicism, and hand politicians and interest groups a wedge with which to lobby news judgments?

Another risk is the association of media performance with the subject of media power. Media elites perceive themselves as holding, and deserving to hold, enormous power (Lichter & Rothman, 1981), but they are understandably loathe to dwell on the subject publicly. Perhaps the safest route to escape various pressures is to deny or simply not discuss media power or media performance.

On the other hand, there are some incentives for more media coverage of media coverage. Large numbers of people—not just scholars and subscribers to journalism reviews—understand media to be a vital ingredient in political campaigns; so, it would seem obtuse for at least the more sophisticated publications to have continued to ignore the subject. There is probably a market for such stories; and, besides, an embargo on media criticism appears self-serving and hypocritical. Airing such evaluations suggests an enlightened and progressive approach (with opportunities to co-opt challenges). Nor should the possibility be ruled out that the feed-back of news analysis might bring changes (maybe even "improvements") in campaign coverage.

Although some media gatekeepers still reject the topic as unnews-worthy or threatening, it clearly received newfound attention in 1980. Developments in network television were small, but the offerings in news-papers were more substantial, and may portend greater changes in future campaigns. Approaches taken by the Knight-Ridder chain, the *New York Times*, and the *Washington Post* in 1980 suggest the extent of develop-ments in many major newspapers.

Knight-Ridder. One of the largest newspaper chains in the US, Knight-Ridder, assigned veteran reporter Frank Greve to write on media coverage of the 1980 campaign. Greve proceeded to develop a remarkably insightful and productive string of over five dozen reports that were car-ried by many large and small newspapers throughout the country. For ex-ample, Greve did a three-part series that effectively updated Edward Epstein in describing the dynamics of nightly network news production. He analyzed the celebrity status of TV newsmen (including Dan Rather's lavish, rented Tudor mansion for the Detroit convention), and he critiqued hyped and boorish interviewing styles. Greve examined the techniques TV reporters used in their concluding remarks (the "closer"), and explained strategies the networks employed at the party conventions. Greve also reported in detail on campaign advertisement tactics. These and other stories were carried in newspapers such as the *Miami Herald, Detroit Free-Press, Philadelphia Inquirer, Charlotte Observer*, and *Tallahassee Democrat*, to name a few. The quality, quantity, and circulation of Frank Greve's work alone would be noteworthy, but there were many solid stories by other reporters as well.

New York Times. For much of 1980, Bernard Weinraub covered media and the presidential campaign for the *New York Times*. Early in the year, Weinraub had a strong series of stories examining the role of television, newspapers, and radio in Iowa, New Hampshire, and other early state contests. Weinraub also did stories on scholarly assessments of TV coverage, including interviews with Thomas Patterson and Michael Robinson. One story highlighted Robinson's finding that coverage in the first 6 months of 1980 had been "extensive, nonpartisan, objective, and superficial" as well as enamored of John Anderson.

The *Times* also ran news stories and columns about media coverage of the campaign by Adam Clymer, Jack Rosenthal, Clyde Haberman, Steven Ratner, Les Brown, Ester Blaustein, Peter Samuels, Tom Wicker, Russell Baker, and William Safire, as well as John O'Connor and Tony Schwartz who regularly wrote about television.

Washington Post.   Overall, the *Post* published more stories on television coverage of the campaign—and featured them even more prominently—than did the *New York Times*. Several of the front-page stories by Robert Kaiser examined newspaper and news magazine coverage along with television. Kaiser analyzed, for example, the media emphasis on Carter's "mean streak," the early October barrage of press criticism of Reagan, and media assessments of the presidential debates. Kaiser's stories had the unmistakable premise that journalists put "spins" on stories which hurt or helped candidates, and that those "spins" were newsworthy and consequential.

Meanwhile, Tom Shales, the TV critic for the *Post*, wrote a remarkable series of critiques, satires, and analyses of television news coverage, including humorous and scathing overnight commentaries on convention coverage. Perhaps his most widely cited columns were those that reviewed several weeks' worth of coverage and concluded, as the titles indicate: "Petty for Teddy: The Anti-Kennedy Bias in TV News" (January 30), and later "The Harassment of Ronald Reagan: TV's Assault on the Candidate" (October 31).

In addition to the work of Kaiser and Shales, the *Post* carried other news stories by reporters such as Richard Harwood, Dan Balz, T. R. Reid, and Dick Dabney, along with columns by David Broder, Henry Fairlie, Bill Greene, John Sears, Haynes Johnson, and others. The *Post* even had editorials on campaign coverage, including one complaining that George Bush's large victory in the Michigan primary had been ignored by the media.

Other Newspapers.   Newspapers around the country also picked up Greve's stories from the Knight-Ridder News Service, as they did those of Weinraub and others from the *New York Times* News Service, and those of Kaiser, Shales, Harry Rosenberg, and others from the *Los Angeles Times-Washington Post* News Service. Fred Barnes of the *Baltimore Sun* and Godfrey Sperling, Jr., of the *Christian Science Monitor* wrote thoughtful columns about television's role in the campaign. And dozens of local TV critics, in addition to the journalists mentioned above, also weighed in with stories for their newspapers. Several syndicated columnists like Patrick Buchanan, Roscoe Drummond, R. Emmett Tyrell, Jr., William Raspberry, and Art Buchwald periodically criticized campaign coverage. Thanks to the widespread availability of so many columns and news stories, most large- and middle-sized dailies carried an impressive number of stories about TV coverage.

Television.   The networks did not begin to match major newspapers, but there were a few interesting developments. Jeff Greenfield on CBS had a regular spot for media commentaries on Robert Northshield's innovative *Sunday Morning*, and he sometimes used the occasion to talk about campaign coverage. On public television, Hodding Carter's program, *Inside Stories*, devoted time to the subject. (Carter's PBS series was the first regularly scheduled program of media criticism to ever be broadcast on US television.) ABC's *Nightline* presented one entire program on television coverage of the campaign which included interviews with Michael Robinson and Tom Shales.

In contrast to newspapers and the small incursion into late-night and early-morning television, the early-evening newscasts had next to nothing to say about media coverage of the 1980 campaign. On CBS, for example, no stories directly on this subject were broadcast during the regular nightly news programs, as data from Michael Robinson's content analysis of CBS coverage demonstrate.

CBS ran a few stories about how candidates pitched their political advertising—most notably, Betsy Aaron's 6-minute exposé about a dramatic TV ad showing Howard Baker confronting an Iranian student (2/8/80). Aaron implied the ad involved questionable ethics and editing. Walter Cronkite reported 3 days later that the Baker campaign had dropped the ad. Political commercials in early primaries were the subject of a few other stories (2/18; 2/21; 3/7), as were NCPAC's anti-Carter ads in the fall (9/23). A few major newspaper endorsements were mentioned (e.g., 3/7). Dan Rather spent 40 seconds on John Anderson's alleged interest in Walter Cronkite as a running mate; Rather quoted Cronkite's denial of interest (4/29). About the closest CBS came to covering media coverage was a quick reference to the increase in journalists' attention to the Iowa caucuses over the previous two elections (1/18).

Stories about news media coverage of the campaign did not penetrate into the nightly newscast line-up. The breakthroughs in 1980 came elsewhere, primarily in major newspapers. The changes may well presage greater coverage in future campaigns.

ACADEMIC RESEARCH ON MEDIA COVERAGE

Months and years after these popular commentaries on campaign coverage, there arrive the products of academic research. This research often addresses a somewhat different set of questions, or may cast similar questions in a different way, and employs different methods of analysis.

Most of the key questions that political communication researchers have raised are treated in the chapters that follow. Chart 1.1 lists some of the central issues involving status conferral, issues and horse-race coverage, campaign events, ideological bias, the electoral process, and homogeneity of media messages.

Chart 1.1
Selected Issues in News Coverage of Presidential Campaigns

1. Status conferral
   - Designations of major contenders
   - Labelling results (victor, moral victor, loser; moribund, surging)
   - Visibility and status granted third and minor party candidates

2. Issues and horse-race coverage
   - Nature of horse-race coverage
   - Thoroughness of issue coverage
   - Selection of campaign issues

3. Campaign event focus
   - Early primaries vs. later primaries and most caucuses
   - Convention and debate coverage
   - Contextual treatment of accompanying Congressional campaigns

4. Ideological bias
   - Major candidate comparability in news volume and placement
   - Content treatment of candidates and campaigns
   - Treatment of parties and constituent groups

5. Electoral process
   - Treatment of the process as democratic and representative
   - Cynical toward political strategies, symbolic politics, and interest aggregation
   - Hypercritical or uncritical toward most candidates

6. Homogeneity of media messages
   - Differences among networks
   - Differences among newspapers and news magazines
   - Differences between broadcast and print news

Status conferral.   One group of issues concerns the sort of status conferred by news attention to political figures, and the lack of status associated with inattention. Especially in the early stages of the campaign when there is a large field of candidates, which ones are identified as "serious" contenders and which ones are dismissed as minor? What kind of logic seems to be employed to make such crucial judgments? How are the results of primaries and caucuses interpreted to ascribe to candidates the status of "victor," "moral victor," or "loser"? In addition to Republicans and Democrats, what standing is allotted to third-party and independent candidates? Are they treated as having a meaningful role or purely as curiosities and potential spoilers?

Public opinion polling has assumed a pivotal place in the process of status conferral, and Anthony Broh's Chapter 3 explains the networks' techniques for using polls to anoint or ignore candidates. Thomas Marshall's Chapter 4 explores both the range of TV labelling of candidates' current status—his term is the media "verdict"—and the power of these verdicts to influence the course of the campaign.

Robert Meadow also touches on the issues of status conferral in Chapter 6 with reference to the power of debates to screen out candidates deemed "minor." Robert Sahr's study in Chapter 8 includes data on which of the 1980 candidates were given some consideration with regard to their views on energy policy. And, the editor's concluding Chapter 10 contains a discussion of the media's power and discretion to determine the credibility of John Anderson's independent candidacy in 1980.

Issues and horse races. Since Thomas Patterson and Robert McClure's (1976) book *The Unseeing Eye,* researchers have been particularly sensitive to the relative paucity of issue coverage and the emphasis on the campaign horse race and hoopla. How much attention goes to assessing "who's ahead and by how much?" How much time is spent in recounting poll figures, analyzing election strategies, dissecting campaign techniques, forecasting future ballot results, and speculating on the eventual outcome? To what degree are policy matters neglected? What is the agenda of policy issues? That is, when issues are cited, which ones are selected? How are those issues presented?

Several chapters in this volume are relevant to these questions. Broh's Chapter 3 documents the extensive and expanding use of opinion surveys to measure the horse race. Marshall's Chapter 4 investigates the importance of those verdicts about the horse race, because, given the lack of issue coverage, voters are offered few other ways in which to evaluate most candidates.

Joe Foote and Tony Rimmer in Chapter 5 observe how horse-race approaches prevail in coverage of party conventions (along with the race among the networks for the latest rumors). Similarly, Meadow's review of news about the debates in Chapter 6 shows the focus on "who won" rather than on the substance of what was said.

Sahr's Chapter 8 concludes that the networks rarely gave any careful exposition of energy policy issues during the campaign. When the topic was mentioned, it was typically shown only as a strategic device manipulated for the sake of the horse race.

The fitting climax to the obsession with horse race, rather than issues, comes on Election Night—the finish line of the horse race. Paul Wilson (Chapter 9) inspects network practices to predict the winner as early as possible (and the controversy over early declarations). In a larger sense, the attempt to forecast the ultimate winner as soon as possible serves as the year-long linchpin of network coverage from the earliest days in Iowa and New Hampshire through to its culmination on Election Day.

Campaign event focus. Which elements of the year-long campaign are given the most visibility, and how are they related? To what extent does coverage heavily front-load Iowa, New Hampshire, and the early primaries in contrast to the later primaries and caucuses? Are caucus states other than Iowa neglected? Are contests in certain states highlighted out of proportion to their weight at the conventions? Are party conventions covered with a magnitude that exceeds their actual importance? What is the nature and magnitude of debate coverage? Is the presidential campaign presented in a near vacuum without real coverage of the accompanying Congressional campaigns?

In this volume, Marshall (Chapter 4) reports the disparities in coverage for various presidential primaries and caucuses, and the emphasis on certain early races to the detriment of those in several large states later in the season. Foote and Rimmer (Chapter 5) appraise the nature of prime-time convention coverage in an era when the conventions' actual news value is questionable. Meadow (Chapter 6) looks at the vaulted place of the debates and, with textual analysis, argues that they are not quite the type of encounters they are billed to be, but are instead rehashed stump speeches.

Ideological bias. Another important set of questions revolves around the possibility of ideological or partisan bias. Robert Lichter and Stanley Rothman (1981) surveyed key decision makers at the networks and within elite print media. These leading journalists were found to have voted overwhelmingly for recent Democratic presidential candidates—87 percent favored Hubert Humphrey in 1968, 79 percent preferred George McGovern in 1972, and 72 percent supported Jimmy Carter in 1976.

Is there a liberal Democratic bias in the news that is selected and shaped by these liberal network personnel? Or do they overcompensate for their own views and give the Democratic candidate the more critical slant? To what extent do they accomplish the difficult feat of neutrality? Are the Democratic and Republican candidates given comparable amounts of coverage, similar levels of criticism, and balanced placement of stories? How are liberal and conservative candidacies portrayed during the primary period? How are the parties depicted in terms of their philosophies, policies, and demographic composition? What are the constituent groups connected to each party, and how are they presented?

Michael Robinson and Margaret Sheehan's (1983) evaluation of CBS coverage determined that treatment of Ronald Reagan and Jimmy Carter was generally comparable. There were periods when the spotlight was on Reagan's "inaccuracies" or on Carter's "meanness," but overall, the ratio of favorable, neutral, and unfavorable coverage was very similar, and the volume of attention given the two-party candidates was identical. (Jonathan Alter (1981) has argued that the personal dislike which many members of the press corps felt toward Carter was a vital ingredient, and it may have offset any ideological antipathy toward Reagan.) Although Robinson and Sheehan did not interpret it as "ideological bias," they did confirm that the most liberal Republican running—John Anderson—received a bonanza of friendly coverage during a key period early in the primary season.

Electoral process.   At a broader level, social scientists want to know more about how the overall electoral process is pictured. Is the process suggested to be democratic in form and in effect? Is it sketched as achieving a reflection of popular sentiments? Are most campaign practices—inevitably involving political strategies, advertisements, symbolic politics, and interest aggregations—shown as nefarious and deceitful, or as legitimate and acceptable? Do campaign stories imply citizen efficacy or futility? Does campaign reporting advance the idea that the American political system merits loyalty and commitment, or that it is less than worthy of such an attachment?

Is coverage relentlessly hypercritical of candidates? This issue of uniformly negative coverage of candidates is included here with "electoral process" issues for the reason that pervasively hostile coverage of all candidates becomes a societal-level question, and reflects on the basic electoral process. Thoroughly uncritical, positive coverage would likewise emerge as a systemic issue.

Much of the research on these questions converges on the conclusion that network journalists give highly cynical accounts of the campaign politics. Robinson and Sheehan delineate in Chapter 2 some of the critical themes they suggest were ubiquitous in coverage of the 1980 campaign. Thomas Benson in Chapter 7 argues that the consistent implicit messages from campaign reports were implications of candidate strategies for manipulation, for image over substance, for hypocritical misrepresentations, and for duplicitous games of symbolic combat.

The degree to which such perspectives may or may not be justified is a separate question; it has become increasingly clear, however, that such perspectives pervade network newscasts. Sahr finds in Chapter 8 that energy issues were almost always presented either as campaign gimmicks or as consistency measures to show presumably insincere policy switches by candidates.

Homogeneity of media messages.   A final series of issues relates to the amount of homogeneity or diversity in the coverage from various news outlets. How similiar are the news packages of ABC, CBS, and NBC? How redundant are various newspaper accounts of the campaign? What is the impact of the *New York Times* and *Washington Post* in setting the news agenda of the networks and the rest of the print media? How alike are the news magazines? In what respects do print and broadcast versions of the campaign differ?

Several chapters are relevant to the inquiry into media homogeneity. Robinson and Sheehan (Chapter 2) contrast in detail CBS and UPI reports of identical campaign events, and discover some crucial distinctions. CBS was found to be "more reactive, more thematic, more personal, more political, more critical, more analytical, and more mediating" than was UPI.

Chapters by Broh (3), Marshall (4), Foote and Rimmer (5), Sahr (8), and Wilson (9) present data on ABC, CBS, and NBC so the reader can gauge the degree of network differences. Usually, but not always, there is a remarkably similar pattern across all three networks.

The editor's concluding chapter contends that much of the debate over "media power" has been marked by a failure to make the necessary analytical separation between the joint impact of print and broadcast media and the unique impacts of each medium. Seven factors are proposed with which to examine the relative influence of television and newspapers on voting—themes, agenda, treatment, endorsements, advertisements, persona, and entertainment. A wide range of previous studies is used to estimate (for elections since 1960) whether voters might have received different messages from TV compared to newspapers on each of these seven factors. In each election, the candidate who appeared to have benefited relatively more, on balance, from television's messages over those of newspapers was found to have received some electoral payoff from certain groups of voters who relied on television.

Other issues.   These six areas encompass some of the more significant research questions about the depiction of campaigns in news media. There are, of course, additional aspects of the media-campaign relationship. For example, related topics, other than strictly news coverage, include the ways campaigns deal with the media (e.g., tactics for improving their coverage, campaign advertising, and the candidate's television persona); the political messages in entertainment (from prime-time television to topical humor in talk shows to political cartoon strips); and editorial endorsements of candidates (separate from news coverage).

Media effects.   Each of the six areas outlined above concerns the content of campaign coverage. Each area has a corresponding field of potential public impact. Content findings in all of these areas may be linked to possible media effects. For example, with regard to status conferral, to what degree does the denial of media status deprive candidates of popular support they might have otherwise acquired?

With respect to the horse race, how does the concentration on bandwagons and on hearses shape voter perceptions of candidates? With regard to campaign events, how does the focus on the early primaries affect subsequent primaries and caucuses? If ideological slants seep into stories, how might they influence the electorate? Media perspectives on the overall electoral process promote what sorts of orientations toward the US political system? Are variations in coverage among news outlets translated into different perceptions of the campaign among people who rely on those different sources?

The potential consequences of news coverage are not confined to the narrow question of whether the winning candidate's victory was caused in part by the media. Other fundamental attitudes may be subject to news media influence—not the least of which includes the quality and tone of political debate, and attitudes toward the responsiveness and worth of the political system and toward the caliber of its leadership.

The chapters that follow are largely devoted to research on TV news content, rather than its effects. Two chapters which do consider effects are Marshall's Chapter 4 study of the aftermath of media verdicts and Adams' Chapter 10 exploration of TV and newspaper influences on voting. It will be apparent to the reader, however, that most of the other chapters —while not strictly speaking "effects studies"—are infused with a belief that the nature of television news content does "matter," and does help mold the character of American political culture.

None of the contributors to this volume contends that TV news alone determines the occupant of the Oval Office or the tenor of national politics. No one suggests that viewers instantly subscribe to everything they are told by the networks. However, the authors of these chapters are obviously informed by the growing body of research which indicates that the news media are one important element in shaping the quality, temper, and dynamics of American political life.

REFERENCES

Alter, Jonathan. 1981. Rooting for Reagan. *Washington Monthly* 12 (January): 12–17.

Efron, Edith. 1971. *The News Twisters.* Los Angeles, Cal.: The Nash Press.

Lichter, S. Robert and Stanley Rothman. 1981. Media and Business Elites. *Public Opinion* 4 (October/November): 42–46, 59–60.

Patterson, Thomas and Robert McClure. 1976. *The Unseeing Eye.* New York: G. P. Putnam's Sons.

Robinson, Michael J. and Margaret Sheehan. 1983. *Over the Wire and on TV.* New York: Basic Books.

APPENDIX A:

Selected Stories About Media Coverage of the 1980 Campaign (Compiled with the assistance of Paula Fischman and Mary Gillespie)

November 5, 1979. Ron Nessen. The Same Old Mistakes, *Newsweek*, 29.

November 11. Haynes Johnson. Arm's-Length Coverage of the Kennedy Campaign, *Washington Post*, 1:3.

November 22. Patrick Buchanan. The News About Morality, *Chicago Tribune*, V:4.

November 27. W. B. Rood. Media Shuns Brown's New England Tour, *Los Angeles Times*, I:14.

December 3. James Q. Wilson. The Media Can Make the Loser the Winner, *US News and World Report*, 42.

December 14. William Raspberry. In the Land of the Blah, Copy is King, *Washington Post*, I:15.

December 23. David S. Broder. 'Tis the Season for Conscience, *Washington Post*, V:7.

January 7, 1980. Adam Clymer. Missing Republican in Iowa, *New York Times*, I:1.

January 9. Bernard Weinraub. Candidates Playing for the Evening TV, *New York Times*, I:17.

January 30. Tom Shales. Petty for Teddy: The Anti-Kennedy Bias in TV News Reporting, *Washington Post*, 2:1.

February 28. Robert Kaiser. CBS' Big Feed: The Primary Pressures, *Washington Post*, 4:1.

March 17. James David Barber. This Year, Why Not the Facts?, *New York Times*, 1:19.

March 25. Art Buchwald. The Boys on the Bus Get Taken for a Ride, *Washington Post*, 3:1.

March 31. Hugh Sidey. The Presidency: The Revolution is Under Way, *Time*, 20.

April 22. Robert Kaiser. 17 Hours of Campaign on TV, *Washington Post*, 1:6.

April 30. Bernard Weinraub. Students of Campaign News Find Hard Issues Neglected, *New York Times*, I:26.

May 13. Tom Shales. Deluge '80: TV's Primary Glut, *Washington Post*, 2:1.

May 25. Editorial. George Bush and Michigan, *Washington Post*, 2:6.

June 3. Robert Kaiser. Covering the Campaign: How a Midwestern Daily Did It, *Washington Post*, 1:3.

June 8. Frank Greve. The Ten Commandments of TV News, *Detroit Free-Press*, 3:1.

June 9. Frank Greve. NBC News: Steered by Instant Decision, *Detroit Free-Press*, 3:1.

June 10. Frank Greve. Anchor is Key to TV News Supremacy, *Detroit Free-Press*, 3:1.

June. George Barton et al. Who Picks the President? *The Washingtonian*, 106–112ff.

July 1. Bernard Weinraub. Study Finds Networks 'Infatuated' With Anderson, *New York Times*, 2:6.

July 6. David S. Brown. How to Predict Presidential Winners, *Washington Post*, 4:2.

July 15. Frank Greve. The Fat Cats: Media Stars Riding High, *Miami Herald*, 1:15.

July 16. Frank Greve. Hyped to Hilt Questions Are the Life of the Party, *Miami Herald*, 5:1.

July 17. Tom Shales. Back to you, CBS, *Washington Post*, 4:1.

July 18. Howard Rosenberg. Networks Nominate the Wrong Rumor, *Los Angeles Times*, 6:1.

July 18. John O'Connor. TV Covering the Big Story, *New York Times*, 1:12.

August 12. Tom Shales. The Lost Hurrah, *Washington Post*, 2:1.

August 15. Tom Shales. Good Night, Walter, *Washington Post*, 3:1.

August 15. Daniel Henninger. The Unblinking Eye on the Democratic Convention, *Wall St. Journal*, 19.

August 28. Robert Kaiser. Reagan's First 10 Days: A Rocky Lesson in the Mass Media, *Washington Post*, 1:3.

September 3. Adam Clymer. TV News and the Campaign, *New York Times*, 2:10.

September 11. Robert Kaiser. Anderson on the Media YoYo, *Washington Post*, 1:1.

September 26. Robert Kaiser. President Carter's 'Low Tide', *Washington Post*, 1:3.

September 30. Donald Baker. TV Reporters with Vice President Seldom Appear on News Shows, *Washington Post*, 1:2.

October 1. Robert Kaiser. Anderson Debilitated by a Flurry of Negative Publicity, *Washington Post*, 1:2.

October 9. William Safire. Stand Up Savants, *New York Times*, 1:35.

October 12. Frank Greve. Behind the Scenes with a Network Team, *Detroit Free Press*, 5:5.

October 17. Frank Greve. TV Gets the Last Word, *Detroit Free Press*, 1:1.

October 18. Robert Kaiser. For Reagan, an Autumnal Media Cold Snap, *Washington Post*, 1:1.

October 25. Robert Kaiser. Just Inches from the Goal, *Washington Post*, 1:2.

October 28. Robert Kaiser. The Hostages' Return to Page 1, *Washington Post*, 1:1.

October 30. Michael Robinson and Margaret Sheehan. The Media's Mean Campaign, *Baltimore Sun*, 1:23.

October 30. Robert Kaiser. Looking for Old Ghosts, *Washington Post*, 1:1.

October 30. John O'Connor. TV Instant Poll Steals Post-Debate Scene, *New York Times*, 3:26.

October 30. John Sears. How Presumptous Can the Press Get, *Washington Post*, 1:23.

October 31. Tom Shales. The Harassment of Ronald Reagan, *Washington Post*, 3:1.

November 3. R. Emmett Tyrell Jr. The Wise and the Wisenheimers, *Washington Post*, 1:21.

November 4. Robert Kaiser. Carter's Last Roll at Big Media Audience Richocheted Into the Ether, *Washington Post*, 1:7.

November 6. Bernard Weinraub. Networks in Dispute on Fast Elections, *New York Times*, 1:32.

2

TRADITIONAL INK VS. MODERN VIDEO VERSIONS OF CAMPAIGN '80

MICHAEL J. ROBINSON
MARGARET SHEEHAN

CARTER'S DAY IN PHILADELPHIA

On September 3, 1980, Jimmy Carter took his campaign to Philadelphia. As usual, the national press went along for the ride. To cover Carter, CBS sent White House correspondent Lesley Stahl; United Press International sent Helen Thomas, UPI's chief White House reporter since 1974.

These women are not cubs—between them Stahl and Thomas have been covering Washington politics for over 30 years. But famous and seasoned as they are, these reporters work for their news organization, not on their own. Although both have a by-line, each represents a news source, if not a news medium.

It was Stahl and CBS together that produced the hard copy about Carter's day in Philadelphia. It was Thomas, writing in the tradition and mode of UPI, who covered those same events for the late-night wire. So comparing their copy tells us less about Stahl and Thomas than about journalism—less about individuals than about traditional American print and contemporary network news.

Our detailed study of 1980 campaign coverage, *Over the Wire and On TV*, documents quantitatively the approaches used by TV news and traditional print. But from the qualitative angle, a case study of Carter's day in Philadelphia reveals vividly the fundamental differences between hard copy filed at the networks and hard copy that goes out over the wire.

Here is a large excerpt of the story Helen Thomas wrote for UPI:

17

After three days on the campaign trail, President Carter is clearly convinced that the once divided Democratic Party is now closing ranks behind his candidacy....

At the windup of a day of campaigning in Philadelphia Wednesday, Carter said in an interview on WPVI-TV that since the political convention last month he has seen "a remarkable coalescing of unity within the Democratic Party."

In the interview at a black Baptist Church, Carter mentioned that Sen. Edward Kennedy, D-Mass., his rival in the primaries, had telephoned to express his hope that the Democratic Party "will be united" in November....

Former Kennedy supporters also have taken their cue and are falling into line. They include Philadelphia Mayor William Green, who never left Carter's side during his visit to drum up votes, particularly among ethnic groups and blacks.

Also Wednesday, Carter won endorsements from three powerful unions that had endorsed other candidates in the primaries....

In his speech from the pulpit to an enthusiastic gathering in Zion Baptist Church in Philadelphia, Carter warned that a Democratic Party divided as it was in 1968 could lead to a Republican victory in November.

During the day, he toured the Italian market, shaking every hand in sight, and had a corned beef and cabbage lunch at an Irish restaurant....

Carter also said he thinks the recession has bottomed out, but he didn't have any good news to report about the immediate prospects for release of the American hostages in Iran.

This is quintessential hard news copy for Thomas and for UPI. In the finest traditions of traditional print, Thomas tells us what Carter said, when he said it, and to whom. It emphasizes the old political factors—party and the working man.

Now for the day's events according to CBS and Lesley Stahl—with introduction and leitmotif provided by subanchor Charles Kuralt:

Kuralt: You remember that great old photograph of Calvin Coolidge wearing a war bonnet. Campaigning politicians need to identify themselves with every segment of the population: the old, the young and the ethnic. It's a tradition. And as Lesley Stahl reports, President Carter stayed busy today—following tradition.

Stahl: What did President Carter do today in Philadelphia? He *posed*, with as many different types of symbols he could *possibly* find.

There was a picture at the day care center. And one during the game of bocce ball with the senior citizens. Click, another picture with a group of teenagers. And then he performed the ultimate media event—a walk through the Italian market.

The point of all this, *obviously*, to get on the local news broadcasts and in the morning newspapers. It appeared that the President's intention was not to say anything controversial....

Simply the intention was to be seen, as he was, and it was photographed, even right before his corned beef and cabbage lunch at an Irish restaurant with the popular mayor Bill Green. . .

There were more symbols at the Zion (black) Baptist church. . . .

Over the past three days the President's campaign has followed a formula—travel into a must-win state, spending only a short time there but ensuring several days of media coverage. . . .

And today the President got a bonus, since the Philadelphia TV markets extend into neighboring New Jersey—another must-win state.

Stahl's piece is not quite so archetypical of *Evening News* as the Thomas piece was for UPI. CBS did not file hard news stories quite like this every day; the color control has been turned up slightly in this CBS case. But despite that fact, these two versions of Carter's day in Philadelphia—wire and electronic—still demonstrate much about national campaign news coverage, old-style and new-fangled.

There were some fundamental similarities. To start with, both these stories were about Jimmy Carter—and so were the plurality of stories in 1980. On CBS and UPI, three quarters of the stories mentioning *any* candidate mentioned Carter at some point. Even excluding all "official" press stories about Carter as President, candidate Carter got far more coverage than anybody else.

Second, however different they may have been, both reports were essentially objective, that is, factually accurate. In fact, almost all of the stories we saw in Campaign '80 were, at a minimum, "objectivistic"— truthful, nonjudgmental as to policies, and based in part on direct attribution. Beyond a shadow of a doubt, Thomas' piece on Carter met all criteria of old-fashioned objectivity. The wire story drew almost no conclusions about Carter without attributing the inference to some legitimate source, usually Carter himself.

The CBS piece came much closer to violating the rules of objectivity. Stahl made two assertions about motive and strategy that went unattributed. The conclusion that the Italian market was the ultimate media event seemed especially "unobjective" given that thousands of reporters had covered the Democratic Convention a month before. But what keeps this piece from being labelled subjective is that no political observers, including the Carter people, think Stahl was wrong in her analysis. Gael Doar, who handled Carter's press advance that day, told us that Stahl's piece "made me cringe—first, because it made the President look as if he had done something wrong, something nobody else does; and second, because she [Stahl] was absolutely right about all the photo opportunities." In American journalism, as in law, truth is its own defense. By that standard, Stahl's piece was clearly "objective" or at least "objectivistic."

A third shared characteristic involves "horse racism." All national media, regardless of their prestige or financial well-being, emphasize the competition—the horse race. Thomas led with the horse race (Carter's prediction that the Democrats were uniting). Half the paragraphs in her original piece dealt directly with electoral competition. Stahl's piece was entirely about campaign strategy—one of the media's higher orders of "horse racism." From start to finish, Stahl's version of Carter's day stressed its use of political symbolism. Both Thomas and Stahl used "winning and losing" to glue together their prose.

But we picked Carter's day in Philadelphia to examine differences in news media, not just similarities. In this case, some of the differences in approach are as obvious as those between South Philly and the Main Line. UPI and CBS covered the same events but in very different ways.

Near the top of the list is the comparative need to "mediate." UPI stories, as this case illustrates, work more on reporting than mediating. The Thomas story basically covered what Carter had said and not why he said it. Seven of 13 paragraphs in the complete, original story were straight paraphrases or quotations from Carter's public remarks that day. CBS, in a longer piece, used Carter's words or ideas only once. As a general rule, CBS did more translation—the wires did more transcription. CBS mediated; UPI reported.

Equally obvious is the difference in the level of interpretation. CBS and UPI both relied on journalism's traditional "Ws": who, what, when, where, and why. But CBS reversed the order of priority. While Thomas talked mostly about "what," Stahl talked mostly about "why" or "how." Sentence by sentence, CBS provided 2½ times as much analysis and interpretation of Carter's trip.

A less obvious difference involves the definition of candidate. Thomas linked Carter to two other traditional political institutions: the Democratic party and the American labor movement. Stahl linked Carter to the media and to symbolism. Typically, the wire related candidates to traditional political forces. Networks made more of the "new politics," the candidate out there by himself, or at best, out there with his pollsters.

This reflects a much more important difference: the affinity of network news for political coverage of the candidate and personal issues. This is not personality journalism. Stahl never touched the subject of Carter's psyche, nor did anyone at *Evening News*. But in Philadelphia, CBS concentrated on the personal issue of campaign style. Thomas did not even bother to mention it.

Least subtle is the difference in criticism. The UPI piece neither said nor implied anything critical about Carter. If anything, the Thomas piece was upbeat: quoting Carter on restored unity in the party, pointing to his three labor union endorsements, his warm reception at the Church, and his phone call from Ted Kennedy. None of that made the *Evening News*. Instead, we have a piece in which Carter is painted as cynical poseur, a practitioner of media-based politics.

This is *not* the kind of report the Carter campaign wanted. After the election, we asked Carter's press secretary Jody Powell about his response at the time. Powell remembered the piece, but pretty much dismissed it. In his words, "by that point, you almost expected that sort of coverage and you just sort of rolled with it." For all practical purposes, Powell had become resigned to this sort of network coverage.

And finally, the question of format. As with most of the wire copy, Helen Thomas filed a news item—not a news story. Her piece had people, places, and events, but it didn't go anywhere much beyond that. Thomas had a "lead" but had no particular theme. The inverted pyramid—building a story from the top down with the basics in the opening paragraph—still lives in the campaign wire copy, especially in hard news coverage. As is usual with traditional print, editors could have easily taken any paragraph out of Thomas' piece and it would have read much the same.

On CBS, Lesley Stahl not only had a theme, she had a *theory*—the Carter formula for exploiting local media. And in a well-coordinated lead-in, Charles Kuralt gave the theme a fitting introduction—a brief preface about the candidates' "need to identify themselves with every segment of the population." Kuralt and Stahl have a lesson for us here, not just about Carter, but also about the less savory aspects of presidential campaign techniques, from Calvin Coolidge to the present.

One difference not yet considered is the inherent difference between a nonstop 24-hour wire service and an all-too-frequently interrupted commercial news program. Thomas actually did several stories that day about the Carter trip, not one; Stahl had just this one piece. The wire goes on and on; *Evening News* has but 30 minutes—22 minutes without the commercials. Can one compare wire copy with news programming in any meaningful way, or is all this an instance of comparing apples and oranges?

Actually, there is nothing wrong with comparing apples and oranges. They compare and contrast just like everything else: baseball and football, the US and the Soviet Union. The rule is that one ought not *add* apples and oranges. This rule does not prohibit comparisons. Despite the distorted cliché, one can and often does compare apples and oranges when deciding which to buy or eat.

There is a larger issue involved here than a frequently expressed mistake about the laws of arithmetic. In fact, apples vs. oranges is the very point we are trying to make. Even if we ignore the audiovisual and concentrate on the sentences and words, we have two very different varieties of news operating here—one variety is "informational," the other "educational." Thomas' story describes; Stahl's piece "teaches."

The case study of Carter's day in Philadelphia can be multiplied several hundred times: Old-style print, as reflected in the wires, and contemporary television, as defined by network news, provide different versions of the same campaign event, and, ultimately, of the whole campaign. CBS and UPI did many things the same, and some things quite well in Campaign '80. Still, the basic differences we found in Philadelphia repeated themselves throughout the year, regardless of reporter, regardless of candidate. Network news was more mediating, more political, more personal, more critical, more thematic than old-style print. Having inspected several thousand campaign stories coming over the wire and on TV, we are convinced that changing the medium clearly changes the message about presidential campaigns, regardless of the candidate involved. Jimmy Carter's major rivals were also treated in these same separate ways by print and video news.

KENNEDY'S DAY IN WASHINGTON

On January 28, 1980, Ted Kennedy made a trip across town from the US Senate to Georgetown University. Kennedy came to deliver what was billed by his staff as a major policy address. But he came with another mission as well. Georgetown was Kennedy's first real attempt, following Jimmy Carter's decisive victory in the Iowa caucuses, to resurrect his presidential campaign.

All the national media gave his Georgetown speech big play. Altogether, his remarks and the reaction to them were given 13 minutes of precious evening news time on ABC, CBS, and NBC—20 percent of that day's total. The *Washington Post* and the *New York Times* put Kennedy's words on their front pages. The speech at Georgetown came over the national wires as highest priority news.

Using media coverage as an indicator, the Georgetown address was the second most important in Kennedy's 1980 campaign. Only his now legendary peroration at the Democratic National Convention in August got Kennedy more play. But for our purposes, media attention to Kennedy at Georgetown serves as another case study in the similarities and contrasts between traditional print and modern electronic journalism.

With CBS News again as our "representative" network, and with United Press International as our surrogate for mainstream American dailies—our symbol of traditional print—the contrast between the world of video and the world of print repeats itself in coverage of that speech.

In one respect, this case study is unrepresentative: The Georgetown speech was covered as a genuine "issues" piece. About three fourths of the news coverage for this event was devoted to issues, as Kennedy outlined them. A solid two-thirds majority of the campaign news in both UPI and

CBS dealt with horse-race news in 1980 and less than 20 percent dealt with issues. Otherwise, the press story out of Georgetown was campaign news coverage writ small.

The UPI story written by Clay Richards is illustrated by the following excerpts:

> Sen. Edward Kennedy, seeking to revitalize his slumping presidential campaign with a dramatic speech, today called for immediate gasoline rationing and mandatory wage and price controls to halt inflation.
>
> In a wide ranging response to President Carter's State of the Union address, Kennedy also said he opposed the Administration's proposal for draft registration.
>
> Kennedy also said in a speech at Georgetown University that he opposes sanctions against Iran for holding American hostages because it will only "propel Iran toward the Soviet orbit."
>
> He said it is time to form a United Nations Commission to investigate the crimes of the deposed Shah of Iran—but that Commission should not begin its probe until all the US hostages are freed.
>
> The Massachusetts Democrat questioned whether the Soviet invasion of Afghanistan is the most serious threat to world peace since World War II and while he said a strong response is warranted, he cautioned against policies which would permanently antagonize Russia.
>
> Blasting what he called the failure of Carter, and calling him a Republican President who ran under the Democratic party label, Kennedy vowed to carry on his battle for the White House despite setbacks in the Iowa caucuses and a lack of campaign funds. . . .
>
> Kennedy complained that the twin crises in Iran and Afghanistan are holding the 1980 presidential elections hostage and he warned:
>
> "Before we permit Brezhnev and Khomeini to pick our president, we should pause to ask who will pay the price."

The CBS treatment of the same event is handled by Walter Cronkite and Phil Jones, with a brief direct quotation from Kennedy:

> *Cronkite:* Senator Edward Kennedy tried today to put back on track the campaign derailed by President Carter in Iowa. In a speech at Georgetown University in Washington, he redefined his candidacy— he accused the President of crossing the threshold of Cold War II and he called for a major price freeze and immediate gasoline rationing. Phil Jones has more.
>
> *Jones:* Some students hung a sign from a building which asked what many have been asking since Kennedy's resounding loss in Iowa, "Ted: Is the Dream Sinking?" But inside it was a fighting Kennedy, but clearly a frustrated candidate.
>
> *Kennedy:* Let me say how much I wish Jimmy Carter were here to debate me now.
>
> *Jones:* And with that Kennedy looked into the teleprompters and read a speech filled with attacks on President Carter and controversial proposals of his own. . . .

> Kennedy said today's speech was to reaffirm his candidacy. Aides said it was a speech to clarify Kennedy and his policies. And one informed source indicated that another speech may come soon, which will be to clarify Kennedy the man. This, says an aide, would provide Kennedy an opportunity to deal with another one of his problems, the lingering Chappaquiddick controversy.

Like the overwhelming majority of campaign news we followed over the wire and on TV, coverage of Kennedy that day was basically hard news—an event recounted, not evaluated. Both wire and electronic stories were, for the most part, neutral in their treatment of the candidate in all respects but one—electability.

Both stories, as is so often the case, explicitly evaluated only the candidate's chances for winning the nomination. Both stories set the speech in a "political" context. In this instance, both stories had similar leads. Each story started out explaining that Georgetown was as much a campaign activity as a policy pronouncement. And, in the end, both stories were more negative than positive in tenor—not so much about Kennedy as about his campaign chances.

The CBS story by Phil Jones and the UPI piece by Clay Richards represent the same shared elements in print and TV news that we saw in coverage of Carter's day in Philadelphia: a scrupulous avoidance of evaluating the candidate's positions on the issues, general factual accuracy with respect to the candidate, subjectivity with respect to the horse race, an electoral explanation or patina for almost everything, and a low-key negativity directed toward the candidate, or at least his campaign. Yet, once again, despite the similar leads and these other shared characteristics, print and television managed to cover the same event but to convey a meaningfully different story.

Although both pieces went long—comparatively speaking—UPI went longer. Print is generally longer than network news, although not so much longer as print journalists generally believe. The Richards story contained 663 words. The Jones piece ran at 532 words—about one fourth less "news" on CBS than on UPI. Moving beyond word count, one also finds that, although UPI was 25 percent longer than CBS, UPI was not that much more issue-oriented than the *Evening News* story of the Kennedy speech. CBS offered an unusually high percentage of "issue" news in its report (73 percent of total time), and UPI went even further in that direction (83 percent of total length). While this was much more issue emphasis than usual for both CBS and UPI, it does illustrate our year-long finding that there was surprisingly little difference in the proportion of issue coverage in each medium.

Yet, in other respects, the wire story and TV piece came up differently. As with the Philadelphia example, the CBS story was more negative.

Richards said nothing about Kennedy as a person; Jones strongly implied that Kennedy was staging his speech for television. Richards commented passingly about Kennedy's political problems; the CBS piece made them quite explicit.

Jones said Kennedy's campaign was now regarded as beyond salvation. Voicing over a shot of a sign saying "Is the dream sinking?" Jones claimed that "many" had been asking that same question since Kennedy's resounding loss in Iowa.

Jones went on to be more analytical; sentence by sentence, he was twice as analytical as the wire story. His CBS account emphasized why and how Kennedy did what he was doing. Such analysis amounts to nearly one third of the CBS report but only one sixth of the item on UPI.

The network story was not merely more critical and more analytical; it was also more personal, more concerned with the candidate per se. In percentage terms, CBS provided four times as much "personal" detail as UPI. So, while Jones painted Kennedy as a fighter, Richards and the wire painted him not at all.

The two stories also contrasted sharply as to structure. The UPI piece was not a story, but a listing of quotes with conjunctions. The last paragraph has an unexciting, less-than-essential quotation lifted directly and entirely from the text—a throw-away quote from Kennedy concerning the Ayatollah.

On CBS, Jones' piece was a real story with an introduction, a center section, and a conclusion. As it turned out, CBS News presented different conclusions in its regular and West Coast editions; but in both instances the Jones piece finished up with a reference to Chappaquiddick. Thus, UPI ended up quoting Kennedy dispassionately on Iran while CBS closed by invoking the issue of Chappaquiddick. In a sense those two endings symbolize almost too perfectly the differences between day-to-day traditional print and night-by-night contemporary TV.

Differences extended beyond the original stories. On the wire the Richards piece appeared in splendid isolation—followed by, of all things, a story on cannibalism in Bangladesh. CBS, on the other hand, followed immediately with an account of responses by the opposition. Coming directly on the heels of the Jones story was Lesley Stahl's reaction story from the White House, a story consuming almost 40 percent as much news time as the original one.

Obviously, the splendid isolation of Kennedy's speech on the wire was "corrected" by editors who put the story back into the campaign section of the newspaper. But, in fact, networks, far more than the wires, consistently followed up hard campaign news with spontaneous reaction —the charge-countercharge form of network news. Here, as throughout 1980, the wire story came across as a simple, discrete event, distinctly on its own. But on the *Evening News,* developments were treated as a Kennedy challenge and a Carter response.

There is another interesting difference between these two stories— an important factor which distinguishes this case from the Carter day example. The CBS story was presented *after* the Georgetown speech; the wire report was filed beforehand! Jones did his piece seven hours after the fact—Richards' copy came across the wire at 10:20 a.m.—40 minutes before Kennedy had even begun to speak.

At first blush, this truth about timing seems to render all our talk about meaningful difference obsolete. Obviously, Richards could not have written anything personal about Kennedy's performance, because Richards could not have known ahead of time how Kennedy had done. Richards could not have incorporated a spontaneous White House response until there had been such a response. Nor could Richards have easily been critical of Kennedy's performance. Candidate performances, after all, are entitled to a presumption of innocence. So UPI had to give Kennedy every benefit of the doubt and play down performance, hoopla, and criticism— and play up context and issues. Given that UPI ran a pre-filed story, while CBS waited for the facts of the case, it looks as if we have an even more classic instance of comparing apples and oranges—not news stories.

But, as it happened, the pre-written piece on the wire and the CBS story that came after the fact make our original comparison even stronger than it was. It is practically inconceivable that network television—given its method of operation and its construction—would ever file with its affiliates a piece of campaign news written before the fact. But wires can, and often do, practice pre-reporting. Pre-reporting of campaign events is not only acceptable in the newspaper business, it is a real advantage, if not a necessity. So, given that the afternoon papers had to have the story before it happened, it isn't at all surprising that Richards obliged by pre-filing. Pre-filing is part of print. But pre-filing means "substance" and "background," as opposed to instant analysis, performance or political response. Substance (the text of the speech) and background (why Kennedy was giving his address) were all that Richards had to work with when he wrote his original report. Print news differed from TV news in this case because they are distinctly different news enterprises, oranges and apples, once again.

Fortunately, at least for us, Clay Richards filed a second story about the Kennedy speech, a piece which followed the original by a full news day. The second story provides an interesting little experiment of sorts— one which helps us put aside the notion that print differs from network news merely as a function of deadlines and filing demands.

Having had the chance to witness Kennedy's speech, having also had at least an opportunity to watch Phil Jones on CBS, Richards filed a second story that came very, very close to his original. Richards' "post-test" report was not quite as "straight" as his first story, but it possessed all the same tendencies. Compared with the CBS story, the second wire account was, as before, heavy on issues, heavy on substance, and light on personality, light on political analysis, light on reactions from others, and light on criticism. Even with a full day to digest Kennedy's performance and to collect lots of negative responses, UPI gave much less play to those aspects than had CBS the night before. The factors that led Stahl to treat Carter differently than did Thomas and that led Jones to report about Kennedy differently than did Richards penetrate much more deeply than simply mechanisms like filing schedules.

Old-style print and new-style video do provide meaningfully different versions of the same campaign—even of the same event. Although we did not find much evidence that network content in 1980 was less issue-oriented than print, the two media differed substantially in other respects. As shown in coverage of Carter's day and Kennedy's day, television is more *reactive,* more *thematic,* more *personal,* more *political,* more *critical,* more *analytical,* and more *mediating* in campaign coverage than is print news. Networks do cover national candidates and their campaigns more insightfully than traditional print, and more incitingly as well.

Differences like these make us wonder not just about the behavior of news media, but about the behavior of the political system as well. Moving from one form of political information—traditional print—and on toward another—contemporary television—means that we have changed the diet on which our political process feeds. It seems logical that by changing the informational menu we may well have changed the process as well; and, if we read recent American history accurately, those characteristics which we have found in abundance in television news—such as increased criticism, greater attention to personality, higher levels of cynicism—seem to be more and more characteristic of our national political life.

3

PRESIDENTIAL PREFERENCE POLLS AND NETWORK NEWS

C. ANTHONY BROH

The malapportionment of delegates to the 1968 Democratic National Convention and the quota system of the 1972 Democratic National Convention created misgivings about the existing procedures for presidential nominations. In 1968, the Democrats appeared to ignore the opinions of citizens who opposed escalation of the war in Vietnam and who supported the candidacies of Robert Kennedy, Eugene McCarthy, and George McGovern. This lack of representation coincided with violent demonstrations in Chicago by disaffected young people, who turned their wrath toward the Democratic Party in the general election. The specter of an unresponsive party convention helped create the image of an irresponsible party candidate. Thus, after the fact, party officials could blame Hubert Humphrey's Election-Day defeat on the failure to conduct orderly nominating procedures.

In 1972, the Democrats appeared to ignore the opinions of party regulars, in favor of the very people left out four years earlier. Democratic party leaders had reformed their party rules by adopting quotas for minorities, women, and young people (see Commission on Party Structure, 1970). Delegations without the proper demographic balance could be and were challenged by the credentials committee. As a consequence of this change in party rules, the 1972 Democratic National Convention had a very high percentage of "newcomers," people with little political experience and, more significantly, a very high percentage of people who did not appear to represent the mainstream of American politics (Kirkpatrick, 1976). Thus it appeared, at least in the media, to be skewed in favor of people concerned about social issues previously unimportant to both Democrats and Republicans. The conservative "excesses" of one convention led to the liberal "excesses" of the next. (For media content analyses of these campaigns, see Meadow, 1973; Frank, 1973; Hofstetter, 1976; Paletz & Elson, 1976.)

As a result of these experiences, party reformers after 1972 returned to the Progressive reforms of the 1910s by instituting presidential primaries throughout the country. Before 1968, less than 40 percent of the delegates to either Democratic or Republican Conventions were selected in presidential primaries (Arterton, 1978). In 1980, 71 percent of both parties delegates were selected in primaries. Clearly the parties sought to earn an image of both responsibility and responsiveness using popular ballots as the main procedure for delegate selection.

The shift of delegate selection from coalition politics (Kessel, 1968) to primaries increased the role of public opinion in the nominating process, often at the expense of party organization. The preferences of large voter blocs, for example, became more important than the ringing endorsement of a party leader. Political bosses no longer controlled convention votes because popularly elected delegates owed their position to the voters.

At the same time that the political parties reformed their delegate-selection procedures, the mass media were changing their campaign coverage. Leaked sources and interviews with party organizers or campaign staff members were no longer especially fruitful for understanding the nominating process. Indicators of public opinion became more useful.

Robert Chandler (1972) notes in describing the history of the CBS News Poll that some news stories "dealt with subjects which virtually cried out for the answers that only survey research could provide." Primary election results were such stories. Polling had been growing at the networks since election results were first projected on the basis of key precincts; but the emphasis on presidential primaries demonstrated the need for networks to obtain systematic descriptions and explanations of voter preferences.

After a one-year experiment with an in-house poll operation in 1969–70, CBS joined forces with the *New York Times* to conduct public opinion polls. NBC and the Associated Press began their cooperative venture into polling at about the same time. For the 1976 election, both ABC and the Public Broadcasting Service commissioned commercial polling houses to conduct their opinion surveys, but both networks insisted on involvement in the planning and analysis of the data. Shortly after the 1980 election, ABC announced the establishment of its in-house polling operation to be cosponsored by the *Washington Post*. While these polling operations at the networks did not develop solely because the presidential preference primaries gained prominence in the nominating process, they clearly provided journalists with a key tool for analyzing the process.

Little data-based research has analyzed this shift in media coverage of presidential nominations from political leaders to public opinion, and thus from interviews to polls. Yet this research is important, because polling can influence the nominating process in several ways. Even if we assume that raw poll data accurately capture public opinion at the time, there can be no such thing as entirely neutral conveying of this information without affecting the election. The timing of polls, their findings, and the networks' presentations and interpretations can affect primaries and popular perceptions of the candidates.

How can the reporting of poll results possibly be completely neutral? Newsmen of necessity make a series of choices in presenting and interpreting poll data, and those choices have political consequences. This is not an issue of overt bias or mistakes; any decision about how to present poll data may have consequences that differ from the consequences of another sort of presentation. Even the initial decision of whether to report and highlight a particular poll is a subjective and significant one. Thus, the media do more than just transmit the public will as they report poll data. This chapter will analyze in more detail televised news of public opinion polls in campaigns for the 1980 presidential nominations.

PRESENTING POLL DATA

The presentation of public opinion polls in the first days of a candidacy can permanently affect the image of a presidential contender. In 1976, for example, Gerald Ford's deficit in the polls prior to the Republican Convention helped create a "no win" image that encouraged Ronald Reagan. This same early deficit was the basis for Ford's apparent "recovery" in the campaign itself. That is, given Ford's low rating in the pre-convention polls, a close Election-Day vote demonstrated exceptional gains in popularity (Broh, 1979).

A similar situation occurred during the 1980 campaign with incumbent Jimmy Carter. Edward Kennedy led Jimmy Carter at one time in the pre-convention period by 30 percent. Events and campaign strategy erased this edge as the campaign progressed, but Carter's image as a weak and unpopular president was difficult—indeed, proved impossible—to overcome during the post-convention period.[1]

---

[1] The juxtaposition of Edward Kennedy's and Jimmy Carter's convention speeches probably reinforced the Carter image. Carter pollster Pat Caddell and Reagan pollster Richard Wirthlin briefed their candidates at length about the Carter image problem. (See Drew, 1981.)

The media not only use polls to help shape candidates' images, but also they tend increasingly to conduct the polls that are then used to shape candidates' images. They create, as well as report, information about public opinion (Cantril, 1980). More polls on television are media-generated than privately initiated. In 1980, news organizations sponsored 73 percent of the polls reported on network evening newscasts from January to the time of the Democratic convention in August. Only 13 percent of the stories were sponsored by other groups such as polling firms, universities, or campaign organizations. (Fourteen percent of the news stories with polls did not report the sponsor or the polling firm.) The 73 percent media sponsorship in 1980 is up from 58 percent in 1976 (Broh, 1980a, p. 519). Clearly, televised poll reports have become the business of news organizations.

The image-building function and the sponsorship of polls create new dangers for journalists as the press takes on new responsibilities. First, a perception of who can win the election is an important criterion for evaluation by party leaders (Polsby & Wildavsky, 1964) and, more important, by contributors. Therefore, releasing an important poll at a crucial point in the campaign may change organized support. In June 1980, ABC news reported a Louis Harris poll that showed 31 percent would vote for third party candidate John Anderson, "if the polls showed that [he] had a real chance of winning the presidential election in November." The appearance of a close three-candidate campaign helped legitimize Anderson's candidacy and, according to press reports at the time, significantly increased volunteer help and campaign contributions. In some instances, critically timed news releases of poll results could produce a "snowball" effect since popularity produces the campaign resources that are required for advertising and news coverage of special events that, in turn, increase popularity. In this sense, polls reinforce as well as respond to existing candidate images.

Second, expectations of who will win a primary or caucus shape opinions about who has won a primary. Candidate success is measured against anticipated results that emerge in the media. Such expectations are generated through public opinion polls, which thus become a benchmark to which a presidential contender's primary support is compared. Sometimes this expectation works in a candidate's favor. For example, George Bush's 33 percent of the delegates in the Iowa caucuses surprised most campaign observers who expected him to receive only about 17 percent as estimated by the *Des Moines Register* poll 10 days before the caucuses. This "victory" propelled his candidacy from that of a minor contender to frontrunner, according to CBS and other network news reports.

At other times, poll-generated expectations become a handicap; a candidate who does not beat the polls is perceived as a loser, regardless of his actual showing. This was the case for George Bush in the New Hampshire primary. CBS began its March 1 report with the following statement:

> By far the most interesting political question of the week has been, "Why did George Bush lose so badly in the New Hampshire primary on Tuesday when the polls taken beforehand had shown him running neck-and-neck with Reagan?"

In other words, Bush suffered defeat in New Hampshire not only because he received fewer votes than Ronald Reagan, but also because he did worse than the "polls taken beforehand had shown."

To answer the question of the week, CBS relied on a follow-up poll. Correspondent Bob Schaffer asserted: "A new CBS-*New York Times* poll suggests at least some of the explanation." Attitude changes in the report were attributed to George Bush's performance during the Nashua Senior High School debates—or "non-debate" as it became known. The significance of the story is that polls provided both the benchwork for comparison and the explanation for defeat of George Bush's primary showing in New Hampshire. Poll standings can deflate as well as boost a candidate.

Third, polls determine the "front-runner." This label is generally desirable, for the candidate with it receives substantial media coverage. Television correspondents continually interviewed Ronald Reagan before the Iowa caucuses even though he did not personally enter the nationally televised Republican debates or the political competition in that state. Reagan was simply ahead in most national polls. As the poll front-runner, he could expect extensive media attention. (See Robinson, Conover & Sheehan, 1980.) At the same time, the "front-runner" is vulnerable to zealous scrutiny by journalists in search of a story. Michael Robinson and Margaret Sheehan (1983) have shown how the news media target front-runners for extra critical coverage.

Whether the label of front-runner is an asset or liability is an empirical question and not analyzed here. Clearly, being the front-runners aided some candidates in 1980 (Ronald Reagan) and for various reasons harmed others (George Bush). The point here is that polls, as interpreted by journalists, now define and bestow the title.

Public opinion polls are subject to interpretation. Polls require explanations. Reporters do not simply transmit information about public opinion—they take an active role in interpreting and assessing it. They become "keepers" rather than "transmitters" of the public will. What should one do with "no responses" and "don't knows?" What are the interpretations of sampling error? What biases exist in the sampling techniques? Are the questions fairly worded? Are screening questions used? These and other questions are crucial to the interpretation of any poll, and journalists usually have neither the training nor the incentives to answer them (Broh, 1980b). Furthermore, the fact that media now commission and create, as well as report, poll findings produces greater interpretive responsibilities for the reporter.

INTERPRETING THE POLLS

The interpretations of poll results on television are usually "reasonable." After all, reporters compare poll results to interviews with political leaders, reports of other journalists, people on the street, their own intuition, Election-Day votes, and other poll results (Crouse, 1972). This procedure creates face validity for the data. However, these reports still must incorporate reporter evaluations and judgments.

An analysis of 131 poll stories presented on television news over a seven-month period in 1980 suggests that news correspondents make many judgments that affect the presentation of the data, the images of the presidential contenders, and ultimately the nomination process itself. More specifically, correspondents and news producers make the following choices about how to present public opinion polls—in addition to the basic decision that a particular poll result is newsworthy:

1. They can present the poll as a "stop action picture" describing only one moment or as a prediction of an election outcome.
2. They can include all candidates or only a few.
3. They can present the poll results as isolated facts or as data for comparison.
4. They can report the absolute level of support for each candidate or other differences in support among candidates.
5. They can focus on the poll data alone or on explanations for the poll results.
6. They can enhance the credibility of the findings or undermine them.

These choices can affect the presidential campaign, and consequently make journalists active participants in the nominating process. To examine these choices more closely, this research draws on the stories about opinion polls broadcast on early-evening network newscasts from the beginning of the presidential nominating process until the Democratic convention—January 7 through August 9.[2] This time period includes all of the major nominating campaign activity.

The unit of analysis is the poll story, or in some instances, the poll report. A news story is defined as a period of news time starting with an

---

[2] The decision about when the presidential campaign begins was the subject of a recent Supreme Court case, CBS vs. FCC. (The political implications of the case are discussed by Broh, 1983.)

introduction by an anchor and including all information about a subject. On most broadcasts, the length of the news story is defined by an "over-the-shoulder" projection symbolizing some aspect of the story (Lichty & Bailey, 1978). A report is a description of a particular political finding about the poll within the story (i.e., the presentation of a single survey question or a single crosstabulation).

FINDINGS

Prediction

Public opinion polls measure attitudes at the time of the survey questions. Indeed, interviewers for polls often present hypothetical situations to find out voters' current preferences. Questions about vote intentions may begin with the phrase, "If the election were held today, ..." Respondents are then asked to state their voting choices.

Journalists have an insatiable urge to project the electoral outcome from the answers to these questions. Poll data represent the reporter's best information about which candidate is likely to win, and since journalism rewards people who describe trends early, correspondents understandably desire to forecast the election results with poll data. On the other hand, wrong predictions are costly to journalists. The forecasts of the *Literary Digest* in 1936 and most commercial polling firms in 1948 provide cautious reminders for reporters to ponder.

In 1980, poll data were used for predictions only rarely. In an ABC story about Illinois polls sponsored by Chicago newspapers, correspondent Brit Hume summarized George Bush's weak showing in the polls this way:

> With John Anderson riding high and Gerald Ford apparently set to enter the race, it is hard to see how George Bush can recover in Illinois and it seems fair to wonder if he ever can.

Hume really made four predictions: First, John Anderson would do well in his home state of Illinois. Second, Ronald Reagan would also do well (mentioned earlier in the report). Third, George Bush would not do well in Illinois. Fourth, Gerald Ford would actively seek the nomination.

The first prediction, along with results of the Massachusetts and Vermont primaries a few days before the broadcast, escalated expectations about John Anderson's popularity. Anderson was described earlier in the year as a nice guy, an effective speaker, but having little chance to win (Robinson, Conover, and Sheehan, 1980). Now, campaign events and some polls suggested he was in contention for significant delegate support, if not the nomination itself.

Failed expectations in Illinois ended John Anderson's bid for the Republican nomination. While the ABC report was not the only factor in raising expectations, poll results helped confirm the reporters' belief that Anderson had a chance. Failure to win one's home state is generally bad for any candidate, but failure to match poll predictions was disastrous for John Anderson in Illinois.

The second prediction in the Illinois primary came true. Ronald Reagan won with 48 percent of the vote to John Anderson's 38 percent. The same day as the ABC story on Illinois, CBS's Bruce Morton reported:

> But Reagan is rolling now. And if he wins Illinois next week, it's hard to imagine anybody—even Gerald Ford—being able to stop him later on.

Reagan did win Illinois, and no one stopped him later on.

The third prediction, regarding George Bush, also came true. He received a paltry 11 percent of the vote. His campaign was already faltering after losses in New Hampshire and Florida. And Bush's victory in Massachusetts had been overshadowed by Anderson's doing better than the polls and pols had predicted in both Vermont and Massachusetts.

The fourth prediction was false. After considering his chances for the Republican nomination with close friends and advisors, Gerald Ford decided not to seek the Republican nomination, even though many polls demonstrated his popularity with Republican rank-and-file.

Predictions using poll data have the potential for affecting the nominating process. Although Anderson never won a primary, his early showings exceeded expectations. Post-primary analyses focused on his "surprising" popularity with voters, and made him a serious candidate for the nomination. The prediction that Ford would enter the race was certainly encouraged by poll results. The possible entry of the former president could have changed strategies, and was thought to have damaged George Bush.

On the other hand, reporters have the option of ignoring their pre-election predictions after the election. NBC reported the dissolution of Edward Kennedy's lead from 68 to 20 percent over President Carter to 56 to 31 percent behind President Carter. Jessica Savitch introduced those results of a *Boston Globe* poll with the statement that "Senator Kennedy's campaign is clearly in trouble in New Hampshire." The story attributed Kennedy's failure in the polls to bad campaign strategy, overconfidence, incoherent speeches, and Jimmy Carter's ability to act "presidential" during the Iranian crisis. The story justified Kennedy's decline in the polls.

In fact, Kennedy did much better in New Hampshire than the predictions of the *Boston Globe* poll. He lost the primary by 51 percent to 39 percent—narrowing the margin to within 12 percentage points instead of the 25 percent margin anticipated by the *Globe*. Moreover, 39 percent of the vote for a candidate challenging an incumbent is certainly not bad; Eugene McCarthy's 42 percent against President Lyndon Johnson in 1968 was treated as a "victory." However, the 1980 contest included a Kennedy, whose family has acquired a mystique among the press and much of the American public. Also, New Hampshire was considered the "backyard" of Kennedy's home state of Massachusetts. Television stories emphasized these facts, and said the New Hampshire vote helped dispel the Kennedy image of invincibility.

In this instance, the prediction that Kennedy would do quite poorly was not entirely supported by Election-Day results. But, reporters chose to ignore their earlier statements and continued to focus on the public's disappointment with Kennedy.

Predictions give correspondents a choice in how to report election returns. The post-election report can emphasize the absolute standing of the candidates or it can emphasize the vote totals in comparison to earlier poll-generated predictions. Both victories and defeats become surprising or expected, depending on the reporter's emphasis of pre-election standing in the polls. The press has a choice to report either context.

The media use several techniques to make predictions. In the cases above, the correspondent or the anchor explicitly forecasts the Election-Day outcome using the poll results. Another technique is to interview a campaign worker. CBS broadcast the words of Tracy Gallagher, Jimmy Carter's Iowa coordinator, shortly before the caucuses in that state:

> It's going to be close. I think the polls, when they do general opinion surveys, are going to find us ahead.

The polls did show Jimmy Carter ahead. CBS balanced its report with a clip from the Kennedy campaign. The network, 10 days before the Iowa caucus, showed Kennedy saying:

> [Kennedy] "I ask all of you to join with us in the final days of this campaign to do the work that needs to be done. . . . And then on the caucus days, we'll show the *Des Moines Register* what a real poll in Iowa really looks like."
>
> —Susan Spencer, CBS News, Des Moines, Iowa

The abrupt end to the report with no analysis by the correspondent had the effect of reporting Kennedy's statement as fact. Of course, the television viewer knows that no one—even Kennedy—can see into the future. Thus, the Kennedy statement, along with the absence of any summary by the correspondent, had the visual impact of a prediction.

In most instances, network news commentators are themselves cautious about making predictions, although sometimes anchors will warn viewers that "it may be hazardous to predict, but. . ."

ABC removed network endorsement of predictions by using Louis Harris during the newscast. Harris would answer the anchor's questions about attitude trends, approaching primaries, and specific breakdowns of the latest poll. He often made causal attributions for a candidate's success or failure in the polls. Harris offered forecasts based on his poll data, and apparently in some cases based on his personal intuitions.

In the 131 poll stories in 1980 analyzed for this study, correspondents or anchors made explicit predictions 19 times. Of these 19 predictions, 7 stated the primary was too close to call or even. Twelve of the predictions stated which candidate was expected to win. Although rare, these predictions created viewer expectations about the candidates' vote totals on primary day and provided a basis for evaluation and interpretation of election returns.

Elimination

Journalists use polls to eliminate candidates with apparently little chance of winning a primary. Just being included in the polls requires a minimum level of name recognition. Consequently, some candidates are not included in polls and are not considered "serious candidates." (Their "potential popularity" remains unknown.)

NBC used its poll data to narrow the field of candidates in its story of February 25. The day before the New Hampshire primary, John Chancellor introduced a poll story with the following statement:

> The Republican race is very close. Ronald Reagan and George Bush, neck and neck.... Howard Baker and John Anderson both running for third.

Garrick Utley's story that followed reflected the poll results. During the 80-second report, Bush or his advisors were shown 33 percent of the time, Ronald Reagan 25 percent of the time, Howard Baker 13 percent of the time, and John Anderson 9 percent of the time; John Connally, Robert Dole, and Phil Crane were mentioned but not shown at all. Utley concluded:

> Despite the seven candidates, this is a two-man race, Bush versus Reagan. A race too close to call with stakes too high to ignore.... For those who are bored by politics or find it too predictable, this primary is a certain cure.

Table 3.1 displays the number of times each network broadcast a campaign report using polls. Candidates do not receive equal treatment during the nominating period. Even discounting that some candidates were dropping out as the campaign progressed, it is clear that several candidates were often ignored. The "also-rans"—Brown, Baker, Connally, Crane, and Dole combined—were mentioned in poll stories less than either Edward Kennedy or John Anderson, not to mention comparison with

Carter or with Reagan. In short, polls and their interpreters can and do eliminate candidates from news coverage.

Table 3.1
Number of News Reports Using Poll Data During the 1980 Pre-Convention Campaign

	ABC	CBS	NBC	Total
Brown	2	7	4	13
Carter	21	32	21	74
Kennedy	10	14	10	34
Anderson	7	22	10	39
Baker	2	4	3	9
Bush	11	14	3	28
Connally	1	4	0	5
Crane	0	3	0	3
Dole	1	2	0	3
Reagan	19	27	13	59
Ford	0	1	1	2
Other	1	4	3	8
No Response	2	6	5	13
TOTALS	77	140	73	290*

* This number is higher than the total number of poll reports because one report might include statements about several candidates.

Comparisons

Polls provide a "snapshot" of public opinion; but, like someone else's picture album, the snapshots are only interesting with an explanation. Journalists explain the political context of polls through comparisons.

The key question in interpreting poll data is: "compared to what?" Does one compare a candidate's popularity to that of other candidates, to a candidate's own earlier popularity, to previous campaigns, or to the intuitions of party leaders, campaign officials, and journalists? All of these points of comparison seem logical and relevant to a candidate's success, but the choice of a comparison can crucially affect a candidate's image.

In 1980, journalists chose many different events and data for points of comparison. In doing so, they created a variety of conclusions about the candidates. Reagan and Bush were "neck-and-neck" in Massachusetts on March 1 even though Bush's percentage in the pre-election polls was much lower than his earlier popularity in the same state. By making a different comparison, reporters could have claimed that Bush was rapidly losing popularity—a very different image than that of an even match between the two favorites.

Journalists sometimes evaluate poll results by interviewing people who are informed about public opinion. For example, one NBC story discounted the polls by comparing the results to knowledgeable sources. Ken Bode reported a pre-primary poll in New Hampshire with the following statement (February 25):

> New Hampshire voters have a long-standing reputation for delivering surprises. At campaign's end, that would seem to be Ted Kennedy and Jerry Brown's best hope.... Top presidential aides work the bars where the press hang out, shaping expectations, promoting the notion that "really it's closer than the polls say".... On his last campaign day, Kennedy shrugged off the polls.

The report had the effect of invalidating the poll data because "New Hampshire voters," "Ted Kennedy," "Jerry Brown," "top presidential aides," the press, and perhaps the bartender for the press must know at least as much as pollsters. It thus made Kennedy's candidacy appear more viable than the stark numbers would have done.

Some uses of graphics compare a candidate's popularity over time. In an early March story about President Carter's handling of foreign affairs, ABC displayed a bar graph of the President's approval rating. The viewer could see the "approve" bar growing taller with each poll, while the "disapprove" bar shrank. The visual image suggested greater strength among Carter supporters. Interestingly, the voice-over report described criticism of the Administration's foreign policy. In this instance, the visual image of growing popularity contradicted the correspondent's report about growing criticism. (See Adams, 1978, on audiovisual discrepancies.) One might speculate that the bar graph presents a sharper, clearer image to the viewer than the words of the correspondent or the "talking heads" that criticized the President.

One danger of comparing poll results is that subtle differences in polling techniques may distort the meaning of such comparisons. This problem is particularly acute when comparing data from two polling agencies. For example, the vote intention question in 1980 for NBC, Center for Political Studies of the University of Michigan, CBS News-*New York Times*, Gallup, Harris, Roper, *Washington Post*, and Yankelovich was slightly different for each agency. In addition, polling agencies gather their findings (1) for different elements of the population (e.g., registered voters vs. likely voters); (2) with different interviewing techniques (telephone vs. door-to-door); (3) by selecting different samples (random digit vs. geographic clustering); (4) with different interview instructions in the field (e.g., probe vs. no follow-up); and (5) with different techniques of analysis (e.g., combine categories of positive rating vs. present all categories). The varying methods of survey research present an exaggerated image of voter volatility (Broh, 1980b, 1981) and, more important here, a possible bias depending on the poll selected for comparison.

Table 3.2 presents the points of comparison selected by network news producers and correspondents during the 1980 pre-convention campaign. In general, they reported the data in isolation of other findings; however, they compared the current poll data to other information in 33 percent of the 185 reports. The most common comparison was to an earlier poll by the same agency. Table 3.2 also shows that the polls were occasionally compared to a variety of other sources, another indication of the discretion and power exercised by correspondents in their interpretations of poll data.

Table 3.2
Comparisons of Poll Reports with Other Data Sources

No Comparison	125
Earlier Poll by Same Agency	41
Reporter's Own Sources	8
Party Leaders	5
Other Polling Agency	3
Previous Years	2
Unspecified	1
TOTAL	185

Subtractions

A technique related to making comparisons is to subtract the popularity of one candidate from the popularity of another. This is a special case of comparisons in election reporting because it explicitly emphasizes the "horse-race" aspect of polling (Broh, 1980a). It remains one of the controversies of presenting poll data.

In 1976, the *New York Times* and CBS presented the results of their polls without mentioning the actual percentage of support for each candidate. The policy de-emphasized the image of elections as sporting competition—or so the *Times* and CBS hoped. However, in virtually all articles and news stories, reporters computed the percentage difference between the two candidates. Thus, the absence of figures may have emphasized journalistic writing about the horse-race image of a campaign, producing an ironic contradiction to the apparent intention of the policy.

Unquestionably, the numerical difference between two leading candidates' pre-primary popularity becomes the main focus of most poll results. A wide poll margin that is narrowed or overcome in a primary can create a sense of increasing support. Furthermore, such newsworthy "surprises" are the grist for lead stories. On the other hand, the expectation of defeat can provide a cushion for a poor showing in the voting booth.

In this circumstance, candidates prefer to trail their opponent slightly in the polls, with the difference small enough to encourage wavering volunteers and contributors. In fact, candidates occasionally learn to use the media's presentation of polls to create such an impression among voters. The Pennsylvania primary demonstrates how candidates can manipulate the media on its own ground. On April 9, CBS reported that results of a Kennedy campaign poll showed the Senator 10 percent behind President Carter in the state. Six days later, on election day in Pennsylvania, Pat Caddell, Jimmy Carter's pollster, leaked the results of a poll to the press suggesting that his candidate was 3 percent behind. The Kennedy campaign objected, as ABC's Katherine Mackin reported:

> Kennedy's people accuse the White House of trying to turn the President into the Pennsylvania underdog, which Kennedy says he is. With claims like these on Election Day, all sides win.

NBC carried a similar analysis on its Election-Night newscast. In this case, the campaign managers could manipulate the networks' predictable tendency to emphasize any differences between poll-based expectations and actual results.

Polls, as the discussion in this section suggests, often place the media in a "double bind." If they report the difference between the candidates in the polls, critics accuse them of encouraging horse-race journalism. If they report the actual percentages of the candidates in the polls, critics again point an accusing finger for horse-race journalism. Pollsters for the media are aware of the problem; but, they argue, responsible journalism requires reporting of candidate popularity—especially in an era when preferential primaries play a role in the nomination process—and polls are the most objective measure available.

Two thirds of the television reports that described polls during the 1980 nomination period did not give the percentage difference between the two candidates. Fifty-seven reports went through the arithmetic calculation of subtracting one candidate's popularity from another. The difficulty in deciding whether or not to report the candidate differences is reflected in the method of the reports. In 33 of the 57 reports, the difference was given only orally; and in 14 of the 57 reports, the difference was given only visually. Thus, television news used its full potential as a sight and sound medium to emphasize candidate differences in only 10 reports, or about 5 percent of all televised poll reports. Although the percentage is small, its existence is another reminder of the range of options available to television correspondents when deciding how to report poll data.

Attribution

The magnitudes of percentages are probably less important in news stories than the explanations journalists attribute to poll findings. Numbers by themselves have little meaning.

In some poll stories, for example, the correspondent rapidly quotes a series of facts and figures, probably leaving viewers with little comprehension about the meaning of the poll. In a story (1/15/80) using the CBS-*New York Times* poll, Bruce Morton reported the results of 28 survey questions in 230 seconds. The extremely rapid pace relied on both the correspondent's amazing verbal facility and on 16 graphics made with the network's newly acquired machine. The story conveyed a lot of information but little analysis—and perhaps little comprehension of the messages.

Stories like the one described above were rare in 1980 in the pre-convention period. Of the 131 stories, only five described answers to four or more questions; and these stories were usually prepared late in the afternoon of a primary election day. More commonly, poll stories reported the results of a single survey question. This was the practice for 59 percent of the stories.

A single poll question takes only a few seconds to report, so such stories spend less time on data than on assessing the reasons for the poll results. Usually poll stories attribute candidate success either to the momentum of the nominating process or to other campaign phenomena. A primary victory in one state often generates favorable publicity that creates good will in another state. George Bush's surprise victory in the Iowa caucuses seemed to prompt an immediate surge in his New Hampshire popularity. Similarly, Howard Baker's poor showing in New Hampshire was followed by lowered poll standings in Massachusetts.

Reporters do more than just attribute poll change to the popularity trends across states. They also explain poll developments using demographic characteristics, media events, or long-term considerations. Explanations of candidate popularity included, to mention a few, the President's Rose Garden strategy, the crisis in Iran, the Nashua Senior High School debate, policy at the United Nations, personality factors, speaking ability, and general feelings of trust. While crosstabulation of these variables with popularity ratings may suggest reasons for voter attitudes, causal attributions are quite difficult to prove and usually require more sophisticated data than are commonly available to even the most responsible reporters.

Polls also seem to encourage attribution. Since campaign strategies in American politics often depend upon ethnic politics, an enterprising reporter will generally want to know how ethnic or social groups feel about a candidate. For example, Florida, with its large Jewish population in the Miami area, provided fodder for stories about the primary in New York, another state with a significant Jewish population. The opinions of Jews in Florida and elsewhere were then attributed to reactions to the "mistaken" anti-Israeli vote by the US at the United Nations. Similarly, reporters often discussed implications of state primary exit polls for the nation as a whole, and announced the types of people that supported each candidate.

That polls encourage attribution is suggested by CBS's polling partner, the *New York Times*, in its leads to three front-page stories on March 26. Discussion of the New York primary attributed victories by Edward Kennedy and Ronald Reagan to events, ethnic groups, and issues. Discussion of the Connecticut primary made no such claims and relied entirely on incomplete voter returns. While New York undoubtedly deserved more coverage than Connecticut,[3] a key difference in the stories was the absence of exit polling in Connecticut.[4]

CBS's evening newscast of March 25 followed the same pattern as the *Times'* front page. There were three stories about New York and Connecticut, lasting 370 seconds altogether. Of this time, only a single sentence described poll-less Connecticut.

Poll stories with attributions emphasize the numerous choices that correspondents must make in reporting a poll story. A survey contains numerous questions, but the correspondent must select which questions to report and how to report them. One powerful consequence of attributions is to make correspondents even more central to interpretations of partisan events. Using polls, broadcast journalists are now prepared to claim that a candidate's trustful personality or an issue stance, for example, "causes" popularity in the polls and in elections.

Validation

"Who knows if the polls are right?" queries Lynn Sherr of ABC news in response to anchorman Sam Davidson's questions about the latest *Boston Globe* poll. Such rhetorical comments raise doubts for the viewers about the validity of polls. With this technique, a reporter can either accept or raise questions about survey findings.

In the 1980 pre-convention period, correspondents raised questions about findings in about 12 percent of the cases. Usually the challenges were not as direct as the one cited above. For example, CBS quoted Tracy Gallagher, a Carter coordinator, in a Maine story (2/8/80) as saying that the sample sizes of polls were too small to tell anything about potential caucus participants. Methodologically, he may be right for several reasons, but the report clearly shakes the viewer's confidence in the polls reported earlier in the program.

Another technique for creating doubt about polls is to treat the campaign and the election story lightly. Television is an entertainment medium

---

[3] While the *New York Times* is obviously a New York newspaper, Connecticut accounts for 7 percent of the *Times'* circulation. Indeed, the Sunday *Times* publishes a regional supplement for distribution in Connecticut only.

---

[4] I am indebted to Michael Kagay for pointing this out. With polls the press could explain voting patterns. Without polls, the press resorted to descriptive generalizations.

and the incentive to be clever as well as informative must be great for correspondents. Also, reporters who follow a candidate day after day, only to hear the same speeches again and again, fight monotony with cynicism and humor. Two of the more inventive stories (2/6/80, 2/3/80) are described below:

Video	*Audio*
Zoom in on pollster employee at bookshelves returning books.	Pollsters agree they all use pretty much the same techniques.
Close-up of telephone directories on shelf.	They all have a lot of telephone directories in the office.
Pan notebooks on shelf.	They do either Democrats or Republicans; not both.
Close-up of notebook with "Nixon, Second Wave, July 1972" on cover.	They have all won some.
Close-up of notebook with "Pres. Ford Codebook" on cover.	And lost some.
Wide-angle shot of entire floor to ceiling library.	Even very good advice in politics is sometimes not enough.
	—Bruce Morton, CBS News, Washington

Video	*Audio*
Wide-angle shot of setting sun over New Hampshire snow-capped pine trees.	With twenty-three bitter February days to go in New Hampshire,
Close-up of horse in a stall.	it is a horse race. Close. . . . George Bush must be regarded as the front-runner.
Horse turns head toward camera and shows head.	by a nose
Wide-angle shot of dark brown horse grazing in field.	over the dark horse, Ronald Reagan who was way out in front last fall.
Telescopic shot of very old car, parked on street with "Baker" painted on side.	The Baker campaign seems to have broken down.
Telephoto view of couple on ski lift, with background of greenish-brown trees and grass.	This has been the driest winter in New Hampshire history. On ski slopes
Zoom in on snow machine in foreground.	the only snow is as synthetic as a paid political commercial.
Pan countryside and zoom to several skiers racing down slope.	The Republican race according to today's poll now is between two men with five also-rans. . . .

Humor challenges the seriousness of news reports. This truism means that correspondents can and do undercut poll findings with an editorial judgment to make the report funny. Once again, we find that correspondents have many techniques to emphasize selected aspects of poll data.

SUMMARY AND CONCLUSIONS

Television news coverage of the presidential nominating process has changed in recent years to reflect the shift in decision making from party elites to the general public through primaries. Simultaneously, reporting has switched to emphasizing public opinion polls and primary election results. The net effect of these two events is that the media, as well as political parties, now interpret public opinion for the purpose of selecting government leaders.

Reporters make choices about poll reports. They can make predictions, exclude some candidate, compare various data, describe relative popularity, attribute the results to specific events, and stress or undermine the survey itself. All of these choices give reporters an active role in the nominating process. Candidates now know that journalists have an independent way of checking their claims of electability or their popularity with a particular group.

A democratic theorist might see the media's new power in primary elections as a new answer to the old issue of who should interpret public opinion. "Responsible party" advocates claim that this is the duty of properly-run political parties; through caucuses, conventions, and primaries, partisans are to express their desires by selecting leaders who are to vie to respond to majority opinion as expressed in the party program.

If news media could simply report poll results without any interpretation, they could be described as transmitters of the public will from the people through the parties and to party leaders. Even then, the timing and very existence of polls—as well as the selection of which polls to report—could affect election results. However, the role of journalists in reporting polls goes beyond transmitting knowledge. As was shown, correspondents cannot avoid making choices about how to present, explain, and frame poll results. These "mediated" polls are central to the horse-race coverage of presidential campaigns and consequently become fundamental elements in the development of candidate images and candidate credibility for the public.

This shift of power from parties to media through polls does give the public a new resource for understanding elections. It further empowers television news correspondents to interpret, analyze, and editorialize about the nominating process. Reporters can affect the outcome of a primary campaign. Neither politicians nor journalists may want the media to have that influence, but the drive to report and interpret poll data means that it cannot be avoided.

Of course, one danger is that the press is not necessarily accountable to its public. Primary elections offer some voter influence in the selection of party leaders and presumably in party policy. How do citizens exert the same influence over the media? Viewer ratings provide some control as do stockholder meetings in network corporations or government broadcast regulations for fairness, equal time, and reasonable treatment. But these are only token forms of participation. If media are taking over some of the role of political parties, perhaps the media, like the parties before them, will need to open their organization and selection processes to greater public scrutiny.

Another danger is that there are no checks on journalists' misinterpretation or distortion of poll results, except their own professional ethics and judgments. But Watergate taught the nation to stop relying solely on ethics in its political leaders; and Janet Cooke's fictitious *Washington Post* story about an 8-year-old drug addict warns us about relying solely on the ethics of journalists.

Public opinion polling by television and other media coincides with the rise of political participation in presidential nominations through primaries. Ironically, the loss in influence by party leaders happened at precisely the same time that the media gained new tools for interpreting campaigns. This capacity to interpret public opinion brought with it additional power and additional responsibilities to the polity.

REFERENCES

Adams, William C. 1978. Visual Analysis of Newscasts. In William C. Adams and Fay Schreibman, eds., *Television Network News: Issues in Content Research.* Washington, D.C.: George Washington University, 155–173.

Arterton, F. Christopher. 1978. The Media Politics of Presidential Campaigns. In James D. Barber, ed., *Race for the Presidency.* Englewood Cliffs, N.J.: Prentice-Hall, 26–54.

Broh, C. Anthony. 1979. "Polling, Prediction, and the Press." Working paper. Durham, N.C.: Institute of Policy Sciences and Public Affairs.

———· 1980a. Horserace Journalism. *Public Opinion Quarterly* 44 (Winter 1980): 514–529.

———· 1980b. The Media's Flawed Reporting of Poll Results. *New York Times* (October 30, 1980): A26.

———· 1981. The Parties Vs. TV. *New York Times* (March 3, 1981): A19.

———· 1983. Reasonable Access to the Airwaves. In John Havick, ed., *Communications Policy and the Political Process.* Westport, Conn.: Greenwood Press.

Cantril, Albert. 1980. *Polling on the Issues.* Cabin John, Md.: Seven Locks Press.

Chandler, Robert. 1972. *Public Opinion.* New York: R. R. Bowker Co.

Commission on Party Structure. 1970. *Mandate for Reform.* Washington, D.C.: Democratic National Committee.

Crouse, Timothy. 1972. *Boys on the Bus.* New York: Random House.

Davis, James W. 1976. *Presidential Primaries: Road to the White House.* New York: Thomas Y. Crowell.

Drew, Elizabeth. 1981. *Portrait of an Election.* New York: Simon & Schuster, Inc.

Frank, Robert S. 1973. *Message Dimensions of Television News.* Lexington, Mass.: Lexington Books.

Hofstetter, C. Richard. 1976. *Bias in the News.* Columbus, Oh.: Ohio State University.

Kessel, John H. 1968. *The Goldwater Coalition.* Indianapolis, Ind.: Bobbs-Merrill.

Kirkpatrick, Jeane. 1976. *The New Presidential Elite.* New York: Russell Sage.

Lichty, Lawrence W. and George A. Bailey. 1978. Reading the Wind. In William C. Adams and Fay Schreibman, eds., *Television Network News: Issues in Content Research.* Washington, D.C.: George Washington University.

Meadow, Robert G. 1973. Cross-media Comparison of Coverage of the 1972 Presidential Campaign. *Journalism Quarterly* 50 (Autumn 1973): 482–488.

Paletz, David and Martha Elson. 1976. Television Coverage of Presidential Conventions. *Political Science Quarterly* 91 (Spring 1976): 109–131.

Polsby, Nelson and Aaron Wildavsky. 1964. *Presidential Elections.* New York: Charles Scribner's Sons.

Robinson, Michael; Nancy Conover; and Margaret Sheehan. 1980. The Media at Mid-Year. *Public Opinion* 3 (June/July 1980): 41–45.

Robinson, Michael and Margaret Sheehan. 1983. *Over the Wire and On TV:* New York: Basic Books.

4

THE NEWS VERDICT AND PUBLIC OPINION DURING THE PRIMARIES

THOMAS R. MARSHALL

The networks and the major nationally oriented newspapers now play a critical role in presidential nominating politics.[1] The national media have this impact even though they seldom show overt biases toward prospective candidates and even though they usually downplay issues in favor of covering the "horserace" aspects of the nominations process (Patterson & McClure, 1976; Robinson, Conover, & Sheehan, 1980; Patterson, 1980a, 1980b).

This chapter argues that the networks and the print media influence the nomination race in two major ways. First, the media focus public attention on a handful of state primaries and caucuses. Second, when the networks, major newspapers, and news magazines report primary and caucus results, they also *evaluate* the vote totals and the delegate counts. In so doing, the media *label* the candidates, declaring some candidates to be "winners" and others "losers."

As the media make their judgments—termed here the "verdict"— donors, volunteers, public opinion polls, and even the candidates themselves usually follow the media's verdict. Within each party, a front-runner and likely nominee emerges early during the primary season. Most other candidates soon withdraw or else drop back to such a weak position

[1] The author would like to acknowledge Renaldo Stowers, Frankie Sims, and Elaine Clay for their assistance in preparing this article. Television video tapes were provided by the Vanderbilt Television News Archive with support from the Television and Politics Study Program at George Washington University. Data analysis was conducted at the academic computing center of the University of Texas at Arlington under a grant from the University's Organized Research Fund.

that they cannot compete effectively for long. As a result, the party nominees tend to emerge long before the national party conventions open in the late summer.

The new power of the media is, by and large, unplanned and unintended—a coincidental byproduct of efforts to reform the nominations process. Recent campaign fund raising and spending reforms, the growing number of presidential primaries and open caucuses, and low levels of involvement or knowledge of the candidates by American adults have all inadvertently increased the importance of the mass media in presidential nomination contests.

CRITICAL MEDIA DECISIONS

Picking key primaries and caucuses.   During the nominations race, the media focus public attention on a handful of presidential primaries and caucuses.[2] Robinson (1977, 1978) and others have documented the extensive coverage given the New Hampshire primary. New Hampshire and a handful of other states dominate the news during the primary season, while most state primaries and caucuses receive only scant coverage.

To assess network coverage in 1980, network newscast time devoted to reporting the results of each state's presidential primary, caucus, or convention was measured. Only regular early-evening newscast time allocated to reporting the primary or caucus results was tabulated. The 10 best-covered state contests for 1980 are listed in Table 4.1, by network, in descending order. Comparable data for the *New York Times* and the *Washington Post* are also presented.[3]

Data presented in Table 4.1 suggest that both the network newscasts and two major American newspapers focus attention on a similar group of state primaries and caucuses. In 1980 the New Hampshire, Pennsylvania, and Illinois presidential primaries led in the amount of network news time received. These three key states averaged 13 to 15 minutes of post-primary coverage on ABC, CBS, and NBC.

By contrast, most other state delegate-selection results merited little time or attention either by the three networks or by the *Times* or *Post*.

---

[2] Although this chapter focuses on the media's role during the primary period, some analysts trace the media's impact to the pre-primary season. They suggest that the media start "screening" contenders long before the earliest primaries and caucuses. (For a description of the "Great Mentioner" argument, see Keech & Matthews, 1977, pp. 12–14.)

[3] For ABC, CBS, and NBC, post-primary, post-caucus, or post-convention newscast time was measured, per state, in seconds. For the *Times* and the *Post,* front-page column inches devoted to reporting the outcome of each state contest were measured. Only post-primary, post-caucus, or post-convention coverage was included. For the two newspapers, the measurement included headlines, text, and pictures. For a description of the importance of the *Times* and the *Post* in American journalism, see Weiss (1974).

Table 4.1
The Ten Most-Covered 1980 Presidential Primary and Caucus Results
(see footnote 3)

Rank	ABC	CBS	NBC	New York Times	Washington Post
1	New Hampshire	Illinois	Illinois	New York	New Hampshire
2	Maine	{ New Hampshire	Wisconsin	Illinois	Pennsylvania
3	Massachusetts	Pennsylvania	Pennsylvania	{ New Hampshire	Illinois
4	Pennsylvania	Massachusetts	New Hampshire	Pennsylvania	South Carolina
5	Illinois	Wisconsin	Massachusetts	South Carolina	Maryland
6	New York	South Carolina	Iowa	Iowa	Maine
7	Wisconsin	Maine	Maine	{ Massachusetts	Ohio
8	Florida	Iowa	New York	Maine	{ New Jersey
9	South Carolina	Texas	Connecticut	Connecticut	Michigan
10	Texas	{ Florida New York	Texas	Michigan	{ Texas Massachusetts

CBS apparently gave no regular early-evening newscast time at all to the primary or caucus results in 10 states; ABC likewise ignored 8 states; NBC overlooked 13 states. In addition, CBS gave only 10 seconds or less of regular newscast time to reporting returns in another 16 states, ABC gave similarly short shrift to another 9 states, and NBC another 6 states. By comparison, both the *Post* and the *Times* allocated no front-page coverage to the primary or caucus results in 24 states. In short, about half the states got little or no attention for their 1980 presidential primary or caucus from each of these five major news sources.

All three networks and the two newspapers surveyed here showed a marked preference for the early contests. Eight of the 11 best-covered states on the CBS regular nightly newscasts held their delegate-selection contests in January, February, or March. On ABC and NBC, 7 of the 10 best-covered state results were also in the first three months of 1980. For the *New York Times* 8 of the 10 most-covered state contests, and for the *Washington Post* 5 of the 11 most-reported contests also fell in the same period. (Not above localism, however, the *Times* did rank the New York primary far higher than did the other news outlets just as the *Post* gave relatively more attention to the Maryland primary.)

Aside from preferring the early primaries and caucuses, the networks and major newspapers also concentrated on primary states rather than caucus-convention states, and on those contests in which one or more candidates might, in their view, be eliminated. They also tended to concentrate on early primaries in a handful of moderately and heavily populated states with the notable exceptions of New Hampshire and Maine.

Naming winners and losers.   In reporting primary or caucus returns, the media also evaluate how well each candidate fared. Most of the lengthier stories reported both the raw vote totals and the projected or actual delegate totals, and then evaluated the meaning of those totals. In most instances, ABC, CBS, NBC, and *Times*, and the *Post* all agreed on how well each candidate fared in each contest.

To measure agreement in picking primary or caucus winners and losers, each network broadcast or front-page newspaper story which reported state primary or caucus results was coded, per candidate, on a scale from + 2 (denoting the greatest success for a candidate), + 1, 0 (denoting neither failure nor success), − 1, or − 2 (the worst outcome for a candidate). This score produced a rough measurement of a candidate's media-judged success in each presidential primary, caucus, or convention, and can be referred to as a candidate's "relative success."

Just as the three networks and two newspapers measured here agreed which state primaries or caucuses were most newsworthy, so, too, did they usually agree on how well each candidate fared in each of the presidential primaries, caucuses, and conventions. In the Iowa caucuses, for example, ABC reported the GOP results as follows (1/22/80):

> Iowa has spoken. The first real test of the '80 campaign is over and the political landscape in this presidential election year has a noticeably different appearance tonight. Here are the latest figures:... In the Republican straw poll, 78 percent complete now, George Bush, with 33 percent, exceeded his hopes and finished well ahead of Ronald Reagan with 27 percent. Third place, but far back in the pack, goes to Senator Howard Baker, with 14 percent...

The ABC coverage was scored as a + 1 for George Bush. And on the same night NBC decribed the Iowa Republican contest this way:

> ... a day when the national political picture has been transformed. The greatest outpouring of voters in the history of the Iowa caucuses produced a landslide win for the president and turned the Republican presidential contest into a close race ...[A]mong the Republicans so far George Bush defeated Ronald Reagan in a straw poll 32 percent to 26 percent, with Howard Baker at 14 percent. Bad news for Ronald Reagan, who had been favored to win here, and something of a triumph for George Bush....

The NBC report was also scored as a + 1 for Bush. CBS, the *New York Times,* and the *Washington Post* also awarded Bush a + 1 appraisal for his first-place showing.

In most cases, the networks and the print media simply name the candidate with the most popular votes or convention delegates as the winner. By so doing, the media avoid controversy and charges of bias, as well as simplify their role in unscrambling the often-complex election returns. By this rule, even a narrow lead counts as a "win" for a candidate—as did, for example, Senator Kennedy's narrow margins in the Michigan and Pennsylvania Democratic primaries. Although a first-place finish usually qualifies as a win, the media may also rely on other rules to judge the magnitude of a primary win or loss, and to evaluate the showing of other candidates.

In addition to a vote plurality, at least five other standards are used to judge how well any candidate fared in a state presidential primary or caucus (Matthews, 1978, Marshall, 1981). First, a candidate who finishes much better than his pre-primary poll standings may be judged to have run well, even if that candidate did not actually place first in the contest. By this standard, John Anderson's second-place finish in the Massachusetts and Vermont GOP primaries was treated as an impressive showing, overshadowing George Bush's actual first-place finish in the Bay State and Ronald Reagan's lead in Vermont. Second, a candidate's performance may be compared to that same candidate's record in the state's primary or caucus in earlier years. Third, the media may evaluate a candidate's vote total or delegate count by comparing it to the amount of time spent, money invested, or pre-primary endorsements collected by a candidate. Fourth, the press usually also assumes that no candidate should lose in his home state or region. Finally, a loss by an incumbent president is always newsworthy—no matter how remote were the president's chances to carry a particular state.

Overall, the similarities in network and newspaper evaluations of candidate success or failure for 1980 were striking. The average intercorrelations between ABC, CBS, NBC, the *Times*, and the *Post* were .86 for George Bush, .80 for Edward Kennedy, .67 for Jimmy Carter, and .57 for Ronald Reagan (all Kendall's Tau). The networks and newspapers also usually agreed on the meaning of presidential primary or caucus returns for the shorter-lived candidacies of GOP contenders John Anderson, Howard Baker, John Connally, Philip Crane, and Robert Dole, and for Democrat Jerry Brown.[4]

The agreement in network and newspaper accounts of candidate success or failure has important implications for the nominations race. As Crouse (1973) and others (Patterson & McClure, 1976; Patterson, 1980a) have suggested, the American news media present a relatively homogenous picture of how the nominations race is progressing. No matter which network or major newspaper an American voter depends upon for news, that reader or viewer will likely receive a similar picture of how each candidate is faring in the nominations struggle.

The verdict. Because the networks and leading newspapers agree, by and large, both on the relative importance of each presidential primary or caucus and also on the relative success of each contender in each state contest, American viewers and readers receive a similar presentation of the nominations race. This account may be described as the media's "verdict." The verdict may be thought of as a combination of two terms: first, the amount of coverage which each state's primary, caucus, or convention receives; and second, the relative success of the candidate in the contest. Expressed as an equation:

$$\begin{array}{ccc} \text{Amount of coverage per} & \text{Relative success} & \\ \text{state primary, caucus} \quad \times & \text{of the candidate} & = \quad \text{The verdict} \\ \text{or convention} & & \end{array}$$

To compute the 1980 verdict for each candidate, the amount of post-primary or post-caucus coverage and the relative success of each candi-

---

[4] The average Kendall's Tau coefficient among the five news sources here was .58 for these six candidates. Because each of these candidates ran in only a few contests, they have been combined for measurement purposes.

date were first measured separately, then combined. The results produced a verdict for each candidate, per each network or newspaper, over the entire pre-convention season. While the verdict for each network or newspaper may be only a rough indicator, it does provide a (ratio-level) test of newscast or newspaper reporting of candidate success or failure. The score may be separately computed for any news source.

If a candidate fares poorly in a well-covered state primary (or caucus), then that candidate's verdict will be large and negative. If a state primary is well-covered and a candidate is judged to have run well, then the candidate's verdict will be large and positive. If a primary or caucus is not covered at all, then a candidate's verdict in that contest will be zero, no matter how the candidate fared.

In most cases, the verdict for each candidate (as scored by ABC, CBS, NBC, the *Times*, or the *Post*) was quite similar. The Reagan verdict for all three networks is shown in Figure 4.1.

As Figure 4.1 indicates, the three networks largely agreed on candidate Reagan's performance throughout the pre-convention season. Each agreed that Reagan fared poorly at the start of the contest but recovered during the early primaries and steadily improved his lead throughout the rest of the primary-caucus season. None of the networks or newspapers disagreed with that pattern.

The CBS verdicts for several major contenders in 1980 are indicated in Figure 4.2. Candidate verdicts by ABC, NBC, the *Times*, and the *Post* were all parallel to the CBS data.[5]

THE MEDIA IMPACT ON NOMINATING POLITICS

Through verdicts the media affect both public opinion and candidate decisions to drop out or to stay in the nominations race. In 1980, much as in 1976 and 1972, the national polls, volunteers, donors, primary voters and caucus-goers, and the candidates themselves all appear to have responded to the media verdicts. The media's impact is usually greatest during the early primary season, upon little-known candidates, and in multicandidate races. The media verdict has a lesser influence in a standoff between two well-known candidates or during the mid- and late-season primaries and caucuses.

---

[5] To test the similarity of candidate verdicts as judged by these five news sources, the verdicts were intercorrelated for five major candidates who ran in several state primaries or caucuses. For Carter, Kennedy, Reagan, Bush, and Anderson, the average intercorrelation of the candidate verdicts was .70 (Kendall's Tau).

Coding was carried out separately by two experienced coders. The average intercoder reliability for the verdict measurement was .77 (Kendall's Tau).

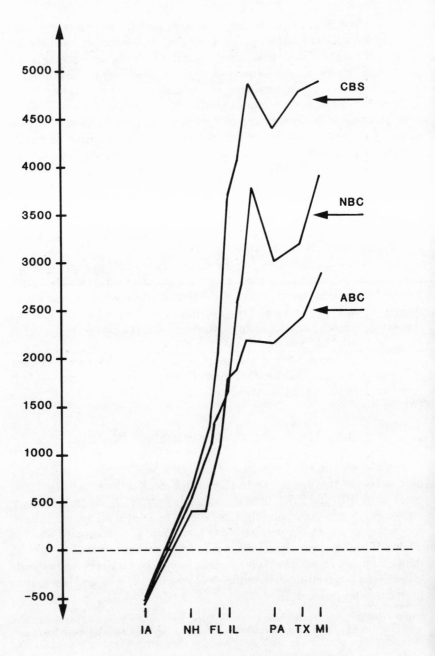

Figure 4.1: Network Verdicts for Reagan, 1980

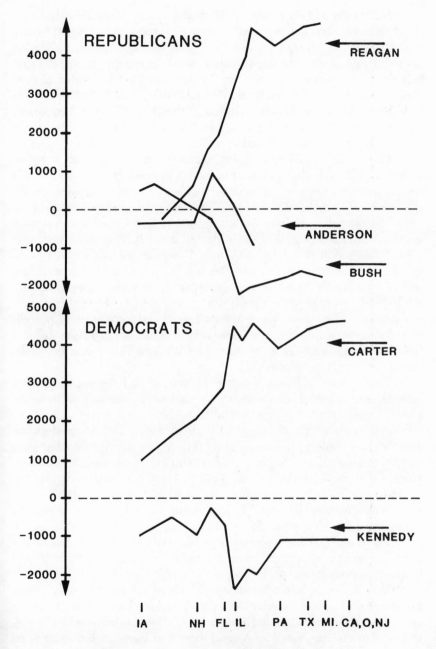

Figure 4.2: CBS Verdicts for Major Candidates, 1980

The verdict and the public. The media verdict often has a dramatic effect on public opinion, especially in crowded races and during the early contests (Marshall, 1981). In 1980, the polls followed the media verdict most dramatically in the Republican contest, especially during the first half dozen primaries and caucuses. In that race, the impact of George Bush's Iowa upset, followed by Ronald Reagan's surprisingly large win in New Hampshire, was clearly reflected in the polls. Figure 4.3 compares the CBS verdict for Bush and Reagan with the CBS-*New York Times* national poll preferences (among Republicans only).

The media verdict and public opinion polls moved closely together during the 1980 Republican race. For each of the major GOP contenders, a similar pattern emerged. All media-designated "losers" lost poll support, while all media-designated "winners" gained public opinion strength.

The candidacy of John Anderson, on the Republican side, provides another dramatic example of the impact of an early, favorable verdict on a candidate's poll standing. Although Anderson did not finish first in either Massachusetts or Vermont, he was judged to have run well and scored a favorable media verdict. Thereafter, he gained substantial national public opinion poll support. Among Repubicans nationally, Anderson rose from 1 percent before Massachusetts and Vermont to 7 percent after those two primaries. A few weeks later Anderson had risen still further—to 10 percent. (Data are from the CBS-*New York Times* telephone surveys among Republicans only.)

The patterns between the media's verdict and the public opinion polls are also reflected in statewide polls, campaign donations, volunteers, and endorsements for a presidential candidate. Candidates who win a favorable verdict typically surge in both statewide and national public opinion polls, collect more campaign funds (especially from small donors through mass mail campaigns), and find volunteers more easily obtained. Media legitimation is most crucial for little-known candidates early in the primary season (such as George Bush and John Anderson in 1980).

Why do the polls, donors, and volunteers all seem to follow the media's verdict? Why does the verdict have its greatest impact during the early races and for little-known hopefuls? The explanation lies in the limited interest and information which most potential voters have toward the nominations race.

Most American adults indicate relatively little interest in the nominations contest. In 1980, for example, only about one in five adult Americans voted in a primary or attended a caucus. Only 1 or 2 percent evidently volunteered to do some work for a candidate, and less than 1 percent of all American adults apparently have given money to any of the presidential contenders in recent years (Alexander, 1976, pp. 82, 248).

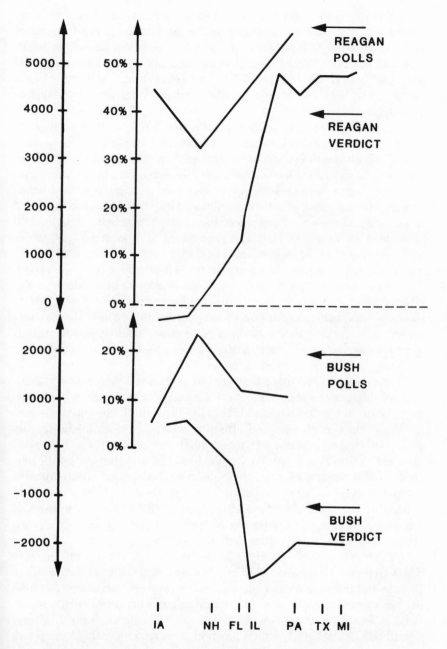

Figure 4.3: CBS Verdicts and CBS/*New York Times* Opinion Poll Standings for Bush and Reagan, 1980

Not only is there limited interest in the nominations race, but many Americans have difficulty recognizing the issue stands or even the names of the candidates. In late 1979, for example, only about half of the adults surveyed could recognize George Bush, and only a quarter recognized John Anderson (Gallup, 12/7–10/79). In recent campaigns, very few contenders have been recognized by nearly all potential primary voters or caucus-goers.

The issue stands of the candidates are rarely very clear to most Americans. Voters are seldom able to agree on the candidates' liberal-conservative positions or even to name correctly many of the candidates' issue positions. In the 1980 Democratic contest between Senator Kennedy and President Carter, for example, voters were unable to agree on the liberal-conservative positions of either candidate. Only half of all adults placed Kennedy left of center; a third placed the Massachusetts Senator to the right of center. For President Carter, disagreement also occurred. Just under half (46 percent) of the respondents put Carter right of center, while nearly that many (37 percent) placed him to the left of center (Gallup, 11/79).

While primary voters and caucus-goers may be more ideologically attuned than non-voters, their vote choices are not strongly related to ideology. Studies of presidential primary voting usually indicate that only a weak relationship exists between a voter's own ideology or issue stands and that voter's choice of candidates (Williams, Weber, Haaland, Mueller, & Craig, 1976; Orren, 1978; Gopoian, 1979).

Most Americans, then, have serious problems in agreeing on candidate ideologies or issue stands, or even in recognizing many of the candidates before the primaries begin. In part, these problems may be due to the slight amount of time and attention which the mass media usually devote to covering the issues (Graber, 1980; Patterson, 1980a; Robinson, Conover, & Sheehan, 1980; Weinraub, 1980). In part, the low public perceptions of candidate issues or ideologies may also be due to contemporary campaign styles which stress personalities or personal qualities instead of issues (Bicker, 1978; Arterton, 1978; Orren, 1978). And, low levels of ideological or issue perception and voting may be due to the public's own chronic low interest in politics (Milbrath & Goel, 1977).

In this climate of a poorly-informed public opinion, the public's tendency to follow the media's verdict is not very surprising. In most cases, a presidential primary winner receives much more extensive coverage than his less successful rivals, and at the same time is endowed with a superficially appealing image. An early primary or caucus victor is always described as a "winner," and his prospects are rated favorably by network newscasts and print journalists alike. Other candidates, by contrast, win little media attention, or else find that journalists focus primarily on their campaign woes.[6]

The verdict and the candidates. Just as the media verdict affects voters, donors, and volunteers, it hits the candidates too. Candidates appear to rely to some extent on the media's verdict in deciding whether to drop out or to remain in the race.

The candidates' reliance on a strong early showing and a favorable verdict is largely a result of recent rules changes, especially fund-raising regulations. Since the mid-1970s, would-be nominees have been sharply limited in the size of donations which they may accept (now $1,000 per individual donor) and in the total amount which they may spend if they accept federal matching funds. At the same time a would-be nominee must compete in more and more state primaries to win enough delegates to capture the party's nomination. Given these two constraints, candidates are confronted with a dilemma: a successful candidate must run in more and more state presidential primaries and open caucuses, but no candidate can expect to raise enough money to fund an adequate nationwide campaign. Instead, each contender must rely heavily on free media exposure, unpaid volunteers, and a steady stream of small donations (plus federal matching funds) to continue a nominations drive through the mid- and late-season state primaries, caucuses, and conventions. Given the new fund-raising rules and rising campaign expenses, it is unlikely that any but the best-organized and most popular of candidates could continue for more than a half dozen or so primaries on the strength of early campaign funds alone. Even well-known and popular contenders must rely on early successes to continue to run a full-scale national campaign.

For all these reasons, perceptions of a candidate's early performance and the early media verdict are critical. A strong showing in the early state contests brings favorable press attention, free exposure on the network newscasts and in the newspapers, and a winner's image. In turn, this may be expected to produce a strong gain in state and national polls, added volunteers and endorsements, and more small donations and the corresponding federal matching funds.

An early poor and negative media verdict, however, will cripple, if not destroy, a candidate. For little-known candidates, the effect of an early negative verdict is usually enough to force a hasty withdrawal from

---

[6] In 1980, just as in 1976 and 1972, candidates who were judged to have run poorly in the early contests found that the press soon focused on their campaign problems. After the 1980 Iowa caucuses, for example, network coverage of Senator Kennedy's campaign quickly focused on the Senator's financial and organizational problems. For other 1980 examples, see ABC reports on January 24, 25, and 29; CBS reports on January 24, and 29; and NBC reports on January 23, 24, 27, and 29.

the field. Even for the best known and organized aspirants, a poor early verdict may force that candidate to concentrate scarce resources on only a very few states, virtually conceding so many delegates that the nomination becomes, at best, a long shot.

⇒ To test how closely the verdict was related to candidate decisions to drop out or stay in the race during the 1980 primary season, the verdict for each major candidate was computed for every state primary or caucus. (See the previous discussion.) Each major candidate could have dropped out or stayed in the race after each primary or group of primaries.[7] Candidate decisions to remain in the race or to drop out could be predicted quite accurately on the basis of the media verdict. For all candidates, the network verdicts were a slightly more accurate predictor than the two newspapers. Using discriminant function analysis, 85 percent of all candidate decisions to stay in the race or to drop out could be predicted correctly from each candidate's verdict as judged by the CBS evening newscasts. ABC and NBC were also highly correlated with candidate decisions—accurately predicting 73 percent or 67 percent of candidate decisions to stay in the race or to drop out. The *New York Times* and the *Washington Post's* combined verdict also predicted 67 percent of the candidate decisions accurately. (See also Marshall, 1981, Appendix C.)

⇒ In sum, the media verdict affects public opinion polls, donors, volunteers, and the candidates themselves during the presidential nominations contest. The media's impact is usually greatest during the early presidential primaries and caucuses, and for initially little-known contenders in a crowded field. In the new nominations system few, if any, candidates can hope to compete effectively for the party's nod without posting an early, favorable media verdict.

⇒ The only candidates with some immunity to this constraint are extremely well-known public figures. In 1980, voters were acquainted with Jimmy Carter and Teddy Kennedy to the extent that the media dynamics operated differently. On the Democratic side, little relationship existed between the media verdict and national preference polls. President Carter's strong early verdict brought only a slight rise in his polls; Senator Kennedy's downs and ups in the media likewise brought little change in his overall poll standings (see Figure 4.4).

---

[7] Candidates included in this analysis were Jimmy Carter, Edward Kennedy, Ronald Reagan, George Bush, Howard Baker, Philip Crane, John Connally, Robert Dole, and John Anderson. For measurement purposes, some presidential primaries or caucuses were grouped together to correspond to the polling periods for the Gallup Poll (for the Democrats) or the CBS-*New York Times* Poll (for the Republicans). Discriminant function analysis was used to test the strength of these relationships (see Marshall, 1981).

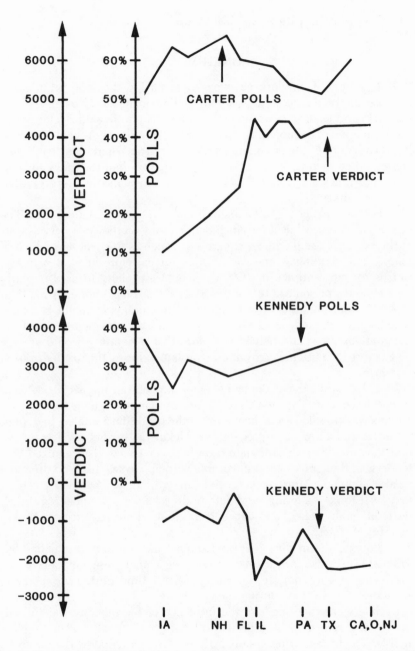

Figure 4.4: CBS Verdicts and Gallup Poll Standings for Carter and Kennedy, 1980

CONCLUSIONS

A review of network news coverage during the 1980 presidential nominations race suggests at least four major conclusions. First, the major networks and leading newspapers provided the public with a remarkably similar picture of the nominations race. Most Americans probably received similar versions of the nominations race no matter where they lived: they were exposed to horse-race coverage ignoring over half the states and emphasizing almost a dozen states, with fairly uniform media interpretations of the outcomes.

Second, the media had a major impact on the nominations race. The media's most critical decisions included focusing on the horse-race aspects of the race, choosing which primaries or caucuses to cover and which to ignore, and naming winners and losers for each presidential primary, caucus, or convention. In 1980, the media especially focused on early state contests, on some of the larger urban states, on primaries rather than caucuses, and on states where one or more candidates might be eliminated. Through these decisions, the media added to the momentum of the nominations race, and helped to ensure that a nominee would emerge long before the national convention—probably during the first half-dozen primaries.

Third, while the media had a major impact, this impact varied from contest to contest. The media's impact was greatest when the field of contenders was crowded and when many of the would-be nominees had slight resources and a low name recognition. The media verdict was less important, however, in two candidate races between two well-recognized contenders; in these races, an unfavorable verdict was less likely to drive the weaker contender from the field. Even here, though, a poor early verdict may well force the losing candidate to drop back to an underdog status, write off many states, and concentrate diminishing resources on only a handful of states.

Fourth, the media's increased impact has been an unintended by-product of recent reforms: party rules changes, increasing numbers of primaries and openly contested caucuses, and new fund-raising and spending regulations. Reformers during the late 1960s and the 1970s gave no sign that they wanted to increase the influence of the mass media; indeed, many party reformers have been critical of, if not openly hostile to, journalists. Yet, by requiring a more open contest, by reducing the resources which any candidate could muster, and by minimizing the power of party elites, recent reforms have inadvertently increased the importance of the media.

The media's influence in contemporary nominations races cannot be measured solely by a content analysis of network coverage. Rather, the impact of the networks and of print journalists must be viewed in the context of changing political realities. In decades past, would-be nominees won the party's nod by wooing the party elite—its governors, senators, big-city mayors, and state party officials. Under the new system, candidates win the presidential nomination by competing in a long series of openly-contested state primaries and caucuses. Candidates must demonstrate an appeal to a public who have, individually, little opportunity to meet the candidates and whose interest in or knowledge of politics is somewhat limited. Candidates no longer have the financial or organizational resources to contact directly all the eligible primary voters or caucusgoers. Instead, voters now rely on the mass media for most of their information about candidates and about how the race is progressing. In turn, candidates depend on the media for free publicity, exposure, and credibility and, to the degree the candidate's image is malleable, the media verdict becomes critical. As a result, the networks and the leading print media have gained a key role in the presidential nominations process.

REFERENCES

Alexander, Herbert. 1976. *Financing Politics: Money, Elections and Political Reform.* Washington, D.C.: Congressional Quarterly Press, 82, 248.

Arterton, F. Christopher. 1978. The Media Politics of Presidential Campaigns. In James D. Barber, ed., *Race for the Presidency.* Englewood Cliffs, N.J.: Prentice-Hall, 26–54.

Bicker, William. 1978. Network Television News and the 1976 Presidential Primaries: A Look from the Network's Side of the Camera. In James D. Barber, ed., *Race for the Presidency.* Englewood Cliffs, N.J.: Prentice-Hall, 79–110.

Crouse, Timothy. 1973. *The Boys on the Bus.* New York: Random House.

Diamond, Edwin. 1976. The New Campaign Journalism. *Columbia Journalism Review* 14 (March/April 1976): 11.

Gallup Opinion Index. 1979. Report No. 172 (November): 3–6.

———. 1979. Report No. 173 (December): 11

Gopoian, David. 1979. Issue voting in the 1976 Presidential Primaries: A Comparative State Analysis. Paper presented at the Southern Political Science Association, Gatlinburg, Tenn.

Graber, Doris. 1980. *Mass Media and American Politics.* Washington, D.C.: Congressional Quarterly Press.

Keech, William and Donald Matthews. 1977. *The Party's Choice.* Washington, D.C.: Brookings Institution.

Marshall, Thomas R. 1981. *Presidential Nominations in a Reform Age.* New York: Praeger Publishers.

Matthews, Donald. 1978. "Winnowing": The News Media and the 1976 Presidential Nomination. In James D. Barber, ed., *Race for the Presidency.* Englewood Cliffs, N.J.: Prentice-Hall: 55–78.

Milbrath, Lester and M. L. Goel. 1977. *Political Participation.* Chicago, Ill: Rand McNally.

Moore, David. 1981. The Manchester Union Leader and the New Hampshire Presidential Primary. Paper presented at the Southwestern Social Science Association, Dallas, March 24–27.

Orren, Gary. 1978. Candidate Style and Voter Alignments in 1976. In Seymour Martin Lipset, ed., *Emerging Coalitions in American Politics.* San Francisco, Cal.: Institute for Contemporary Studies.

Patterson, Thomas. 1980a. *The Mass Media Election.* New York: Praeger Publishers.

———. 1980b. The Miscast Institution: The Press in Presidential Politics. *Public Opinion* 3 (June/July 1980): 46–51.

Patterson, Thomas and Robert McClure. 1976. *The Unseeing Eye.* New York: G. P. Putnam's Sons.

Robinson, Michael. 1977. The TV Primaries. *The Wilson Quarterly* 1 (Spring 1977): 80–83.

————. 1978. TV's Newest Program: The "Presidential Nominations Game." *Public Opinion* 1 (May/June 1978): 41–46.

Robinson, Michael; Nancy Conover; and Margaret Sheehan. 1980. The Media at Mid-Year: A Bad Year for McLuhanities. *Public Opinion* 3 (June/July 1980): 41–45.

Weinraub, Bernard. 1980. Students of Campaign News Find Hard Issues Neglected. *New York Times* (April 30, 1980): A26.

Weiss, Carol. 1974. What America's Leaders Read. *Public Opinion Quarterly* 38 (Spring 1974): 1–22.

Williams, Daniel; Stephen Weber; Gordon Haaland; Ronald Mueller; and Robert Craig. 1976. Voter Decision-Making in a Primary Election: An Evaluation of Three Models of Choice. *American Journal of Political Science* 20 (February 1976): 37–49.

Witcover, Jules. 1972. William Loeb and The New Hampshire Primary: A Question of Ethics. *Columbia Journalism Review* 11 (May/June 1972): 14–27.

5

THE RITUAL OF CONVENTION COVERAGE IN 1980

JOE FOOTE
TONY RIMMER

Since 1952, when the networks began full-scale coverage of the Democratic and Republican National Conventions, these quadrennial political meetings have become synonymous with television campaign coverage.[1] Although Nielsen ratings showed that in 1980 less than half of all those watching television tuned to the Republican National Convention and just slightly more than half watched the Democratic Convention, network commitments to coverage actually increased that year (Viewers, 1980). In 1980, for the first time in 12 years, all three networks devoted almost continuous prime-time coverage to the two conventions, using more than 2,000 employees, and spending an estimated $40 million—twice the amount spent 20 years earlier (Hickey, 1980a).

Against this rising allocation of resources runs a steady decline in the importance of party conventions to the electoral system. With presidential nominees being chosen largely through a series of primaries and pre-convention caucuses held early in the political year, the conventions have almost become anachronisms. But, the networks' interests in conventions have not yet diminished.

Organizationally, political conventions fit the mold of a commissioned event, whereby television resources are committed long before the convention's news value can be ascertained (Epstein, 1973). Once the conventions are included in the network budgets, they are imbued with a video life and momentum all of their own. By the time the convention

[1] The authors wish to thank the University of Oklahoma and the University of Texas at Austin for funding and facilities assistance.

draws near, a dazzling electronic support system is already in place. Thus, to a significant extent, patterns of coverage are already dictated. While this infrastructure is designed to support the coverage of a newsworthy event, the initial allocation of network resources helps guarantee its "newsworthiness" and high visibility. What sort of coverage results?

Paletz and Elson (1976) found the networks drifting further away from coverage of official proceedings and closer to their own interpretations of convention events. They noted that more innovative, fast-paced coverage required greater emphasis on the functions of anchormen "to link, synthesize, explain, and analyze convention activities and events." Womack and Hoar (1981) found that the attention given leading candidates was disproportionate to the delegate strength of those candidates when they entered the convention, suggesting that factors other than delegate strength were important determinants of interview attention. Fant (1980) concluded that a reciprocal relationship between the major parties and the networks has altered the structure and function of the conventions, and that network rivalry is a major factor behind convention coverage.

When ambitious network commitments are directed toward a lackluster convention, the resulting news value can, of course, be exaggerated. Such appeared to have been the case in 1980 when network executives and correspondents freely admitted the presence of a newsworthiness gap. Among the most outspoken at the Republican Convention was CBS News President William Leonard:

> There's nothing here so newsworthy that it couldn't be televised in a single day—perhaps in a single hour—rather than taking up four nights of prime time. We've built this elephant gun and we have aimed it squarely at a gnat (Hickey, 1980b).

As opinion grew that the networks had overcovered the 1980 conventions, CBS President Thomas Wyman later announced that his network planned to abandon gavel-to-gavel coverage of the 1984 conventions in favor of summaries and highlights. In explaining his decision, Wyman (1981) said:

> Unfortunately, over the years the conventions have become far less significant political events and we must ask ourselves whether the public is well served by the availability of long hours when the political process is embarrassed by triviality. The viewers say no. They are watching other programs. We have been responsible for handling an important step in the political process, and we have done it badly when we were on the air with low-content broadcasts. All of us have witnessed the embarrassment of anchormen struggling in a desperate effort to create broadcasts out of non-events.

Wyman's statement marks one of the rare occasions when network executives have confessed the fallibility of their independent news judgment. Historically, the networks have denied any kind of organizational bias and have contended that they simply hold a mirror to reality and objectively reflect that image to the viewing public (Epstein, 1973). In the case of convention coverage, however, it would seem that the impact of resources and organizational norms have clearly had an effect upon the news product that even network executives will acknowledge—especially when their convention ratings are down.

While grumblings about the resources dedicated to 1980 convention programming were widespread, some network officials viewed the coverage as a huge public service announcement. NBC News President William Small defended the extensive convention coverage as a means of helping a citizen prepare for "the most important thing he can do—vote properly." He said, "Those who watched the conventions learned a lot about where Democrats stand and where they differ from Republicans" (Playing, 1980). Walter Cronkite of CBS called the conventions an important "civics lesson," while NBC producer Gordon Manning cited the entertainment value: "Americans love a parade, and this is a carnival" (Merry, 1980).

Another factor in convention coverage is the role of network competition in what has been called the "Olympics of television journalism."[2] NBC producer Lester Crystal said, "We feel each other's presence. It's one of the few times that we go head-to-head on the same story" (Hickey, 1980a). While the incentive for competition among the networks appears great, the opportunities for clear-cut victories are not. After observing the convention coverage process, journalist Daniel Henninger (1980) wrote:

> The three networks don't have too many ways they can compete at these conventions; to the average viewer one network's coverage looks pretty much like another's. What they can do is report breaking news before the competition gets it. This is basically the way newspapers compete with each other, but papers measure their victories with each 24-hour edition. On television, such victories are measured in seconds and minutes, and the TV floor reporters are told instantly if a competing network has pushed a breaking story ahead even an inch. It's then their job to leapfrog the competition and fast.

---

[2] There is also testing and competition among the reporters as well as among the networks. Convention observers have speculated that the conventions serve as a rite of passage for younger journalists and a reunion for the veterans. Frequently, young talent has been tested in the competitive convention atmosphere as a prelude to their advancing to high visibility positions. For example, Chris Wallace, a floor correspondent for NBC, was credited with being the first reporter to break the story that George Bush was Ronald Reagan's vice-presidential nominee. Wallace later became a White House correspondent. Being selected or not selected as a floor reporter or anchor can also be a test of "first-string" status for veteran correspondents. Walter Cronkite's career was thought to be seriously jeopardized when he was replaced as an anchor during one of the 1964 conventions. In 1980, Dan Rather, who had just been designated as Cronkite's successor in the anchor desk on the *CBS Evening News*, was put on camera with interviews or commentary from the floor more than twice as often as any other CBS reporter.

This chapter examines the networks' portrayals of the 1980 party conventions that emerge from this complex mix of organizational constraints and commitments, public service goals, and network rivalry. The premise underlying this study is that a gap between the newsworthiness of the conventions and the network resources allocated to covering them has developed which influences coverage through organizationally based constraints. Specifically addressed were the following research questions:

1. To what extent does network-generated convention coverage overshadow coverage of official proceedings?
2. Does the coverage of official proceedings, floor interviews and reports, and anchor booth analysis vary greatly from network to network and convention to convention?
3. What kinds of story lines and coverage rhythms are observable, and how do they appear to influence coverage?

METHODOLOGY

One night of prime-time coverage for the Democratic and Republican National Conventions on ABC, CBS, and NBC was taped. Each evening encompassed approximately 3½ hours of programming per network (except for CBS's three hours of coverage of the second Democratic session). Included in each of the ABC tapes from both conventions was an hour-long special edition of the news magazine *20/20* which usually did not relate directly to the conventions and was not coded.

Coverage of the second convention sessions was chosen for analysis because the choice of nominees was still unresolved and time would not be given to the actual presidential nominations or to acceptance speeches. The second-session convention broadcasts have generally been limited to debate on the party platform and party loyalists speaking to the convention. Given the limited content of second session broadcasts, they represent especially appropriate cases for examining convention coverage in the absence of an obvious news peg.

Three main categories of content, similar to those used by Paletz and Elson (1976), were coded for analysis: (1) official proceedings; (2) anchor analysis; and (3) correspondent reports and interviews. Segments were delineated as essentially uninterrupted appearances by individual subjects (e.g., correspondent report, correspondent interview, anchor interview, anchor segue, anchor analysis, convention speech). During official proceedings, crowd reaction shots and brief demonstrations were included in the segment of the podium speaker.

Segments were coded according to the video content. Voice-over commentary by the network anchor was coded as official proceedings when the cameras remained focused on the convention floor. Each entry also recorded the network identification, length of segment, and identity of participants. For each interviewee, additional information was recorded regarding political affiliation, convention role, minority status, issue orientation, and story-line relevance.

OFFICIAL PROCEEDINGS

Paletz and Elson's (1976) study of NBC's coverage of the 1972 Democratic National Convention reported a shift away from official proceedings and toward network-originated interviews and analysis. This approach, Paletz and Elson contended, denied viewers a comprehensive, accurate view of the convention proceedings in their entirety. The networks maintained, however, that their mission was to "report" a convention, rather than "carry" it, and to keep the program visually interesting.

Table 5.1 compares the Paletz and Elson data from 1972 to our 1980 findings. Considering the wide differences in news content between the 1972 Democratic and 1980 conventions, the data are strikingly similar— implying the presence of a framework for coverage which remained relatively static despite changes in political news. Coverage consistently showed official proceedings about half of the time, and devoted a third of air time to correspondent reports, with the balance going to anchor analysis.

This similarity is further corroborated by Table 5.2, which shows no major differences in types of coverage among the networks. While ABC devoted less time overall to convention broadcasts, ABC's percentages of time were nearly equivalent to CBS and NBC, the networks with continuous convention coverage. (Out of the nearly 48,000 seconds of coded coverage, there was only 84 seconds difference between the amount of time CBS and NBC gave to coverage of official proceedings.)

Table 5.3 further indicates that these basic patterns were reflected in coverage of both the Republican and the Democratic conventions. Coverage of the second sessions broke down into nearly identical approaches, with direct coverage of the floor and podium of the Democrats in New York City only three percentage points greater than that given the Republicans in Detroit.

With only half of convention coverage focusing on official proceedings, network producers have become selective in their use of podium-based action. Climactic moments such as presidential and vice-presidential nominations, acceptance speeches, and floor fights over rules, credentials,

Table 5.1
Comparison of Coverage of 1972 and 1980 Conventions

	1972 Democratic Convention (NBC)*	1980 Second Session Demo. and Rep. Conventions (ABC, CBS, NBC)
Official Proceedings	47%	52%
Correspondent Reports/Interviews	34	32
Anchor Analysis	19	16
	100%	100%

	Second Session Democratic Convention (NBC only)	
	1972*	1980
Official Proceedings	44%	52%
Correspondent Reports/Interviews	34	27
Anchor Analysis	22	21
	100%	100%

* 1972 Source: Paletz and Elson (1976).

Table 5.2
Comparison of 1980 Second Session Coverage by Network

	ABC		CBS		NBC		Total	
	Seconds	Percent	Seconds	Percent	Seconds	Percent	Seconds	Percent
Official Proceedings	5981	49%	9286	55%	9370	50%	24637	52%
Correspondent Reports/Interviews	4159	34	5186	30	6090	33	15435	32
Anchor Analysis	2014	17	2525	15	3107	17	7646	16
Total	12154	100%	16997	100%	18567	100%	47718	100%

Table 5.3
Comparison of 1980 Second Session Coverage by Party

	Republican		Democrat		Total	
	Seconds	Percent	Seconds	Percent	Seconds	Percent
Official Proceedings	12706	50%	11931	53%	24637	52%
Correspondent Reports/Interviews	8210	33	7225	32	15435	32
Anchor Analysis	4400	17	3246	15	7646	16
Total	25316	100%	22402	100%	47718	100%

or platforms have generally dominated such coverage. Likewise, convention organizers have become more intent on scheduling events in prime time that promote party unity and downplay controversy. The parties have also shortened speeches and streamlined procedures in an effort to lure the cameras toward the official proceedings of the conventions (Fant, 1980).

During second sessions, which historically have not been as newsworthy as the third and fourth, both producers and convention organizers have been challenged to make the coverage interesting. At the 1980 Republican convention, for example, delegates routinely ratified the platform before prime-time coverage began, filling the convention program with a cavalcade of Republican speakers methodically extolling the virtues of their party. Aside from speculation over the vice-presidential nominee, only the last minute inclusion to the program of a speech by NAACP leader Benjamin Hooks concerning the status of blacks in America and in the Republican Party provided a solid news angle.

At the Democratic Convention's second session, on the other hand, a lively platform fight over the jobs plank was climaxed by Senator Edward Kennedy's speech to the convention. The early part of the evening had a strong air of drama. The emotion of the Kennedy supporters provided a good backdrop for coverage of the Kennedy speech and subsequent platform votes.

Despite the apparent difference in newsworthiness between the second sessions of the two conventions, the amount of continuous coverage which CBS and NBC spent on official proceedings was very similar (Table 5.4). Coverage of speeches at both conventions fit into the 6- and 8-minute range including beginning and ending applause. Speeches that exceeded that range were likely to be either joined in progress or terminated before their conclusion.

By inserting 20/20 broadcasts periodically during the convention, ABC producers retained some flexibility and diversity in their evening programming. The decision on where to include the hour-long program, however, had to be made in advance, so that the spontaneity of the broadcast was constrained. By inserting 20/20 at the beginning of the Republican second session, ABC missed all but the last 6 minutes of Benjamin Hooks' unscheduled speech; CBS broadcast the entire 13 minutes.

While Hooks' speech at the GOP Convention seemed to catch producers by surprise, ABC was able to split 20/20 into two parts in order to carry the dramatic speech by Senator Edward Kennedy during the second session of the Democratic Convention. This maneuver allowed for coverage of the speech itself, but caused ABC to miss much of the emotional build-up to the Kennedy speech. CBS and NBC viewers received a 30-minute preview of the controversy surrounding the economic jobs plank to

Table 5.4
Coverage of Official Proceedings in 1980 Second Sessions, by Party and by Network

	Republican				Democrat			
	Seconds of Proceedings	Percent of Total Coverage	Number of Segments	Average Length	Seconds of Proceedings	Percent of Total Coverage	Number of Segments	Average Length
ABC	3636	61%	7	8'30"	2345	39%	5	7'45"
CBS	4663	50	11	7'0"	4623	50	12	6'25"
NBC	4407	47	9	8'5"	4963	53	11	7'30"
Total	12,706	52%	27	7'50"	11,931	48%	28	7"10"

the Democratic platform and the role Senator Kennedy played in this fight. They saw Andrew Young pleading for the President's position, interviews with a number of delegates on both sides of the issue, and the intense emotion of the Kennedy delegates contrasted with the less enthusiastic response of the Carter delegates. The spirited introduction of Senator Kennedy and the exuberant demonstration that followed eluded ABC viewers, who went directly from *20/20* to the podium as the Senator began his speech, missing much of the mood of the occasion.

Overall, ABC viewers were exposed to more than one third fewer podium speakers during the second sessions and more truncated versions of other speeches. The coverage differences were far more pronounced during the early parts of the broadcasts when the *20/20* interruptions occurred. Later in the evening, ABC's coverage fell in line with its competitors. While offering less coverage, ABC increased its ratings during the excursions away from the convention hall. During both of the second-session broadcasts, ABC's audience surged when it shifted to *20/20* programming.

Our analysis of TV audience trends shows that during both conventions *20/20* was the highest rated program segment. In the case of the Republican Convention, the advantage of screening *20/20* was considerable. Between 8:30 and 9:00 p.m. (EDT), ABC led all the networks with a 21 audience share—seven percentage points over CBS and eight percentage points over NBC.

The *20/20* advantage was not as large during the Democratic Convention. ABC's first segment of *20/20*, while giving the network a ratings advantage early in the evening, did not position ABC well for the Kennedy speech. With their closer attention to the convention early in the evening, CBS and NBC were able to exploit anticipation of Senator Kennedy's scheduled appearance. The short-term ratings gain by inserting "magazine" programming into convention coverage did not guarantee a continued large audience for ABC later in the evening.

At least since convention organizers began to schedule "spontaneous" demonstrations, the networks have been wary of being used by partisan interests. The networks have become particularly skeptical of using material that is pre-packaged by the parties and intended solely for self-promotion before the television audience. Still, the networks have continued to broadcast at least parts of films produced by the parties. At the 1980 Democratic Convention, NBC carried more than 10 minutes of a film eulogizing former Vice President Hubert Humphrey while CBS ran 4½ minutes of it. ABC produced its own 4-minute profile of Humphrey.

By dimming the lights in the convention halls for films, convention organizers can make it difficult for the networks to conduct floor interviews. In the case of the Humphrey film, however, ABC filled most of the blackout time with the second half of *20/20* while CBS shifted to its studio for reminiscences of Hubert Humphrey by its three guest commentators. The Humphrey film was the major place in which CBS and NBC differed in their coverage of official proceedings. Otherwise, both networks carried exactly the same speakers, and showed them for about the same amounts of time.

NETWORK-GENERATED COVERAGE

As the news value of the conventions has decreased, the networks have intensified their efforts to fill the void with their own brand of coverage through anchor and correspondent initiatives which now account for half of network convention air time. Aiding the networks in their efforts is a sophisticated communications system which gives television immediate access to almost any convention location:

> The nerve centers. . . are four control rooms. . . Central, Remote, Perimiter and Auxiliary. . . 52 television screens lining the walls. . . minicam crews. . . all connected to the various control rooms by miles of cable and by microwave relay. . . intercom systems, radio communications with base stations and walkie-talkies. . . about 750 different telephone instruments and close to 500 different centrex lines (Henninger, 1980).

Paletz and Elson (1976) found that more than 83 percent of the delegates interviewed said the convention they attended was more orderly than conventions they had seen on television. The researchers concluded that production norms and techniques gave the appearance of conflict and disorder. The networks acknowledge a burden they place on themselves to keep coverage lively and entertaining, especially when the news value is lacking.

During the 1980 convention, ABC was said to have called up a director from its *Monday Night Football* broadcast to energize the technical capabilities of coverage. After the first night of Democratic coverage, Ernest Leiser, CBS's Vice President for Special Events and Political Coverage, lamented that, "It will tax our ingenuity to keep the next three nights interesting" (Playing, 1980). As the networks have relied increasingly on anchor analysis, correspondent interviews and reports, pre-packaged taped segments, and guest commentators to round out their convention coverage, each has strived to package a unique blend of these ingredients that will satisfy the viewers' tastes.

ANCHOR ANALYSIS

Historically, network convention coverage has been structured around an anchorman who serves as a focal point for coverage. Broadcasters like

Walter Cronkite and David Brinkley have been relied on to provide a high visibility focus to coverage and enhance the credibility of the broadcasts. Endowed with celebrity status, these veteran anchors can sometimes overshadow events they are employed to cover. This star phenomenon is encouraged by a flurry of personality-based promotional announcements designed to draw viewers to their anchor and correspondent team. These promotional vignettes focus on the network personnel rather than on conventions as news. And the key interpreters of events of the day are the American leaders at the three networks, not the American leaders of the two political parties.

During the final session of the 1980 Democratic Convention, the celebration of Walter Cronkite's retirement became a media event when NBC focused its cameras on the CBS anchor booth for a tribute, momentarily overshadowing coverage of the convention. This was not too surprising as Cronkite probably had a stronger public identity than most of the political figures who paraded before television screens during the week. Even the physical presence of the anchors is impressive during a convention. The four visually dominating features of the hall are the podium and the three brightly lit booths where anchors assume a commanding position atop their electronic perches.

Producers are adept at wrapping coverage around anchors in a way that brings out the network's organizational strengths. CBS, for example, placed Walter Cronkite clearly in the spotlight for his final convention appearance in 1980. NBC emphasized the relationship between its two veteran anchors, David Brinkley and John Chancellor, allowing them to lapse frequently into extended, casual colloquies. ABC, meanwhile, with a slightly less experienced anchor team of Frank Reynolds and Ted Koppel, used its anchors in a somewhat more abbreviated form to link disparate elements of coverage together.

These observations about the relative emphasis of the networks on anchormen were supported by the data. The average anchor segment on ABC was 35 seconds, compared to 49 and 46 seconds, respectively, on CBS and NBC. However, the use of anchors was very similar at each convention. Most of the anchor segments were bridges to commercials or to other types of coverage.

On several occasions all three networks used anchor interludes to offer commentary and put events in perspective. NBC's seasoned anchor team of Brinkley and Chancellor indulged themselves in lengthy commentaries far more than their competition. At the second sessions of both conventions, ABC and CBS anchors each ventured past the 2-minute mark only once, but NBC's pair did so nine times. For example, Chancellor and Brinkley speculated for over three minutes about whether Senator Kennedy might have been able to win the nomination after his powerful speech had the majority of the delegates not been bound by party rules to vote for President Carter.

In addition to their functions as linkers and synthesizers, anchors often set the tone for convention coverage and the agenda. At the 1980 conventions, anchors voiced early in the evening the story lines their networks followed. Walter Cronkite began the second session of the Republican Convention by saying, "The only suspense left in this convention is who Ronald Reagan will pick as a running mate." Accordingly, CBS devoted more than twice as much air time to this subject during the first hour than the other two networks.

At the Democratic second session, Frank Reynolds of ABC began his broadcast by saying, "If you think all the excitement went out of this convention last night with the adoption of the binding delegate rule, you were probably right." Viewers appeared to agree with this assessment as ABC ratings began a steady decline throughout the evening. Reynolds, however, seemed to try to resurrect interest in the convention throughout the rest of the evening: "A quick swing around the floor shows that all is not peace and harmony." "There is still a great deal of dissension." "There is still no peace." "This looks like a bossed convention."

In concert with Frank Reynolds' "disunity" theme, ABC correspondents busily hustled eight Carter defectors on the jobs plank to the microphones, reinforcing the idea of a bitter split in the party. Meanwhile, NBC conducted only two interviews with Carter defectors and CBS none. The ABC disunity theme was further advanced by interviewing five of the eight Carter defectors within a 10-minute period.

CORRESPONDENT INTERVIEWS AND REPORTS

Since 1952, when portable cameras were introduced to political conventions, network correspondents have possessed the mobility to monitor reaction to podium events instantly, making the coverage of conventions two-dimensional. The networks' technological ability to cover convention events has almost outpaced their ability to assimilate information.

During the 1980 conventions, network officials were quoted as being concerned about the lack of time available to apply rigorous journalistic screening to the numerous reports coming into the control rooms. NBC Producer Lester Crystal acknowledged that it was easy to "get swept up into something in the heat of the moment." "We don't have time to go over the interviews with a blue pencil," Crystal conceded (Merry, 1980).

The networks place a premium on competition and on breaking a story. However, at best, one network might get a small jump on a story that everyone would know anyway within an hour. With so many correspondents running after so few stories, it is easy to see how the drive of rivalry aided by technology can leave correspondents relentlessly chasing (and spreading) rumors. The third session of the Republican Convention provided a good case study in competitive pressures among the networks.

Conjectures over Ronald Reagan's choice for his vice presidential running mate became so chaotic that NBC anchorman John Chancellor called it "politics out of control in the electionic age." Chancellor said that rumors were flying "with the speed of light" and that "in general, everyone got a little off the mark." "It was not," he concluded, "the finest hour for journalism" (Schardt, 1980).

The drama began early Wednesday evening when CBS's Dan Rather suggested that Gerald Ford would be Ronald Reagan's choice as the vice-presidential nominee, a notion advanced by Ford himself in network interviews. After heightened speculation, CBS's Walter Cronkite announced at 10:10 p.m.:

> CBS News has learned that there is a definite plan for Ronald Reagan and the former President of the United States, Gerald Ford, who will be selected as his running mate, an unparalleled, unprecedented situation in American politics...to appear together in this platform for Ronald Reagan to announce that Ford will run with him (Schardt, 1980).

It was nearly two hours later that NBC correspondent Chris Wallace learned from a man running down one of the convention aisles that the vice-presidential nominee was actually George Bush. CBS announced the news less than a minute later; ABC followed 5 minutes later.

After NBC's "triumph," Chris Wallace was singled out for high praise as a result of his minute lead over the competition. One publication named him the "hero" of the Detroit coverage, and Wallace called the experience "one of the most remarkable moments of my life" (Smith, 1980). NBC purchased full-page ads in five newspapers proclaiming that "while some reporters were jumping to conclusions, NBC hung in there with extraordinary calm." In an even more revealing show of competitive one-upmanship, CBS ran full-page advertisements in the *New York Times* and the *Washington Post* claiming that CBS was "on top of the story...just where you'd expect us to be."

In post-convention interviews, CBS's Dan Rather, who promoted the Ford story much of the evening, was strongly defensive of CBS. Rather insisted that CBS "had more of the story and had more of it right than anyone else" and that NBC "didn't have a clue" as to what was happening earlier in the evening (Beating, 1980). Asked if he wished he had been more cautious, Rather replied: "There have been times in the past when I've felt that way—but not this time. If I hadn't had this story and my competition had had it, I would have wept" (Anderson, 1980).

As this episode at the Republican National Convention indicates, competitive pressure is a key organizational factor in convention coverage. Three separate armies of TV journalists and their machines go against each other in structured combat; competitive edge is rewarded and every lapse in vigilance is punished. Intramural competitiveness can emerge as the primary motivation, rather than an unavoidable by-product in the treatment of a particular story. Conventions have become arenas for video combat between network gladiators.

The excitement associated with trying to "get the jump" on the network competition is further enhanced by the use of quick-paced production techniques. Paletz and Elson (1976) found that production norms and techniques gave the appearance of conflict and disorder in 1972 conventions. In 1980, such techniques were common. NBC, in particular, used the technique of clustering several brief, quick floor reports without an intervening anchor segue. After NAACP Executive Director Benjamin Hooks' speech to the Republican Convention, for example, viewers saw a rapid-fire succession of a black Iowa delegate, a black Connecticut delegate, Senator Strom Thurmond of South Carolina, and a white Mississippi delegate commenting on Hooks' speech. NBC used this type of interview clustering 12 times during second-session coverage, 6 times at each convention.

The NBC technique seemed to have its greatest utility during the second session of the Democratic Convention after Senator Kennedy's emotional speech. NBC presented two four-report clusters immediately following the speech to gauge reaction and show what looked to be the beginning of a Kennedy surge. Reports in the first cluster averaged only 42 seconds, including a 22-second interview with Detroit Mayor Coleman Young. Interviews in the second cluster averaged 74 seconds. Many times when the interview cluster technique was used, correspondents seemed pressured to terminate the interview and hand coverage to another correspondent even when there did not appear to be a compelling reason, other than fast pacing, for doing so.

The NBC penchant for round-robin correspondent reports appeared with such regularity at both conventions that it must be considered a special organizational practice. Womack and Hoar (1981) found in their study of the 1972 Democratic Convention that NBC broadcast 78 percent of all interviews. At the 1980 second sessions, NBC interviewed as many participants as the other two networks combined. Thus, it would appear that NBC has established a pattern of relying heavily on floor reporter interviews to amplify its convention coverage and has chosen to enhance the visual effect of those interviews and the pacing of coverage by clustering them together.

Table 5.5 shows network interviews at both conventions to have run at a lively pace. ABC and NBC interviews averaged less than 1½ minutes while CBS's carried slightly past the two-minute mark overall. Even though conventions represent one of the few times when networks have control of an entire evening of prime time, their time restrictions for interviews appeared to be as strict as those on 30-minute evening newscasts.

An exception to the pattern of brief interviews occurred when the interview was conducted in the anchor booth high above the noise of the convention floor. In this environment, the pace was more leisurely. During the second session of the Democratic Convention, for example, only four persons, including two members of President Carter's family, were accorded this privilege: CBS—Lillian Carter (4:01), Ruth Carter Stapleton (3:55); NBC—Lillian Carter (4:50); ABC—Carl Wagner, Kennedy Floor Director (3:30). These interviews lasted an average of 4 minutes and 5 seconds compared with 1 minute and 35 seconds for all other convention interviews. An invitation to the network anchor booth guarantees much more exposure than an exchange on the convention floor.

Table 5.5 shows that CBS and NBC were fairly similar overall (as was also the case with official proceeding and anchor data) although CBS used much longer segments. ABC continued to show an opposite trend, due to the inclusion of *20/20* programming. ABC's flow of coverage was disrupted in different parts of each convention, causing a change in the coverage of official proceedings in one case, and in correspondent reports and interviews in the other case.

Coverage in 1980 employed increased use of pre-taped reports and guest commentators. Network producers point to these video aids as a means of increased flexibility, especially when the newsworthiness of the convention is suspect. ABC prepared 100 pre-recorded segments for the Republican Convention and used about 20. Many of these inserts on ABC were personality profiles to introduce convention speakers to the audience in lieu of the partisan introduction. NBC used taped issue interviews with Ronald Reagan as a counterpoint for floor interviews. CBS sent Charles Osgood to the film library for flashbacks of previous conventions and Andy Rooney to his typewriter for humorous convention observations.

Table 5.5
Coverage Using Correspondent Reports/Interviews During 1980 Second Sessions, by Part

	Republican			Democrat		
	Seconds	No. of Segments	Average Length	Seconds	No. of Segments	Average Length
ABC	1685	17	99"	2474	34	72"
CBS	2927	26	112"	2259	16	141"
NBC	3598	40	89"	2492	29	85"
Total	8210	83	99"	7225	79	91"

The networks used these pre-recorded vignettes twice as much during the second session of the Republican Convention as they did during the Democratic Convention. Presumably, the more volatile, spontaneous atmosphere at the Democratic Convention that evening lessened the need for this type of artificial coverage.

In addition to network-generated tapes, outside commentators were used by all three networks. Most commentators were well-known newspaper columnists, but NBC selected prominent members of the opposite party for rebuttals. Carter campaign official Robert Strauss and Democratic Senators Paul Tsongas and Lawton Chiles manned the microphones for the Republican Convention, while National GOP Chairman William Brock and Republican Senator William Roth did so during the Democratic Convention.

Democratic "critics" at the GOP Convention (second session) were given four opportunities for comments totalling over 9 minutes and averaging 2 minutes, 17 seconds for each segment. However, NBC only broadcast one segment of Republican critics during the second session of the Democratic Convention; it ran 2 minutes, 15 seconds. This disparity was presumably due to the greater perceived newsworthiness of the Democratic session and the lessened need for fillers.

Commentaries on all three networks averaged 2 minutes and 59 seconds at the Republican Convention and 2 minutes and 58 seconds at the Democratic Convention, although more were broadcast at the Republican second session. Altogether, 26 of the non-floor-related segments were used during the second sessions, averaging 1 minute, 40 seconds each. These segments ran longer than the interviews originating from the convention floor and tended to be used during periods when the newsworthiness of the convention proceedings was questionable. Thus, the networks were prepared to fill substantial amounts of air time with non-convention programming; this air time was often devoted to network interpretations of recent political history and took viewers far away from the convention floor.

THE NETWORK HORSE RACE
AND THE NOMINATION'S HORSE RACE

Patterson (1980) argued that campaign reporting on television is limited by an obsession journalists have with the "horse-race" aspects of the campaign. The competitive and strategic positions of the candidates are highlighted rather than more substantive policy issues. The electoral process is treated on television in win-loss terms.

The story lines throughout the 1980 conventions seemed to follow Patterson's horse-race formula. At the Republican Convention, the general story line remained constant: "Who will be Reagan's vice-presidential running mate?" What changed were the names of the candidates on whom speculation focused, with TV's "front-runner" changing daily.

At the Democratic Convention the following four stories were pursued, roughly one for each day:

1. Can Senator Kennedy win the vote on Rules Minority Report Number 5, eliminating the rule binding delegates, and boosting his chances of winning the nomination?

2. Can Senator Kennedy and his supporters humiliate President Carter by winning the vote to include a stronger jobs plank in the party platform?

3. Will Senator Kennedy join President Carter on the platform after President Carter's acceptance speech?

4. Will President Carter be able to unite the Democrats after the bloody battles with Senator Kennedy?

These themes were revealing, because they confirm the depth of the network focus on "horse race," that is, on the issue of who is going to win. Network news personnel often claim that the constraints of time on the half-hour nightly newscasts prevent more substantive coverage of issues. Yet, with as much as 3½ hours each night for several nights, the networks still stressed the horse race, and speculation about the horse race, while devoting little serious attention to issues. The coverage even retained, to a remarkable degree, the rapid pacing of the nightly news, with its reliance on 90-second stories.

During the time most TV content was directed to the nomination horse races, the networks were pursuing another sort of horse race—the race with each other. That rivalry gave every evidence of driving the struggle to convert dramatic rumors into network-confirmed facts as many seconds as possible before the other networks.

Despite this network competition and despite variation in the newsworthiness of the conventions, there was a remarkable degree of uniformity in the basic structure of coverage on all three networks. The 1980 figures on the share of time given to official proceedings and network-generated coverage coincided with data from coverage of a 1972 convention. Furthermore, the 1980 data showed only a few differences between the continuous coverage networks (CBS and NBC), or between conventions. The results suggest strongly ingrained expectations or rituals for convention coverage. (Only when ABC opted out of coverage for an hour each evening were the patterns somewhat different.)

Although official proceedings still account for about half of broadcast coverage, the networks' own interpretation of convention events dominates coverage. All three networks rely heavily on floor correspondent reports, interviews, anchor analyses and commentaries. Official convention proceedings are dispensed to viewers in 6- to 8-minute segments. Attempts by the convention organizers to adapt their agendas to accommodate (and manipulate) the networks appear to be a source of amusement to TV anchors and pundits.

All three networks also used sophisticated production techniques, pre-recorded material, and a wide-ranging array of interviews to quicken the pace and variety of coverage and to try to keep it interesting. Although news producers controlled an entire evening of prime-time programming, coverage often resembled the clipped format of a ½-hour nightly newscast.

Within the similar basic frameworks, there were some network differences. Anchor reliance, for example, was more prominent on NBC and CBS: ABC initiated more pre-recorded segments; and NBC used distinctive floor-interview formats.

It had appeared that 1980 might have been a watershed year for broadcast coverage of American political conventions. Network news executives publicly questioned the model used for the past three decades and admitted there was a gap between the amount of actual news and the volume of network resources at the two conventions. Of course that gap provides a special temptation to "discover" drama and controversy where they are lacking.

Sensitive to this newsworthiness gap, a new coverage model might be developed for 1984, although the tradition of continuous convention coverage may be difficult to break. There is also some chance that future conventions may do more than merely ratify preordained selections. The Democratic Party has moved to eliminate the rule requiring delegates to vote for the candidate to whom they were originally pledged and to create 550 additional uncommitted voting delegates chosen from elected and party officials. Such changes would inject more uncertainty into the convention process and could create a deliberate forum in which a significant number of delegates might be open to persuasion and wheeling and dealing. It would be ironic if the networks—after having given extensive coverage to a series of relatively routine, predetermined conventions—decided to experiment with minimal convention coverage in a year when the conventions might regain much of their lost power.

REFERENCES

Adams, William and Fay Schreibman, eds. 1978. *Television Network News: Issues in Content Research.* Washington, D.C.: George Washington University.

Anderson, Christopher P. 1980. Is Television the Real Power at the Conventions? *People* (August 1980): 37–45.

Beating Around the Bush-Ford Story. 1980. *Broadcasting* 99 (July 28, 1980): 28–30.

Epstein, Edward J. 1973. *News from Nowhere.* New York: Vintage Books.

Evans, Katherine. 1981. A Conversation with David Brinkley. *Washington Journalism Review* 3 (November 1981): 15–18.

Fant, Charles H. 1980. Televising Presidential Conventions, 1952–1980. *Journal of Communication* 30 (Autumn 1980): 130–139.

Henninger, Daniel. 1980. The Night the TV News Dam Broke. *Wall Street Journal* (July 18, 1980): 28.

Hickey, Ed. 1980a. It's a $40-million Circus. *TV Guide* (July 12, 1980): 4–8.

———. 1980b. Overkill at Detroit May Mark Final Year of Full Coverage. *TV Guide* (July 26, 1980): 1–2.

Merry, Robert W. 1980. For a TV Producer, Covering Convention is a Series of Challenges. *Wall Street Journal* (July 17, 1980): 1.

Paletz, David and Martha Elson. 1976. Television Coverage of Presidential Conventions: Now You See It, Now You Don't. *Political Science Quarterly* 91 (Spring 1976): 109–131.

Patterson, Thomas E. 1980. *The Mass Media Election.* New York: Praeger Publishers.

Playing Out the News Hand in New York. 1980. *Broadcasting* 99 (August 18, 24–29.

Reeves, Richard. 1977. *Convention.* New York: Harcourt Brace Jovanovich, Inc.

Schardt, Arlie. 1980. TV's Rush to Judgment. *Newsweek* 96 (July 28, 1980): 72–75.

Smith, Stephen. 1980. A Convention House of Mirrors. *Time* 116 (July 28, 1980): 54–55.

Viewers Abstain. 1980. *Broadcasting* 99 (August 18, 1980): 25.

Weisman, John and Sally Bedell. 1980. How They Covered a Convention That Was Over Before It Started. *TV Guide* (August 23, 1980): 3–4.

Womack, David and Jere R. Hoar. 1981. Treatment of Candidates in Convention Floor Interviews. *Journalism Quarterly* 58 (Summer 1981): 300–302.

Wyman's Rifle-Shot Approach to Broadcast Journalism. 1981. *Broadcasting* 101 (October 12, 1981): 78–82.

6

TELEVISED CAMPAIGN DEBATES
AS WHISTLE-STOP SPEECHES

ROBERT G. MEADOW

Despite the absence of consistent, convincing evidence on the effects of presidential debates, a number of myths concerning the debates have arisen. For candidates, myth has it that debates have spelled the difference between winning and losing elections. Kennedy "won" the 1960 debates and the election because he appeared mature, clean-cut, and articulate. Ford lost the 1976 debates and the election because he allegedly made a "gaffe" on Eastern Europe, and Reagan "won" both the 1980 debate and the election with his casual and easy manner. How beneficial the debates are for candidates, of course, is subject to considerable variation. Regardless of what forensic experts or even respondents to post-debate opinion polls say, there ultimately is only one victor: the candidate who wins the election. For the winner, the decision to debate was a good one, for the loser the decision was less sound.

For American voters, presidential debates have several important implications. During debates, the usual media gatekeepers are bypassed; pre-edited stories do not confine the audience to the second-hand reports of campaign hoopla that characterize the evening news (Hofstetter, 1976; Patterson & McClure, 1976; Patterson, 1980). Debates thus offer voters the opportunity to see and hear the candidates directly. Second, to the extent they pay close attention to the debates, voters are given an opportunity to determine some of the issue positions of the candidates. Third, debates serve symbolic and system-supportive functions by presenting shared political events which offer voters an opportunity to reaffirm and renew their faith in "open," competitive, democratic politics. In 1980, according to *New York Times* estimates (9/23; 10/30), 55 million Americans watched the September 21st debate between John Anderson and Ronald Reagan, and about 120 million viewed the October 28th debate between Jimmy Carter and Ronald Reagan.

Journalists have also stressed the significance of the debates, despite the loss of some gatekeeping power. Debates are the events during the campaign when the war, sport, and fight metaphors that journalists love so much seem actually to apply; debates *are* contests. Less acknowledged, though also important, debates offer electronic journalists and television networks an occasion to legitimize themselves by performing a public service, at substantial loss of advertising revenue.

In the period following the 1976 debates, surveys found that up to 66 percent of the respondents favored debates in 1980 (Kraus, 1979). Some observers (cf. Ranney, 1979) went beyond merely calling them important; some even proposed a new constitutional amendment to require candidates to debate. As an alternative, they should be forced to agree publicly at the nominating conventions that they would be willing to participate in a debate. Indeed, one debate moderator in 1980 (Bill Moyers) had stated on the air during his concluding remarks that he "would like to see such meetings become a regular and frequent part of every presidential campaign." This view has been shared by some academic researchers with long experience in debate analysis (Kraus, 1979). Yet before the Constitution is amended or party nomination rituals changed, it is important to understand the ostensible purposes of the debate and to determine whether or not those purposes are served.

The manifest purpose of debates, as expressed in the opening remarks by Frank McGee in the second 1960 debate, was "for the candidates to present their philosophies and programs directly to the people and for the people to compare these and the candidates." In 1976, according to Edwin Newman, moderator of the first 1976 debate, the purpose was to promote "a wider and better informed participation by the American people in the election in November." For the second debate, moderator Pauline Frederick claimed the League of Women Voters' Education Fund hoped "to help voters become better informed on the issues and to generate greater voter turnout." In the third presidential debate of 1976, Barbara Walters, the moderator, proclaimed the League sponsored the events to provide viewers "with the information you will need to choose wisely." This information function carried through to 1980, when Ruth Hinerfeld, opening the Reagan-Anderson debate, remarked that the debates were presented to "provide citizens an opportunity to see and hear the candidates state their positions on important issues of concern to us all." Overall, then, it appears as if debate sponsors seek primarily to inform voters about candidate stands on the issues.

The latent functions are less obvious, but hardly insignificant. Debates serve first to legitimize candidates. No clearer example can be found than Jimmy Carter's refusal to debate with John Anderson. Popular political pundits summarized the Carter position: Why should Carter give Anderson any credibility by appearing on the same platform as Anderson? Carter's decision was supported by one television network (ABC) which refused to air the Reagan-Anderson debate. Apparently the absence of the President made the debate less than "real." When Reagan ultimately did meet Carter, Anderson was denied a platform and faded from view.

Candidates can quickly become non-candidates by being excluded from the debate roster, and access to the national platform is denied to minor party candidates. Yet debates still offer the opportunity to foster the impression of system openness. At times, debates preserve myths of openness by merely allowing the major candidates to address people directly through national television. At other times debates explicitly call attention to participatory values, as Barbara Walters did when she declared them "a truly remarkable exercise in democracy." Second, debates enable candidates to define the issues of the campaign in their own terms rather than those imposed by news analysts and reporters who summarize the candidates' view night after night. Third, debates offer opportunities for journalists to enhance their professional prestige and status (as well as the profession as a whole) by being selected as presidential inquisitors. Fourth, debates placate the desires of the audience for a contest—a need undoubtedly enhanced by the horse-race orientation that dominates election coverage (Carter, 1978; Broh, 1980). Fifth, debates offer the viewers a chance to observe "history," be it the event itself as history or the possibility that a candidate will make a verbal error, stumble, or otherwise appear less than presidential.

Perhaps the most important function of television presidential debates is to enhance the images of the party nominees. In debate, participants demonstrate their stamina and skills by presenting themselves to the camera for an hour or more of purportedly tough questions, by demonstrating an ability to think on their feet, and by responding to questions on the array of government activities. On the assumption that verbal skill is highly valued by voters, candidates have clearly tried to polish that skill. This has led to the development of techniques in debate that have diminished the utility and spontaneity of debates. The result is that debates offer candidates an opportunity to offer prepared remarks of the whistle-stop variety under the guise of a debate. This chapter addresses the question of spontaneity—or its absence—in a debate, and its implications for candidates, citizens, and journalists.

On the surface, debates are presented as spontaneous events. In the best tradition of electronic journalism, they are broadcast live. The audience is told by the moderator, somewhat erroneously, that the candidates have no prepared remarks with them. What is meant, however, is that candidates have no *written* notes with them. In an effort to stress an extemporaneous setting, Frank McGee, in the second 1960 debate said, "neither the questions from the reporters nor the answers you heard from Senator John F. Kennedy or Vice President Richard Nixon were rehearsed." Similarly, Edwin Newman, when opening the first 1976 debate, declared, "President Ford and Governor Carter do not have any notes or prepared remarks with them this evening." Similar statements were made by Pauline Frederick and Barbara Walters when opening the second and third debates.

These opening disclaimers are clearly inconsistent with accounts that emanated from campaign headquarters. Thick briefing notebooks were prepared by campaign or White House staffers, answers to possible questions were rehearsed to fit the allotted time, mock-up studios were built in the White House, and rehearsal debates were conducted to simulate television studio and debate conditions. Perhaps recognizing this rehearsal, the moderators in 1980 were somewhat more careful in their wording of the preparedness of the candidates. Bill Moyers stated only that "None of the questions has been submitted in advance." Howard K. Smith, moderating the Carter-Reagan debate, indicated that "the candidates are not permitted to bring prepared notes to the podium." Still, the debates are staged in such a way to appear simply as live events where anything can happen.

In reality, the debates conform little to this image. Jackson-Beeck and Meadow (1979) have argued there are three agendas during presidential debates. First, voters have issues that they would like to see the candidates address. Second, journalists have an interest in the debates. They get to ask the questions that presumably correspond to their own and their profession's issue priorities. Yet the questions they ask may not be answered by the candidates, who have a third agenda. Candidates, after waiting patiently for journalists to ask questions, proceed to try to make the points they want voters to hear.

Rarely do these three agendas converge. Given the different agendas and the format of the debates, it is not surprising that the debates exhibit little spontaneity. For journalists, formulating questions requires considerable forethought. So, the questions are at least mentally rehearsed. Moreover, evidence (Jackson-Beeck & Meadow, 1979) from content analysis of the 1960 and 1976 debates suggests that less than half of the utterances by candidates directly addressed questions raised by journalists or even by the opposing candidate. In other words, candidates get to say what they want, and, of course, candidates have previously decided what they "want" to say. Their desired message is embodied in the standard campaign speech, the so-called "whistle-stop," "stump," or "stock" speech that is used throughout the campaign during the candidate's personal appearances.

Although there are considerable differences between a national audience, such as that viewing a presidential debate, and a local audience for a campaign rally, campaign speeches rarely undergo major alterations for new audiences. In part, this is attributable to the quantity of speeches that must be made. At the same time, all speeches are actually addressing national audiences because electronic journalists record campaign rallies for broadcast on the network news. Undoubtedly, the desire to avoid a gaffe or an inconsistency motivates the candidates and their staffs, but the result is that candidates are essentially programmed for speeches and for responding to questions in ways that minimize creative thought. This does more than just limit the expression of original thoughts during a campaign. First, as will be explained in more detail, this approach has important implications for the conduct and meaning of the debates. Second, it will be argued that journalists, particularly electronic journalists, are co-conspirators in the debate ritual and continue to perpetuate the images of spontaneity and the gamesmanship dimensions of televised debates—despite their knowledge that much of the debaters' rhetoric is derived from the campaign stump speech.

METHODS

Without detailed knowledge of the preparations of the candidates for the debates or of the stock speech, it is impossible to determine the extent of spontaneity in debate. Although the *New York Times* published a version of the stock speeches of each of the candidates during the primary election season, none were available for the general election. However, through a close analysis of the content of the debate, one can look for evidence of prepared remarks in the form of stock phrases, repeated thoughts, and parallel rhetoric between the debates. Because Carter and Anderson participated in only one debate, no comparisons can be made for them. Reagan appeared in two debates, permitting comparison across the debates. It could be argued that isolating Reagan for analysis is unwise because, as a professional actor, he is more skilled than the average candidate in learning lines. However, all candidates develop these skills during the course of a campaign.

Research on the 1976 debates (Jackson-Beeck & Meadow, 1978) suggested that the *New York Times* transcripts contained several errors of omission and commission including missing words and phrases. To facilitate the analysis, a transcript of each 1980 debate was prepared from video tapes of the events. The transcripts were entered into word processing equipment with the capability of searching for common patterns of words. Computer-identified patterns were then supplemented with researcher observations to verify the patterns and to isolate similar but nonexact phrasing by the candidate. In addition, television news coverage of the debates for the two days following the Carter-Reagan debate were analyzed for, among other things, references to the candidates' originality —or lack thereof—in debate. Editions of the early-evening ABC, CBS, and NBC network newscasts loaned from the Vanderbilt Television News Archive were used for this purpose.

RESULTS

By looking at the questions posed to the candidates in both debates, the preparation of the journalists is obvious. The format of the debates offered the candidates an opportunity to reply to the same questions. Unless the journalists had extraordinary recall abilities, this required that journalists prepare their questions and write them out completely before their turn to ask questions. Out of the six different questions asked in the Anderson-Reagan debate, three were repeated verbatim, two were repeated with one or two word modifications, and one was repeated with only minor modifications. Only the often lengthy introductory remarks that preceded the actual questions were omitted when the question was repeated for the second candidate. In the Carter-Reagan debate, eight different questions and seven different follow-up questions were asked. Excepting changes required by direct address or grammar, four of the questions were repeated verbatim, three had one or two word changes, and one had several minor wording changes. These findings provide strong suggestive evidence of the preparation of the journalists.

The questions also showed that the journalists did indeed have their own agendas. At no time did one journalist follow up the question raised by another journalist—a common practice in news interviews, press conferences, and other events more spontaneous than debates. During the Anderson-Reagan debate, the topics included inflation, energy, the military draft, urban problems, economic policy, and church-state relations. In the Carter-Reagan debate, the topics were the use of military power, inflation, urban problems, terrorism, Salt II negotiations, energy policy, social security, and the qualifications of the candidates. The limited number of questions touched on relatively predictable policy areas, offering the candidates opportunities to respond with prepared remarks.

Evidence of candidate preparation is seen in several responses by Reagan to questions raised in debate. In response to a question on inflation in the debate with Anderson, Reagan said:

And when you are reducing productivity at the same time that you are turning out printing press money in excessive amounts, you're causing inflation.

In response to a similar question during the Carter-Reagan debate, he replied:

You can lick inflation by increasing productivity and decreasing the cost of government to the place that we no longer have unbalanced budgets and are no longer grinding out printing press money flooding the market.

This is an example of similar, although not precisely the same remarks made several weeks apart. Both offer solutions to inflation that are rooted in the concept of "printing press" money.

In response to a question on inflation in the first debate, Reagan said:

Now I know this has been called inflationary by the man who isn't here tonight. But I don't see where it is inflationary to have people keep more of their earnings and spend it, and it isn't inflationary for government to take that money away from them and spend it on the things it wants to spend it on.

In the second debate, in response to a question on cutbacks in government spending, Reagan's words are remarkably similar. Given all the possible configurations of words in his vocabulary, it is difficult to conclude that Reagan's response was not prepared:

And the idea that my tax cut proposal is inflationary. I would like to ask the president why it is inflationary to let people keep more of their money and spend it the way they'd like, and it isn't inflationary to let him take that money and spend it the way he wants.

Another similarity emerges in Reagan's economic forecasts. During the debate with Anderson, Reagan commented:

And I believe the plan I have submitted with detailed backing and which has been approved by a number of our leading economists in the country based on projections, conservative projections out for the next five years—that indicate that this plan would by 1983 result in a balanced budget.

Over one month later, Reagan responded to a question on his budget with a similar vocabulary:

I have submitted an economic plan that I've worked out in concert with a number of fine economists in this country, all of whom approve it, and believe that over a five-year projection this plan can permit the extra spending for needed refurbishing of our defense posture, that it can provide for a balanced budget in 1983.

Reagan was given an unusual opportunity to present the same anecdote in his debates with both Anderson and Carter, because both debates contained questions on urban problems. The first time, while debating Anderson, the anecdote was told as follows:

> Stand in the South Bronx as I did, in the spot where Jimmy Carter made his promise that he was going to—with multibillion dollar programs—refurbish that area that looks like bombed out London in World War Two. I stood there and I met the people.

The second time the anecdote was told, during the debate with Carter, it was fleshed out with more drama:

> I stood in the South Bronx on the exact spot where President Carter stood in 1977. You have to see it to believe it. It looks like a bombed-out city. Great gaunt skeletons of buildings, windows smashed out. Painted on one of them "unkept promises," on another, "despair." And this is the spot where President Carter had promised that he was going to bring in a vast program to rebuild this department, this area.

On occasion, twice in the same debate, repeated phrases are found. During the debate with Anderson, in response to a question on energy, Reagan said:

> There are hundreds of millions of acres of land that have been taken out of circulation by the government, for whatever reasons they have.

A few moments later, Reagan declared:

> When you stop to think that the government has taken over one hundred million acres of land out of circulation in Alaska.

Six weeks later, in response to an energy question, a similar answer was given:

> Our government has in the last year or so, taken out of multiple use millions of acres of public lands.

Also on the subject of energy, Reagan noted in the debate with Anderson:

> All of these things can be done, be done when you stop and think that we are only drilling on two percent, at least only two percent of the possibility for oil of the whole continental shelf around the US.

Twice in the debate with Carter, Reagan made references to the drilling areas:

> The other thing is that we have only leased out and begun to explore two percent of our outer continental shelf for oil.

Later in the same debate he said:

As for offshore drilling, only two percent is now leased and producing oil.

The most convincing evidence of the whistle-stop dimension of presidential debates comes from comparing the responses given to questions with statements made in closing remarks. In theory, and according to debate moderators offering the rules of the debates, the candidates have no prepared remarks with them. Yet it seems more than coincidental that in the debate with Anderson—when presumably the candidate has no control—spontaneous responses to questions are virtually the same as closing remarks made in the debate with Carter five weeks later. During the debate with Anderson, for example, Reagan responded to a question on economic forecasts in part by saying:

> Now I speak with some confidence of our plan, because I took over a state—California—ten percent of the population of this nation—a state that if it were a nation would be the seventh ranking economic power in the world.

In his closing statement against Carter, he said:

> But I think in being Governor of California—the most populous state in the union—if it were a nation it would be the seventh-ranking power of the world—. . . .

This same pattern is repeated elsewhere. Against Anderson, Reagan states:

> We cut the rate of increase in spending in half, but at the same time we gave back to the people of California, in tax rebates, tax credits, tax cuts, five point seven billion dollars.

Concluding his remarks against Carter, Reagan's defense of his California policies remains the same:

> We cut the cost, the increased cost of government, in half over eight years. We returned five point seven billion dollars in tax rebates, credits, and cuts to our people.

These quotations indicate the preparation and stump-speech characteristics of the rhetoric in presidential debates. Yet the newscasts in the days following the Carter-Reagan debate largely overlooked the similarities with Reagan's remarks in the debate with Anderson, or with candidates' standard campaign speeches.

On the day following the Carter-Reagan debate, ABC broadcast seven debate-related items plus one debate tease before a commercial break. These items totalled 11 minues and 55 seconds—more than half of the newscast that day. However, all but one of these news stories had a primary focus on the ongoing campaign in general or some other related news item, rather than the debate per se. Anchor and film reports on Carter's and Reagan's campaigning during the day contained brief candidate claims of victory in the debates, while the Anderson story made reference to his exclusion from the debate. These stories totalled 7 minutes, 10 seconds. Another item was a 45-second tongue-in-cheek film report in which Amy Carter was interviewed on her role in policy-making, with reference to Carter's remark in the debate that Amy thought the most important issue facing America was nuclear proliferation. One story about courtroom testimony by Richard Nixon included a five-second interview in which Nixon praised Reagan's performance. Finally a 10-second tease and a 3-minute, 45-second report on voter reaction to the debate was broadcast. This item reported on the results of a nationwide post-debate telephone "call-in" sponsored by ABC in which voters were to indicate (after paying a 50 cent toll charge) "who gained the most from the debate." Figures on Reagan's relative success were presented, but the focus of the story was on the logistics of establishing a nationwide call-in network and on the methodological limits of the "survey"—an enterprise for which ABC was widely criticized. Thus, only the story on Amy Carter addressed the substance of the debate, and even then, very superficially and not seriously.

The evening news on NBC opened with a 20-second anchor report on the candidates' claims of victory, which served as an introduction to the day's campaign events of Carter, Reagan, and Anderson. There were references to the outcome of the debate in each of these reports, but again the emphasis was on the activity of the candidate rather than on a debate post-mortem. These reports lasted a total of 4 minutes, 40 seconds. Only one story focused directly on the debate—a 1-minute, 50-second report on the audience reaction to the debate. In a film report narrated by Tom Petit, the size of the audience and the reactions of one household were cited. Edited clips from the debate were the Amy quote from Carter and Reagan's reference to the witch doctor. In the only analytic portion of the report, Petit quoted the headlines from several major newspapers in which the debate was reported as a sporting event.

CBS reported seven debate-related stories, totalling 9 minutes, 15 seconds. Two of the stories addressed the debates directly, one of which was the lead story. This report, lasting 2½ minutes, concerned a CBS poll on who won the debate, and the extent to which voters might be influenced by the results. This was followed by a 45-second report on Nixon's view of the debate and the winner. Film reports on the activities of the candidates mentioned the debate performances of the candidates and the claims of their aides regarding the outcome, strengths, and weaknesses of the candidates. For Carter and Reagan, these totalled 3 minutes, while a 10-second desk report indicated Anderson's views on being excluded. Another anchor report noted a State Department clarification of a comment made by Carter during the debate.

The final story of this CBS newscast was the most analytical of all the network reports. In a 2-minute, 5-second report, Bruce Morton presented edited clips of the candidates repeating themes that he claimed their advisors had urged to be stressed. Through a mini-content analysis, Morton revealed that Carter called Reagan "disturbing" or "dangerous" 7 times, referred to himself as a Democrat 8 times, and to his status as President 10 times. Reagan referred to "peace" 6 times, and said he was misquoted by the President a total of 7 different times. In addition, the Amy quote and the reference by Reagan to witch doctors were presented on video tape. The point of the analysis was to suggest that the candidates had specific themes, but no reference was made to the implications this had for the lack of spontaneity, nor were references made to substantive redundancy or stump-speech characteristics of the debate.

On the second day after the debate, broadcast journalists moved on to other topics. There were no reports on the debate on CBS or NBC, although there were some very brief references to the debate as a critical event during the final campaign week. Eighteen minutes into the broadcast, ABC had a 1-minute, 45-second report on the ABC-Harris poll, including the results of questions on who did better, and who would best handle the economy and issues of war and peace. These data were compared with those reported by other media polls.

Overall coverage was consistent. The debate was another event, albeit an important one, during the course of the campaign. It seems clear that the electronic media learned little from their experience, and even less from research on the 1960 and 1976 debates. They continued to focus on the question of "who won" the debate in both their direct reports and in their reviews of the campaign in the day following the debate. With the exception of the Bruce Morton report, they failed to explore the strategies and tactics of the debaters. What is more significant, perhaps, is that the networks failed to examine the contribution of the debates to the discourse of the campaign and to examine the extent to which the justification for holding the debates (as expressed by the sponsors and moderators of the debates) could have been met.

The quotes from Reagan represent a fraction of the total words spoken by the candidate during the debates. And, although the patterns presented refer to only a single candidate, one who was experienced in memorizing lines, they are suggestive of a serious problem in televised presidential debates. Rather than offering the public a chance to observe candidates in a true debate, the events offer the candidates an opportunity to address the nation, while being guided only marginally by questions. It is interesting that this phenomenon is not lost on the journalists who, despite their recognition of the problem, continue to play the game (for reasons mentioned earlier in this paper). Early in the Reagan-Anderson debate, after the candidates had the opportunity to reply to only one question, Daniel Greenberg, a syndicated columnist and one of the questioners, noted before asking his question:

> Gentlemen, what I'd like to say first is I think the panel and the audience would appreciate responsiveness to the questions rather than repetitions of your campaign addresses.

From his position as a reporter following the candidates on the campaign trail, such an observation was simple. For viewers at home, the stump-speech quality of the replies was less obvious.

Greenberg was the only panelist to remark on the character of the debates. Several questioners pleaded with the candidates to respond with examples or to be more specific. Only one, Barbara Walters, was critical, reviewing the candidates' responses by saying:

> Well, I would like to say that neither candidate answered specifically the question of a specific policy for dealing with terrorists.

This emphasis on the failure of candidates to be specific should direct viewers—and journalists—toward criticism of the debates rooted in the recitations of excerpts from stock speeches. Nonetheless, we have seen how broadcast journalists failed to follow through on this in their newscasts following the debates.

A number of proposals for changing debate formats have been offered that would eliminate the panel of journalists or would require candidates to address a specific issue. It is not at all certain, however, that removing the journalists would result in debaters addressing one another or the issues at hand. Most concerns are directed toward the lack of specificity by the candidates; the stump-speech dimensions of the debates go largely unnoticed.

Implications of the whistle-stop debating presented in this chapter are significant for a number of reasons. Debates begin to take on the characteristics of game shows. Questions posed by journalists, no matter how complex and specific, are culled by the candidate for a buzz-word—"draft" or "inflation" or "SALT II"—which serves much as a bell did for Pavlov's dogs. Such terms release a flow of information that candidates have developed during the campaign season. Thus, debates take on the characteristics of television game shows rather than forums for high-level discourse. In this format, debates have little to offer voters who are looking for new and creative approaches to government. Instead of getting responses to questions, voters receive a fragment from a set speech.

If voters are going to be given a prepared speech, debates become little more than free campaign advertisements. Regardless of who sponsors the debates, if the debates are prepared speeches rather than bona fide newsworthy events, there are clear implications for the equal-time requirements imposed on broadcasters. Indeed, the real message of debates may be to demonstrate how easy it is for candidates to avoid appearing on platforms with minor-party candidates and how simple it is for candidates from major political parties to circumvent the equal-time rules.

There may well be some utility both in allowing the candidates unedited air time to make their separate cases in a joint forum, and in having one major televised event that is not filtered entirely by network news departments. However, the illusions perpetuated by the pretense of a debate—and largely echoed by its network coverage—are misleading.

One solution, of course, would be to eliminate debates, but this cannot be done because of the ever stronger popular perception that candidates ought to debate and because of the need for high political drama during the course of a political campaign. Reforms are needed. Otherwise, as experience with debates accumulates, debaters will continue to play it safe, which means more rehearsing and memorizing, less spontaneity, and ultimately less information for voters and fewer insights into the candidates for the presidency.

REFERENCES

Broh, C. Anthony. 1980. Horse Race Journalism: Reporting the Polls in the 1976 Presidential Election. *Public Opinion Quarterly* 44 (Winter 1980): 514–529.

Carter, Richard F. 1978. A Very Peculiar Horse Race. In George F. Bishop, Robert G. Meadow, and Marilyn Jackson-Beeck, eds., *The Presidential Debates: Media, Policy and Electoral Perspectives*. New York: Praeger Publishers.

Hofstetter, C. Richard. 1976. *Bias in the News*. Columbus, Oh.: Ohio State University.

Jackson-Beeck, Marilyn and Robert G. Meadow. 1978. Analysis of Debate Transcripts. In George F. Bishop, Robert G. Meadow, and Marilyn Jackson-Beeck, eds., *The Presidential Debates: Media, Policy and Electoral Perspectives*. New York: Praeger Publishers.

Jackson-Beeck, Marilyn and Robert G. Meadow. 1979. The Triple Agenda of Presidential Debates. *Public Opinion Quarterly* 43 (Summer 1979): 173–180.

Kraus, Sidney, ed. 1979. *The Great Debates: Carter vs. Ford, 1976*. Bloomington, Ind.: Indiana University.

Patterson, Thomas E. 1980. *The Mass Media Election*. New York: Praeger Publishers.

Patterson, Thomas E. and Robert D. McClure. 1976. *The Unseeing Eye*. New York: G. P. Putnam's Sons.

Ranney, Austin, ed. 1979. *The Past and Future of Presidential Debates*. Washington, D.C.: American Enterprise Institute.

7

IMPLICIT COMMUNICATION THEORY IN CAMPAIGN COVERAGE

THOMAS W. BENSON

All television news reporting of politics is, necessarily, reporting about and through a system of communication. The news is a communication system reporting to viewers about the symbolic actions of politicians and their associates in campaigns, speeches, hearings, press conferences, annouce-ments, and so on. Hence, every description of politics—and especially of political campaigning—is also largely a description of communication as symbolic action. Conversely, every description of political communication is also an implied description of politics itself, with political rhetoric and communication as the visible evidence of politics and government.

Politics is formed partly as a result of our views about it. In this sense, it is a self-fulfilling prophecy. Thus, the way television reports about politics and political communication affects not only our understandings of politics, but our political actions as well. Politics and television are mutually constraining systems.

A detailed study of CBS television news coverage of the 1980 Presidential campaign was undertaken in order to discover how television reports and employs political communication.[1] To investigate CBS coverage

[1] This study sought to extend and verify a series of tentative and unpublished findings that resulted from a detailed study of television coverage of the 1976 Presidential campaign by ABC, CBS, and NBC, supported in part by the College of Liberal Arts, The Pennsylvania State University. The current study was supported in part by a grant from the Television and Politics Study Program, School of Public and International Affairs, George Washington University. Tapes were obtained from the Vanderbilt Television News Archive. In addition, broadcasts from earlier in the campaign were studied through the facilities of the Department of Speech Communication, The Pennsylvania State University.

of the campaign as political communication, the perspective of "implicit communication theory" was chosen.

IMPLICIT COMMUNICATION THEORY

Implicit communication theory is a research paradigm still in its infancy, but one which shows signs of providing considerable insight into how human beings communicate. Simply put, implicit communication theory refers to the collections of ideas that lay practitioners hold about the way they and others communicate. Such ideas are theoretical because they relate to one another and to generalized views of the world, though they do not necessarily exhibit internal consistency. Such ideas are implicit because, although they are often displayed in talk, they are seldom stated as generalized theoretical formulations. Human beings hold implicit "theories" about a wide variety of matters that constrain human action in the world. Such theories are typically common sense understandings about such matters as time, space, causality, motion, action, and motivation. At times our implicit theories seem to be built into our language and culture; at other times theories may relate more specifically to groups, individuals, or situations.

We use implicit theories to help us interpret, enact, and evaluate our actions and those of others. Experience does not speak to us directly. Instead, we perceive and interpret experience through the filter of our theories.

Social scientists first studied implicit theories as a way of understanding psychological processes. Implicit psychologies, sometimes called "naive" or "lay" theories, were understood as ways in which individuals constructed a picture of how they and others behaved. Wegner and Vallacher (1977, p. 36) describe nonscientists as amateur builders of

> a cognitive representation of both physical and social reality. This implicit construction is similar to the theories developed by scientists and psychologists. Although less explicit than formal theories, the layman's theories are similarly motivated by needs for understanding, prediction, and control.

Other scholars have reported on implicit theories about personality, in such areas as first impressions, personal constructs, and attribution theory (Jones, 1954; Schneider, 1973; Kelly, 1955).

More recently, in a research paradigm that parallels implicit psychological theory, scholars have begun to report on implicit communication theory and implicit rhetorical theory. The first use of the term "implicit communication theory" seems to have been made by Johnson (1972). As Johnson pointed out in her review of the literature, however, other scholars had addressed the general question under other names (White, 1963; Zyskind, 1968; Scott, 1968). Scholars in speech communication not cited by Johnson had also investigated the theoretical implications of nonscientific views of communication (Stelzner, 1965; Benson, 1968). Since Johnson's dissertation in 1972, other scholars in communications (some of them independently of her work, apparently) have begun to investigate implicit communication theory (Blankenship, 1976; Wish & Kaplan, 1977; Benson, 1978; Benson & Barton, 1979; Benson, 1980a; Ellis, 1980; Harrison, 1981).

How can implicit communication patterns be identified? For a researcher there is the problem of circularity. Should the researcher establish a definition of communication, its elements and processes, and then look for references to those elements and processes in a naive theorist? Or should the researcher put aside all preconceptions about definitions and look for references to what the naive theorist seems to define as communication? Researchers may discover rather different descriptions of communication as it is understood and experienced, depending upon the choice of approaches.

If we start with our own definition of communication, and look for references to that domain in our subject, we may very well be imposing our own theory on our subject at the outset. But if we do not start with a definition of communication, we may not have any clear idea of what to look for. In this investigation, an attempt was made to employ both methods, singly and together: to abstract a network of activities and elements from several theories of communication, and to look for references to them in television descriptions of campaigns.

METHOD OF ANALYSIS

Reports of the 1980 Presidential campaign on CBS evening newscasts were studied for all references to communication. News coverage on all networks was monitored selectively from before the primaries through the election, with intensive analysis of the last three weeks of the campaign. Video-tape recordings and transcripts of the content were subjected to critical scrutiny.

Visual and audio portions of each broadcast were searched for explicit and implicit references to key terms in communication theory drawn from classical rhetoric (Aristotle, 1932; Benson & Prosser, 1969); contemporary rhetorical theory (Burke, 1969a, 1969b; Johannesen, 1971; Ehninger, 1972; Benson, 1974; Benson, 1980b; Brock & Scott, 1980); communication theory (Aranguren, 1967; Dance, 1967; Sereno & Mortensen, 1970; Littlejohn, 1978; Mortensen, 1979; Bormann, 1980; Pearce & Cronen, 1980); and semiology (Barthes, 1970, 1972; Eco, 1976; Sebeok, 1977, 1978).

Because the approach was qualitative and critical rather than quantitative, I did not simply establish a list of key terms and search for occurrences. Rather, I searched for instances in which understandings of key elements and processes seemed to be implied or evoked. The method was qualitative and critical, rather than quantitative, because for a first survey it seemed desirable to discover the implied categories, dimensions, and relations, rather than count the numbers of television descriptions of political communication (Wegner & Vallacher, 1977, pp. 284-293).

This chapter describes an implied theory of communication in television news coverage of the presidential campaign. Such a study of content, though providing important clues to the ways in which political understandings are voiced, is necessarily incomplete. The method does not allow us to allege that the messages in the news entirely reveal the beliefs of the professional newspeople, nor can we be certain that general audiences would understand or even agree with the implicit content as extracted by the analyst. At best, this research can develop a critical argument about the view of political communication that is broadcast. Other research will need to investigate the extent to which these findings, if they seem persuasive, represent (1) the actual beliefs of the newspeople and their organizations; (2) the understandings of general audiences who watch the news broadcasts; (3) fair conclusions about the political processes being described in the broadcasts; or even (4) the generality of television descriptions of political communication.

This study is also limited by its choice of the narrowest definition of political communication: the Presidential campaign. An adequate investigation of television descriptions of political communication must reach beyond this narrow circle to the ever larger concentric rings of political communication represented by (1) other political campaigns; (2) other political communication; (3) an understanding of all of politics and government as symbolic action; and (4) an understanding that everything on television, even when it does not refer to politics and government, is "political" in that it operates as part of a system of political and economic arrangements, and assumes a world view that is the context of political communication.

CBS COVERAGE

From the perspective of communication and rhetorical theory, CBS television coverage of the Presidential campaign presented a striking and paradoxical picture of political communication. *Contrary to the conventional wisdom, television news reports draw attention not to what is most obvious from looking at concrete visual images, but to what is not evident.*

Most striking is the emphasis on hidden motivations and future contingencies. Much of the political process itself is treated as a fundamentally deceptive, cynical, and illegitimate enterprise, although, paradoxically, it is worth continuing daily attention and conventional signs of respect.

For a striking example of implicit communication theory as it applies to politics, let us examine in some detail a climactic report that CBS broadcast near the end of the campaign, on the day after the Carter-Reagan debate of October 28. Near the end of newscast on October 29, Walter Cronkite introduced a report by Bruce Morton that is characteristic—though somewhat exaggerated—in its depiction of political communication. The following transcript was made from the video tape of that important broadcast:

CBS EVENING NEWS: WEDNESDAY, OCTOBER 29, 1980

VISUAL	AUDIO
1 MCU of Walter Cronkite speaking to camera.	[Walter Cronkite]: For our last word on last night's Presidential debate, at least today, here's Bruce Morton, who followed it as attentively as he has followed the whole campaign.
2 LS from high overhead of stage on which debate took place the night before. Both candidates are on stage, and the debate is apparently about to begin. Ronald Reagan is at Jimmy Carter's podium. Reagan extends his hand, and they shake hands.	[Bruce Morton]: The two tigers showed good moves, good coaching.
3 MS from behind the candidates. Reagan finishes shaking hands and moves screen left, towards his own podium.	Each was supposed to hit some key words, key themes.
4 CU of Jimmy Carter; shot zooms out slowly and pans slightly right to reveal Reagan at screen right, in foreground. Carter looks at Reagan. Reagan is speaking, and gestures with his left hand, sweeping it left to right.	Each did. "Remember, Mr. President," Carter's handlers must have told him, "the other guy is scary. Dangerous. Disturbing." Right.
5 CU of Carter speaking. Then freeze frame, and wipe to:	[Carter]: There is a disturbing pattern in the attitude of Governor Reagan.

6 CU of Carter, speaking. Then freeze frame, and wipe to:

[Carter]: This attitude is extremely dangerous and belligerent in its tone.

[Morton]: Carter called Reagan's positions "dangerous" and "disturbing" a total of seven times.

7 CU of Ronald Reagan.

[Morton]: The Reagan strategists for their part must have said, "Listen,

8 LS Carter and Reagan. Carter is in left foreground, Reagan in right background, both facing screen right.

you've gotta convince people you don't want to push the button. Talk like a peacenik." Right again.

9 CU Reagan, speaking. Then freeze frame and wipe to:

[Reagan]: I believe with all my heart that our first priority must be world peace.

10 CU Reagan, speaking. Then freeze frame and wipe to:

[Reagan]: The burden of maintaining the peace falls on us.

[Morton]: Reagan used the word "peace" six times.

11 LS of the two candidates on stage, from behind the panel of questioners, who are seated in a row facing the stage.

[Morton]: Neither wandered far from basic themes.

Reagan mentioned witch doctors.

12 CU Reagan, speaking.

[Reagan]: It's like the witch doctor that gets mad when a good doctor comes along with a cure that'll work.

13 CU Carter.

[Morton]: Carter introduced a new national security advisor.

[Carter]: I had a discussion with my daughter Amy the other day before I came here to ask her what the most important issue was. She said she thought nuclear weaponry.

14 LS from overhead and slightly in front of the stage; candidates at their lecterns.

[Morton]: But mostly they stuck to their themes: "Don't let them misquote you."

15 MLS of the two candidates at podiums, from eye level. Reagan in foreground, Carter in background, both facing left. At end of audio, freeze frame and wipe to:

[Reagan]: Well, that just isn't true.

16 MLS of candidates, at podiums, facing right. Carter in foreground, screen left;

[Reagan]: That's a misstatement, of course, of my position. I just have...[fades out]

Reagan in background, screen right. Freeze frame and wipe to:	[Morton]: Reagan did that seven times.
17 LS Carter from front, with backs of interviewers visible at bottom of screen.	[Morton]: "Remind us you are the President.
18 CU Carter.	Talk about
	your office."
	[Carter]: Mr. Stone, I've had to make thousands of decisions since I've been President, serving in the Oval Office...
Jump cut to:	
19 CU Carter.	...in that Oval Office...
Jump cut to:	
20 CU Carter. Freeze frame; wipe to:	...in the Oval Office...
	[Morton]: Carter did that ten times.
21 LS from overhead, candidates at lecterns facing screen left. Camera zooms out slowly, revealing the panel of inter-viewers.	[Morton]: And he was careful to insist that he was part of the Democratic tradition, in the Democratic mainstream, work-ing with the Democratic Congress. There were eight references to that.
22 MCU Bruce Morton, speak-ing to camera. Behind him a bank of television monitors.	So they each had their themes, and stuck to them. They fol-lowed their game plans. They don't, for some reason, seem to have changed very many minds. Bruce Morton, CBS News, New York.
23 MCU Walter Cronkite. He looks from lower screen left up to camera and speaks directly to it.	And that's the way it is, Wed-nesday, October twenty-ninth, 1980, the 361st day of captivity for the American hostages in Iran. This is Walter Cronkite, CBS News. Good night.

Morton's report, and most of the CBS coverage, includes a number of significant implications and assumptions:

(1) *Political communication is not "normal discourse" but a form of combat.* Morton opens with a reference to the candidates as "the two tigers," a double metaphor to the candidates as boxers and to boxers as beasts of prey. The metaphor is extended in the use of boxing metaphors in the phrases "good moves, good coaching," which are spoken over a visual image of the two candidates shaking hands. There is a later refer-ence to "Carter's handlers."

(2) The candidates are manipulated by behind-the-scenes strategists.
Morton refers to the "good coaching," and notes that the candidates were "supposed to hit some key words, key themes." Morton even fictionalizes the behind-the-scenes manipulation by "quoting" the presumed directions that advisors gave the candidates. The structure of Morton's whole story depends upon his totally unsupported assumption that the candidates are motivated and manipulated by hidden forces of which he has knowledge. If there was a basis for that knowledge, it was never presented.

By the end of the story, the fictional language goes so far as to get inside a candidate's mind, when, in shot #21, Morton asserts that Carter "was careful to insist." Morton could know what Carter was careful about only by seeing into (or being told about) Carter's personal motives. This attribution by Morton is consistent with the language of television journalism, which typically discerns what politicians "believe" and not just what they "say."

(3) Political rhetoric and television news both function as symbolic being, knowing, and doing, but with important differences. Political talk is often a matter of image-building, but television penetrates the mask and reveals the inner politician. Political talk may be true or false, but television can reveal its degree of truth. The strategic design of political talk is to persuade (by identifying a politician with voters' opinions and interests), but the role of television news is to inform people. (Cf. Benson, 1974.) This cluster of statements of implicit theory suggests television news' presentation of itself as insightful and resistant to manipulation, and underscores the manipulative intent of political rhetoric.

(4) The candidates are afraid to really debate each other. Morton describes two debaters who repeated themselves, rather than develop new ground. The repetition quickly becomes a joke and a grievance, supported by visual editing that freeze frames on a close-up and wipes to another example.

(5) Candidates rely on metaphor and sentiment rather than fact and argument. Reagan calls Carter a witch doctor, and Carter mentions his daughter's fears about nuclear war.

(6) Candidates are more interested in image than in substance. Carter attacks Reagan as dangerous and disturbing and promotes himself as "presidential" with references to the Oval Office. Reagan attacks Carter as a witch doctor and a liar, and promotes himself as a "peacenik."

(7) Candidates understand that the situation requires them to hypocritically misrepresent themselves, running against the grain of popular perceptions. Reagan calls himself a peace advocate, and Carter portrays himself as decisive and as a traditional, mainstream Democrat.

(8) Candidates reduce complicated matters to fragmented key words and themes. This charge is made explicitly, and is supported implicitly throughout the story by the cutting method, which shows us bits and pieces of the debate.

(9) The public is too smart to be taken in by the candidates. "They don't," says Morton, "seem to have changed very many minds."

(10) The CBS story of the debate is a factual and objective account of what happened, and certainly does not contain any evaluation or "implicit theory." "And that's the way it is," says Cronkite, implicitly joining in Bruce Morton's deniable disapproval of the quality of the debate.

This list could continue, but perhaps the point has been made that if viewers are to understand Morton's story, they must accept Morton's unstated but implicit views about how campaign communication functions. In addition, the viewer is presumed to accept an implicit theory about how television news covers an event like the presidential debate. Throughout the Morton report, a competent decoder would be able to share—at least provisionally—Morton's implicit theory about how politicians and television can and do communicate.

This extended example indicates something about the way a viewer would be likely to experience the implicit communication theory communicated by television news. The example suggests how implicit theory becomes imbedded in and communicated by television news stories. One illustration does not of course amount to a convincing demonstration that this story is representative or even that viewers would understand it exactly as it is described here. Additional research will be required to investigate the scope and nature of implicit theory, and to understand the formal and organizational constraints that lead to stories like this one.

Despite these limitations, continued viewing of many hours of television news reports of the campaign has convinced the author that there is a more or less repeated—if contradictory and paradoxical—implicit theory of communication being transmitted. In story after story, correspondents file a brief description of a candidate's speech, and then, facing the camera themselves to wrap up the story, describe "the real reason" behind the speech; and the real reason usually has to do with hidden political strategies planned by behind-the-scenes advisors. Then, correspondents often spend precious television time speculating about future events that will, in any case, be known within days or weeks, instead of conveying political information and actions that can help viewers decide for themselves how to influence the outcome.

I have no wish to speculate about the motives of news correspondents, whom I regard as well-informed and hard-working, but it is impossible not to notice a curious symmetry between the constraints of television news as a medium and the repeatedly expressed frustrations of news correspondents about political communication.

Bruce Morton suggests that the candidates fragmented the real issues, and reduced them to a few key words. But, with the exception of the debates and a few parts of the nominating convention, political speeches are *reported* as fragments. One seldom hears, in television news reports of campaigns, anything like a whole argument. Instead, one hears a report of a promise, a slogan, or an accusation understood to operate as strategic goads to opponents, or as brief appeals to views or interests of voters (as when a candidate is shown defending social security in a retirement community).

If one were to ask, not even as a proposal but just as a method of gaining perspective on formulas, whether television news could not, say, once a week, report an entire speech by every candidate from somewhere on the road, one would be told that it was impossible. The "impossibility" of reporting more than fragments of candidates' speeches is yet another part of the implicit theory of communication that governs television news.

Television news formulas constrain correspondents to describe campaign rhetoric as a series of disjointed and dubiously motivated fragments, and then to complain about fragmentation and motivation. This fragmentation and reduction are more than mere gatekeeping: the reshaping of candidates' talk through the dramatic fictions of television news change our political information and the context within which we can come to understand it. We do not simply hear a *part* of the objective world. Synecdoche (the part representing the whole) is transformed into metaphor (what we see stands for a symbolic entity unlike itself).

Reporters' continual references to hidden motivations bear a similar relation to television film's inability to record what the reporter thinks we ought to know. And so the reporter works against the grain of his own story, showing us one thing, and then telling us that it is not the way it seems, that there are hidden forces at work. The reporter tells us that what we have seen and heard did happen (this is, after all, CBS news), but that it is not the truth. The locus of the untruth is not, as the reporter describes it, in the medium itself but in the duplicity of the political candidate about whom the story is reporting. The focus on the motivations of the candidates creates an ongoing story of bad faith. And, what might be reported as "we are not showing you the whole truth" becomes "they are not telling you the truth."

All symbolic communication carries implicit assumptions about communication. This chapter recounts the results of part of a critical analysis of CBS television news coverage of the 1980 Presidential campaign. The aim has been to illustrate the benefits of investigating implicit communication theory in television reporting about politics. The conclusions offered here are partial, tentative, and qualitative; and they are meant to interest fellow scholars in pursuing this line of research by a variety of methods. If we were able to articulate a theory of television and of political communication that broadcasters would recognize as their own, it would have an advantage over implicit theories, because it could be subjected, by broadcasters and their critics, to inspection, analysis, and possible modification. When the implicit is made explicit it becomes arguable. The difficulty, of course, is that the better an implicit theory is the more complex it is likely to be; and a complex implicit theory resists explicit description. Furthermore, most of us operate from day to day on the basis of common sense, implicit theories that we might even deny if they were to be stated explicitly. Television's implicit communication theory may or may not be a source of wisdom, rather than of error.

Television's implicit theory of political communication is filtered through its theories of television as communication, with paradoxical effects. Television news reports in their structure and content de-legitimate politics and deprecate political performance and, at the same time, assume the inevitability of the structure and content of both politics and television.

REFERENCES

Aranguren, J. L. 1967. *Human Communication*. New York: McGraw-Hill.

Aristotle. 1932. *The Rhetoric of Aristotle*. Translated by Lane Cooper. New York: Appleton-Century-Crofts.

Barthes, Roland. 1970. *Writing Degree Zero and Elements of Semiology*. Translated by Annette Lavers and Colin Smith. Boston, Mass.: Beacon Press.

————. 1972. *Mythologies*. Translated by Annette Lavers. New York: Hill and Wang.

Benson, Thomas W. 1968. Poisoned Minds. *Southern Speech Journal* 34 (Fall 1968): 54–61.

————. 1974. Rhetoric and Autobiography: The Case of Malcolm X. *The Quarterly Journal of Speech* 60 (February 1974): 1–13.

————. 1975. Videology: Space and Time in Political Television. *The Pennsylvania Speech Communication Annual* 31 (1975): 23–38.

————. 1978. The Senses of Rhetoric: A Topical System for Critics. *The Central States Speech Journal* 29 (Winter 1978): 237–250.

————. 1980a. The Rhetorical Structure of Frederick Wiseman's *High School*. *Communication Monographs* 47 (November 1980): 233–261.

————. 1980b. "Rhetoric As a Way of Being." Unpublished paper, The Pennsylvania State University.

————. 1981. Another Shooting in Cowtown. *The Quarterly Journal of Speech* 67 (November 1981).

———— and Michael Prosser. 1969. *Readings in Classical Rhetoric*. Boston, Mass.: Allyn and Bacon.

———— and Richard Barton. 1979. Television As Politics: The British View. *The Quarterly Journal of Speech* 65 (December 1979): 439–457.

Blankenship, Jane. 1976. The Search for the 1972 Democratic Nomination: A Metaphorical Perspective. In Jane Blankenship and Herman G. Stelzner, eds. *Rhetoric and Communication: Studies in the University of Illinois Tradition*. Urbana, Ill.: University of Illinois.

Bormann, Ernest G. 1980. *Communication Theory*. New York: Holt, Rinehart and Winston.

Brock, Bernard L., and Robert L. Scott, eds. 1980. *Methods of Rhetorical Criticism: A Twentieth-Century Perspective*, 2nd ed. Detroit, Mich.: Wayne State University.

Burke, Kenneth. 1969a. *A Grammar of Motives*. 1945, rpt. Berkeley, Cal.: University of California.

————. 1969b. *A Rhetoric of Motives*. 1950, rpt. Berkeley, Cal.: University of California.

Dance, Frank E. X. ed. 1967. *Human Communication Theory: Original Essays*. New York: Holt, Rinehart and Winston.

Eco, Umberto. 1976. *A Theory of Semiotics*. Bloomington, Ind.: Indiana University.

Edelman, Murray. 1964. *The Symbolic Uses of Politics.* Urbana, Ill.: University of Illinois.

Ehninger, Douglas, ed. 1972. *Contemporary Rhetoric: A Reader's Coursebook.* Glenview, Ill.: Scott, Foresman.

Ellis, Donald G. 1980. Some Effects of Task Context on Implicit Communication Theory. *Communication Quarterly* 28 (Winter 1980): 11–19.

Harrison, Robert Dale. 1981. "Heckling As Rhetoric." Dissertation, The Pennsylvania State University.

Johannesen, Richard L., ed. 1971. *Contemporary Theories of Rhetoric: Selected Readings.* New York: Harper & Row.

Johnson, Bonnie McDaniel. 1972. "Implicit Communication Theory in Images of Organized Countergroups." Dissertation, State University of New York at Buffalo.

Johnson, Bonnie McDaniel. 1975. Images of the Enemy in Intergroup Conflict. *Central States Speech Journal* 26 (1975): 84–92.

Jones, Edward E. 1954. Authoritarianism As a Determinant of First-Impression Formation. *Journal of Personality* 23 (1954): 107–127.

Kelly, George A. 1955. *The Psychology of Personal Constructs.* New York: W. W. Norton.

Littlejohn, Stephen W. 1978. *Theories of Human Communication.* Columbus, Oh.: Charles E. Merrill.

Mortensen, C. David. 1979. *Basic Readings in Communication Theory,* 2nd ed. New York: Harper & Row.

Pearce, W. Barnett, and Vernon E. Cronen. 1980. *Communication, Action, and Meaning: The Creation of Social Realities.* New York: Praeger Publishers.

Schneider, David J. 1973. Implicit Personality Theory: A Review. *Psychological Bulletin* 79 (May 1973): 294–309.

Scott, Robert L. 1968. A Rhetoric of Facts: Arthur Larson's Stance As a Persuader. *Speech Monographs* 35 (June 1968): 109–121.

Sebeok, Thomas A., ed. 1977. *A Perfusion of Signs.* Bloomington, Ind.: Indiana University Press.

———, ed. 1978. *Sight, Sound, and Sense.* Bloomington, Ind.: Indiana University Press.

Sereno, Kenneth K. and C. David Mortensen. 1970. *Foundations of Communication Theory.* New York: Harper & Row.

Smith, Robert Rutherford. 1979. Mythic Elements in Television News. *Journal of Communication* 29 (Winter 1979): 75–82.

Stelzner, Hermann G. 1965. Analysis by Metaphor. *The Quarterly Journal of Speech* 51 (February 1965): 52–61.

Wegner, Daniel M. and Robin R. Vallacher. 1977. *Implicit Psychology: A Introduction to Social Cognition.* New York: Oxford University Press.

White, Eugene F. 1963. Cotton Mathers' *Manductio ad Ministerium. The Quarterly Journal of Speech* 49 (October 1963): 308–319.

Wish, Myron and Susan J. Kaplan. 1977. Toward an Implicit Theory of Interpersonal Communication. *Sociometry* 40 (September 1977): 234-246.

Zyskind, Harold. 1968. A Case Study in Philosophic Rhetoric: Theodore Roosevelt. *Philosophy and Rhetoric* 1 (1968): 228-254.

8

ENERGY AS A NON-ISSUE IN 1980 COVERAGE

ROBERT C. SAHR

Energy was not a central issue in the 1980 presidential election campaign. Yet such a bald statement is deceptive. Energy considerations underlay several important foreign policy and economic issues, and both candidates and news personnel called attention to those connections. In addition, many elements of President Carter's energy policy made news during 1980 and constituted at least an indirect part of the campaign. Finally, the candidates did take positions on energy issues, and energy policy sparked one of the few explicit exchanges about a particular policy during the entire campaign.

To examine television news coverage of energy in relation to the 1980 presidential election campaign, the Vanderbilt *Television News Index and Abstracts* issues for January through October 1980 were carefully reviewed. Video tapes of stories that appeared to have the most direct bearing on energy in relation to the campaign were obtained from the Vanderbilt Television News Archive for coding and detailed analysis.[1]

GENERAL NEWS ABOUT ENERGY IN 1980

Table 8.1 shows general, non-policy (i.e., not related to specific public policy proposals or actions) coverage of energy on early-evening network television newscasts during the period of January through Octo-

[1] I would like to thank James Pilkington, director of the Vanderbilt Television News Archive, for all his help during this project, and William Adams and the Television and Politics Study Program at the George Washington University for financial support of this study.

117

Table 8.1
Non-policy Energy Coverage by Network News,
January–October 1980

Topic	ABC		CBS		NBC	
	Number	Time	Number	Time	Number	Time
Oil						
OPEC	17*	24:00	21*	18:50	21*	17:40
Profits	7	6:10	20	18:00	8	4:20
Prices	17*	15:10	17*	14:40	8*	4:30
Fraud	2	0:40	4	4:30	4	1:10
Other	24	33:50	41	53:40	29	41:20
Nuclear						
TMI**	23	29:30	28	25:30	20	24:10
Other	15	9:20	26	31:20	17	24:00
Other energy	10	17:40	18	22:00	9	18:00
Totals	115	136:20	175	188:30	116	135:10

* Excluding passing mention in stories on the economy.
**Related to Three Mile Island nuclear accident.

ber 1980. Energy was mentioned incidentally in other stories as well, particularly in those about the economy. Nearly all general energy stories during that period focused on either oil or nuclear power, with oil far outdistancing nuclear. Solar energy, coal, and other general energy topics received much less attention.

Oil stories were especially related to the US economy. Tables 8.1 and 8.2 show the nature of this emphasis on oil. Most of the coverage of oil came early in the year when oil prices were a major factor in inflation. Similarly, much of the coverage in the later period focused on OPEC.

Television coverage emphasized changes in the price of oil and oil products, particularly gasoline. TV news also stressed the improved profits of oil companies during this period. Reports nearly always compared profits only with those of the same period the previous year, a practice which oil company officials and many energy economists say is deceptive or at least inadequate for examining trends. CBS was quite concerned

Table 8.2
Coverage of Non-policy Oil Topics, Number of Stories by Period

Topic	Early (January-May)			Late (June-October)		
	ABC	CBS	NBC	ABC	CBS	NBC
Prices	14	16	7	3	1	1
OPEC	4	11	5	13	10	15
Profits	7	16	6	0	4	2
Fraud	1	4	4	1	0	0
Other oil	14	23	14	10	18	15
Totals	40	70	36	27	33	35

Table 8.3
Contribution of Energy Price Increases to the Consumer Price Index

A. Yearly increase in energy prices

1976	1977	1978	1979	1980*
6.2%	8.2%	7.5%	36.5%	18.9%

*November 1979–November 1980.

B. Change in consumer price index, energy and all items, by quarter

	1979-IV	1980-I	1980-II	1980-III
All items	13.7%	16.9%	13.6%	7.2%
Energy	25.6	53.3	22.5	3.8

Source: Economic Report of the President, 1981, pp. 149–150.

with oil company profits, spotlighting this subject with more stories and more time than the other two networks combined.

With high inflation fueled by energy costs, the incumbent president running for reelection might have enjoyed the implication of oil company profiteering and surely wanted to blame OPEC as well. In several stories, President Carter was shown or quoted as blaming OPEC for a big part of the rise in prices. One early example was a White House interview with Frank Reynolds (ABC, 1/3/80).

Talking to Reynolds, President Carter said inflation was "almost completely attributable to OPEC," over which the United States has no control. Subtracting the OPEC-stimulated increase in prices, he argued, inflation would have been similar to earlier rates of 7 or 8 percent.[2] Frank Reynolds continued to push the President to explain why he had not used his high recent standing in the polls to "solve the dependence on foreign oil" (a phrasing filled with strong policy assumptions). When Carter turned to the high rise in prices and their impact, Reynolds continued to ask if Americans had been pushed "as hard as they can go."

Reynolds' theme in this interview was, transparently, leadership; energy was a vehicle for that subject. This was the first, but not the last, time in 1980 that TV news used energy this way. Nevertheless, the interview did give the president his best opportunity on television to state precisely his view of the relationship between OPEC price increases and changes in the inflation rate.

Related to the Middle East were two other major news subjects during the campaign period that probably reinforced the oil-inflation-Presi-

[2] Such precision can be risky. A few days later (1/25/80) ABC's Sam Donaldson focused on a *Washington Post* headline reading: "Carter Erred. . ." Donaldson reported the *Post's* conclusion that Carter had incorrectly attributed virtually all of the increased inflation rate to the surge in energy prices. The measurement issues are complex, however, and, for certain months and quarters, Carter's statement was not such an exaggeration; see the data in *Economic Report of the President, 1981*, p. 294.

dent Carter association: Iranian events (throughout 1979 and 1980) and Billy Carter's relationship with the government of Libya (especially during July, August, and September of 1980). (See Adams & Heyl, 1981.) Because earlier changes in Iranian oil supply had affected oil prices, the continuing reference to Iran during 1980 may have recalled this connection, particularly early in the year when oil prices were rising. The seeming inability of the Carter Administration to resolve the hostage crisis may also have reinforced questions about the President's ability to deal with the Middle East, oil prices, and energy in general. Of course, President Carter maintained that OPEC price rises were the chief cause of inflation and that, in dealing with OPEC (as quoted by Dan Rather, CBS, 2/26/80), "we are caught up in circumstances over which we have very little control." But this posture might well have reinforced—in the context of Iran—perceptions of the Administration's weakness or lack of competence or both.

An exact account of the amount of attention newscasts devoted to energy in relation to the economy throughout the year is difficult to obtain because so many of the references were in economy stories that only briefly mentioned energy. Nevertheless, it is clear from Table 8.1 that since most of the energy stories considered oil, the energy-inflation connection was made explicitly and implicitly throughout much of the year. It is also clear that, going into the election year, Americans already had an overwhelmingly negative impression of Carter's skill with energy issues. The President was given only a 19 percent approval rating on his ability to handle the nation's energy problems (ABC-Harris poll, Fall 1979, cited in Foley, Britton, & Everett, 1980, p. 73). It is in this context that the President offered his energy policy proposals.

ENERGY PROPOSALS OF THE CARTER ADMINISTRATION

A number of Administration energy policy proposals were the focus of television coverage in 1980 (Table 8.4). The "windfall profits" tax, energy mobilization board, and synthetic fuels proposals all had been introduced by the President in 1979. Gas rationing powers had been a continuing issue, though most of the specific proposals on that topic were new in 1980. Proposals concerning gasohol, nuclear waste, the oil import fee, and the sale of nuclear fuels to India were essentially new in 1980; the first three made news between January and June and the last in June and September.

Television news essentially ignored the continuing policy proposals until Congress acted definitively on them.[3] The first of the three proposals from 1979 to be resolved by Congress in 1980 was the windfall profits tax.

---

[3] For a review of television and news magazine coverage of Carter's energy proposals in 1977 and 1979, see Sahr and Gladstone (1981).

Table 8.4
Coverage of Carter Administration Energy Policy Proposals,
January-October 1980

	ABC		CBS		NBC	
pic	Number	Time	Number	Time	Number	Time
sohol	2*	2:20	2*	1:20	1*	2:00
s rationing plan	4	2:30	4	6:40	3	0:50
indfall profits tax	3	3:00	7	8:50	5	4:00
clear waste storage	1	3:00	1	1:50	1	0:30
e on imported oil/ gasoline	5*	10:40	7*	9:20	9*	12:30
ergy Mobilization Board	1	2:00	1	2:00	1	2:00
nthetic fuels	3	3:40	2	6:20	2	1:50
clear fuel sale to India	2	1:00	4	3:20	4	1:20
Totals	22	28:10	28	39:40	26	25:00

n addition to passing mention in stories on the economy, etc.

When the Senate approved this tax on March 27, all three networks devoted at least two minutes discussing the bill's passage. ABC and NBC opened with this story as the lead.

Both CBS and NBC presented essentially similar stories, though both were about two minutes instead of ABC's four. The CBS story was 10 minutes into the program. Both CBS and NBC emphasized the "overwhelmingly final approval" and that "President Carter may have lost two primaries this week but he won a big victory" by a 2:1 margin in the Senate. Both showed how the revenues would be used and quoted several senators, including Senator Robert Dole who called it a "big, big, tax." Carole Simpson of NBC closed by calling the action "maybe the biggest legislative victory of the Carter administration." On ABC, the Senate result was also presented as a victory for the President, although it was trailed by a story suggesting higher oil prices.

The next round of network attention to energy legislation came when Congress voted on the Energy Mobilization Board (EMB), proposed by the President back in 1979 to speed the approval process for future energy facilities. The House rejected the proposal, and the surprising nature of the loss was emphasized by all three news programs in similar 2-minute stories on June 27. References to the EMB defeat were repeated in June 30 stories about President Carter's ceremonial signing of the synthetic fuels bill (the Energy Security Act).

During this period, one correspondent made probably the year's most sympathetic statement about President Carter and energy policy. Jack Smith, who narrated ABC's reporting of Carter's victory on synfuels and the windfall profits tax, and his defeat on EMB and the gasoline fee, pointed out that energy appeared to be an unfortunate issue for the President because, despite its importance, "Congress does not take it very seriously." The attitude of Congress also formed the basis for perhaps the least sympathetic closing assessment when Lesley Stahl noted that the President had gone out of his way to involve Congress in the synfuels bill ceremony. She said there was White House concern because Democrats were not following the President; some actually seemed to "enjoy embarrassing him." The two statements, and the tone in which they were spoken, gave rather different impressions of the responsibility and actions of the President and the Congress.

Most of the energy proposals initiated in 1980 were not too controversial on network news. The White House's proposals in early January to increase gasohol production were presented on television—consistent with the Administration's rationale—as a response to the potential effect of the embargo of grain sales to the Soviet Union. Each network outlined the Administration's goals and the difficulties of meeting them in the short time projected.

When the Administration put forth on February 12 its proposals for dealing with nuclear waste, ABC gave 3 minutes to the story, CBS gave 70 seconds, and NBC 30 seconds. President Carter's coal proposals received even less attention: 20 seconds each on CBS and NBC, none on ABC.[4] None of the networks mentioned either of these proposals again during the period studied here.

Two more controversial proposals were the gasoline rationing plan and the sale of nuclear fuel to India. (The gas rationing plans of President Carter had generated considerable controversy in 1979; see Goodwin, 1981, pp. 606–608.) In 1980, all three networks devoted one story to the Department of Energy's gasoline conservation/rationing plan in early February. Then in early June, each devoted two or three stories to the issue when President Carter sent his proposals to Congress. CBS consistently devoted the most time to the topic: four stories of 1½ to 2 minutes each, as contrasted with three June stories of 30 seconds each on ABC (which had a 1-minute, 20-second story in February) and three 10- or 20-second stories on NBC. CBS presented some of the issues, showed then-representative David Stockman raising some mild questions about the proposal, and suggested that there was little outright opposition because the plan would become law automatically, unless specifically rejected by Congress.

The issue of nuclear fuel sales to India arose in September. In June, President Carter proposed the sale; and in September, the Senate finally

---

[4] A very different interpretation, or emphasis, on the political importance of coal policy in relation to President Carter's reelection is given in Kirschten (1980).

approved it, after being satisfied that fuel sales would increase rather than decrease US control over India's use of nuclear power for peaceful purposes. Though this was a potentially difficult issue for the Administration, only CBS devoted much attention to it, and then only 3½ minutes, mostly in June.

The energy proposal that received the most attention, both in Congress and in television news programs, was the $4.62 per barrel fee on imported oil. This fee would have increased gasoline prices by about 10 cents per gallon. This was also the energy proposal which may have been most politically damaging to the President in 1980. When it was introduced, all the networks described the plan as part of the President's anti-inflation package (3/14/80). They then mentioned it occasionally in relation to other energy or economic issues. But the next "news peg" upon which to hang a complete story about the import fee/gasoline fee came when a federal judge held up the use of the fee just two days before it was to go into effect. Both ABC and NBC treated that action as the lead story and devoted significant program time to it: 4 minutes and 3 minutes, 20 seconds, respectively (5/13/81). CBS, on the other hand, devoted only 10 seconds to the story and placed it later in the program.

The proposal was, in the words of NBC's Andrea Mitchell, "an issue that Congress loves to hate," and members of Congress quickly intensified efforts to block the fee. News coverage logically shifted to actions by the Congress: the policy issue had become a real drama. All networks showed Administration spokesmen before Congress on May 14, with comments by assorted members of Congress in the hearings. On Thursday, May 15, CBS and NBC quoted President Carter in 20-second stories as saying that Congressional leaders in March had encouraged him to propose an import fee but that members of Congress were backing away under the pressures of an election year.

CBS initially had emphasized the issue less than the other networks, but that changed. Nelson Benton of CBS devoted 90 seconds on May 31 to continued opposition of Congress to the fee and to revenue effects of its passage or defeat. On June 4, when House rejection of the fee was reported, ABC and NBC both placed the story about 20 minutes into their news programs. CBS, however, placed it in the lead position, even though the newscast was the day following the "Super Tuesday" presidential primaries.

The three networks reported the 376–30 vote and pointed out that there were sufficient votes to override a veto. All used televised tapes of the House floor debate to show Representative Vanik of Ohio arguing passionately for the proposal. Vanik was shown saying that because he was retiring from Congress, he could afford to vote for it more than could other members of Congress. Each network also showed Representative

Shannon; ABC and NBC used the part of his speech where he called the proposal a "gold-plated turkey." All three stories emphasized the political significance of the vote for President Carter, and showed him promising to veto the legislation. CBS, devoting the most time to the President, presented him stating that it "is not popular to increase prices in an election year," but that it "is right for the country, right for holding down future consumption—even if I don't get one vote, I intend to veto...because it's right."

The next two days brought the drama to its foreordained—according to news reports—conclusion: President Carter vetoed the legislation and the House and Senate both overrode his veto by more than the required two thirds majority. (Only CBS showed the President's comment that it does "not help to stand up and give speeches...unless they can take the heat.") Before or after (or both) the Senate vote, all the networks emphasized the historic significance—the first Democratic president since Harry Truman to have a veto overridden—and the political significance in an election year.

ABC and NBC emphasized the mood of the House—"uproarious" (Brit Hume of ABC) and "hardly a dignified moment" when the message arrived (Andrea Mitchell of NBC). Hume suggested before the votes that the Republicans supported repeal because they hoped to embarrass the President. After the votes, he said the "Democratic Congress seemed almost eager to hand the President a humiliating defeat." Andrea Mitchell recalled that a member of Congress had told her that it was "not only a defeat but a warning for the President. He has the votes to be renominated but still does not understand what's happening out there in America." So, she said, "the fee was overturned and the President damaged."

Michael Robinson (1981, pp. 180–181; and also Robinson & Sheehan, 1981) has suggested there was a sharp shift in the media stereotype of President Carter that began during the spring. Carter's portrayal changed from the image of the "decent man in over his head" to the "J. R. Ewing candidate" who was "mean, vindictive, manipulative, and petty."

One example of the start of the Ewingesque portrayal came on March 23. On that date, all three networks devoted one to two minutes to President Carter's criticism of Mobil Oil for being the only oil company to refuse to take corrective action in relation to price guideline violations. All three put a political twist on the report. ABC's Sam Donaldson emphasized the White House hope that the President's stance would be seen as "tough." CBS's Lesley Stahl suggested that Carter's statement that even an election year was "no time for political cowardice or demagoguery'.... seemed to be a jab at his political opponent," Edward Kennedy. NBC's Judy Woodruff suggested that the intent was "to minimize criticism of the President on inflation."

By autumn, Carter was entirely transformed, as Robinson discovered, into a wiley, manipulative incumbent. For example, one story, ostensibly about energy proposals by Judy Woodruff (NBC, 10/9/80), was used to illustrate the use of incumbency by President Carter. The story reported the President's White House ceremony that day announcing hydroelectric projects in 17 states. She pointed out that these states were all electorally close. His signing of a bill in Niagara Falls, his activities regarding Chicago, and his upcoming tour of a synfuels plant were all discussed along with his recent news conference, the first "eight minutes of which were spent on trumpeting" his accomplishments. Reference to his town meetings and the use of his cabinet officers—who were to be spending a total of 110 days in October campaigning—concluded that he "continues to take full advantage of the office." The energy opening was only a peg for the angle of crass electioneering.

Despite this transition in the fall, during June and earlier—at least with regard to energy initiatives—coverage was still much more concerned with the President's leadership and competence than with meanness and motives. The issues of leadership and competence seem to have been particularly reinforced by the following elements of energy coverage: (1) rising energy prices were presented as partly caused by President Carter's actions in 1979; (2) the President was shown to be (and indeed admitted to being) powerless to do anything about many energy problems, especially those related to OPEC and Iran; (3) when President Carter finally did try to be more bold, he selected a policy that was said to increase inflation and probably would not have much, if any, impact on oil imports; and, (4) probably most damaging (in coverage of the oil import fee), Jimmy Carter was shown as not even having the respect, must less the support, of the Congress of his own party.

Although weak, Carter was not sketched as a cunning J. R. Ewing in the first half of the year. In fact, the one key positive note that surfaced was the depiction of Carter as a principled person working for what he believes is correct in spite of political and other obstacles, especially in CBS coverage. While the CBS treatment was not overly sympathetic, more than the others it allowed the President to give relatively detailed justification for his actions.

Generally, the coverage of his policy actions—most clearly in relation to the oil import fee—simply reinforced stereotypes that had arisen earlier in relation to President Carter. Hess (1981, p. 99) and Grossman and Kumar (1981) argue that stories about the President are often funneled through Congress. In instances of Congress-President interaction, such as the import fee, news stories may well have accurately reflected views of President Carter held by many of those in Congress. "But if the story was a reflection of reality, it also contributed to the reality of the story," as Grossman and Kumar observed (1981, p. 317). "Carter's reputation, as shaped and hardened by the media, contributed to his difficulties in getting control of his office" and presumably in his reelection efforts as well.

ENERGY AS A CAMPAIGN ISSUE

It would be misleading to tabulate all of the "energy campaign stories" in 1980 because, with very few exceptions, energy was not considered in isolation. Stories examining the positions of candidates or their records sometimes included energy, occasionally in detail but usually with only a brief reference. Interviews with candidates sometimes made a brief mention of energy.

When energy policy was part of campaign coverage, it was nearly always treated in one of two ways: first, as a campaign "vehicle" (which need not be examined for its merits and practicality) or, second, as a consistency measure for stories examining candidate positions over time (with changes of view taken to be politically motivated). With both approaches, the substantive content of energy issues was far less important than the political context.

So many candidates were running in the early primaries that detailed examination of the issue positions of all of them was apparently not considered practical on television news programs. (Special campaign programs may devote more time to this but they are also generally seen by a much smaller audience than the evening news programs.) As a result, Patterson (1980, p. 168) suggests, "very little actual learning about issues occurs during the first four months" of a campaign. "Issue material is but a rivulet in the news flow during the primaries, and what is there is almost completely diluted by information about the race." An example of this is a 5-minute story by ABC's Barry Serafin just prior to the New Hampshire primary. Serafin surveyed the domestic issue positions of candidates Anderson, Baker, Brown, Bush, Connally, Crane, Dole, Kennedy, and Reagan—5 minutes to cover all nine candidates on all domestic issues. Because nuclear power was an issue in New Hampshire, 30 seconds were devoted to the information that Kennedy and Brown opposed nuclear power and all the Republicans favored it. John Connally was shown saying that nuclear power was the "cheapest, safest" form of energy.

Somewhat more detailed examination of issue positions had to wait until later when more candidates had been "winnowed out"—not much help to voters in the early primaries. When the number of candidates had been reduced, then television could begin to give some attention to the issue positions of those who remained. Indeed, the only candidates whose energy positions received much coverage were Carter, Reagan, and Anderson ("survivors" of the primary process), and their energy views received little attention relative to other issues.

Coverage of the winnowed candidates was apt to stress energy issues as either a "campaign vehicle" or a "consistency measure," or both. For example, Anderson's views on a variety of topics, including energy, were examined in a two-minute report on ABC (4/24/80) and in a six-minute story on NBC (7/3/80). The ABC story by Lynn Sherr said nothing about the substance of the candidate's position on energy; instead, Sherr mentioned the political effect of his views. She insisted that Anderson is "always good on energy, but ABC polls show that voters never decide on the basis of energy."

The longer NBC examination of Anderson's views emphasized his changes ("about face") on a variety of issues, including energy: he supported nuclear power and the breeder reactor, but "today he sounds like he opposes it" (then Anderson is shown saying nuclear power policy "does not make much sense"); and "in 1975 he voted against a 20 cent per gallon gasoline tax," though "now he supports a 50 cents per gallon gasoline tax." This NBC "Special Segment" was one of many network stories that looked at campaign issues strictly in terms of candidate consistency.

Probably the most famous 1980 examination of a candidate's shifts was Bill Plante's analysis of "Reagan's shift to the center" on October 7. The CBS graphics showed Reagan's face covered with a large "X" each time Plante noted a moderated position. That report mentioned, in relation to energy, only that Reagan no longer emphasized abolishing the Department of Energy as much as he had previously.

Other stories examining Reagan's record did include more discussion of his energy positions, including reports in late spring about Reagan's "errors." ABC's James Wooten (4/11/80) showed Reagan's views on energy, especially in relation to the oil companies, and then presented an Energy Action spokesman who challenged those views.

Bill Plante of CBS spent almost 7 minutes on another "error" story, of which about two minutes were on energy. He focused particularly on Reagan's use of figures concerning American oil reserves, and argued that Reagan had misemphasized the figures or had used reports that were no longer supported by their authors, and that he had never checked the accuracy of his use of the reports with their authors. Don Oliver of NBC on May 6 mentioned in 10 seconds of his 4-minute report that Reagan exaggerated oil reserve figures.

Both Plante and Wooten softened the "accuracy" question by pointing out that "it may be just a matter of style" to "support his view that 'less is generally better' in relation to government." Wooten suggested with regard to "style over substance" that "so far it's working" as it "worked four years ago for Carter." The question in the election campaign may be "who's the better practitioner of the art" of style over substance. Only NBC's Don Oliver did not soften the conclusion. He concluded: "The criticism is that he often takes questionable information. . . and uses it as the basis" for policy proposals. "If the facts are wrong, the solutions don't exist."

Occasionally, when the candidates were interviewed, their views on energy were part of the discussion. In January, Walter Cronkite interviewed Reagan and elicited this discussion of energy:

> CRONKITE: . . . Reagan's answer to the energy crisis is equally straight-forward.
>
> REAGAN: Well, I think, like inflation, government is to blame. We had the cheapest energy of anyone in the world from the time that that first oil well was drilled in 1859 in Pennsylvania up to 1971. In 1971, we put government price-fixing and regulations on the oil industry. In '54, we had done it to natural gas. And since 1971, look at how the price of oil has—and gasoline has skyrocketed.
>
> CRONKITE: Do you think de-control then basically can solve the entire energy problem?
>
> REAGAN: I had one man, an independent in this business and one of the top men in that field, tell me that he believed we could be self-sufficient in five years with de-control.
>
> CRONKITE: Let me get just one thing straight, if I may, Governor. Are you saying that US federal regulations controlling prices are more responsible for our high prices today and our shortages than the Arab price increases, the OPEC price increases?
>
> REAGAN: Yes, plus our depreciating value of the dollar.
>
> CRONKITE: Of the other front runners, only Connally agrees with him in opposing windfall profits taxes, though all want de-control. . . .

Although later Reagan was to tone down his conclusions concerning self-sufficiency, this January interview, as brief as it was, probably gave the most complete statements of Reagan's approach to energy shown during the entire year on early-evening network newscasts.

On October 21, Cronkite was shown conducting parallel interviews with Reagan and Carter. In the six-minute segment, about 30 seconds were devoted to energy. Carter said he thought it was largely a task for the private sector; that was why he said he moved to de-regulate oil price controls, over time to prevent shock to the economy.[5] Reagan stated his

---

[5] The usual argument, though rarely fully explained on TV news, is that price controls on domestic oil production keep the average price of oil down but reduce domestic exploration and production and also stimulate the importing of oil. Removal of price controls would raise the average price of oil, and thus reduce overall oil use, resulting in less need for imports, while simultaneously stimulating domestic production. According to a former Department of Energy official I interviewed in Washington, in June 1981, one of the largest gaps between energy experts and the public is that the public sees price as the major part of the energy problem, while experts both in and out of government tend to see price as part of the solution. See, for example, Stobaugh and Yergin (1980). Television news, with its emphasis on prices, has not made the task of explaining this to the public any easier.

opposition to the "windfall profits" tax. This segment appears to have been the longest general examination of the energy positions of the two candidates on nightly network news programs during the fall.

The following night NBC's John Chancellor interviewed both candidates, also in parallel interviews, on their views of the environment in Alaska, including the impact of oil. In a 2½-minute interview, the philosophies of each man were put forward relatively clearly.

Carter's record as President was the subject of several news stories, some of which mentioned energy. In a five-minute review of Carter as President, Sam Donaldson of ABC (2/19/80) spent one minute on an examination of his energy actions:[6] Carter had promised a policy on a problem which was the "moral equivalent of war"; Congress did not pass the key tax on oil; so the President acted alone with phased de-control plus a windfall profits tax, while emphasizing conservation and nuclear power. "The bottom line: use less oil and pay more for it."

NBC's review of Carter's record with some reference to energy was broadcast May 22. This 6-minute report devoted about 30 seconds to energy. The organization for this "Special Segment" ("Jimmy Carter: The Record") was promises, examining those kept and those not kept. Energy policy involved both promises kept and those not kept: promises kept included natural gas price de-control and the formation of the Department of Energy. On the other side, "on the economy he has not done as well," and he has blamed OPEC. "A promise yet to be kept: a comprehensive energy plan. The centerpiece windfall profits tax" has been signed into law "but the others are still pending. After three years of wrangling," there is still no comprehensive energy policy.[7]

Bruce Morton of CBS (10/17/80) also focused on promises, more then 600 of them made in the 1976 campaign. The sole mention of energy was in relation to the promised removal of price controls on oil.

The only energy news that contained potentially good news from the Carter Administration's perspective was NBC's report on September 6 that the Secretary of Energy had announced American imports of foreign oil were down 37 percent over the previous year. NBC also reported that Gulf, Texaco, and Atlantic Richfield were lowering their wholesale gasoline prices. In the days that followed, none of the networks appear to have followed up this 30-second pair of stories with analyses of the role, if any, of Carter Administration policies in bringing about the changes.

---

[6] "Soon after his defeat by Ronald Reagan, Jimmy Carter told reporters that there were two things he'd be delighted to bequeath to the new President: ABC-TV's abrasive Sam Donaldson and Israel's stubborn Menachem Begin" (House, 1981). According to Alter (1981), most Carter aides despised Donaldson.

[7] For a more systematic examination of Carter's record on energy, see Cowan (1980). Carter's views on the deregulation of natural gas appear to have changed over time; see Congressional Quarterly (1979, p. 15). Regarding a comprehensive energy program, see Pelham (1980) and Corrigan and Kirschten (1980).

SKIMMING THE SURFACE

A consistent and careful viewer of any network news program during 1980 probably would have had some general idea about the energy positions of at least Anderson, Carter, and Reagan, with Anderson's "50 cent per gallon gasoline tax" probably the best known. But none of the policy positions were examined in detail or subjected to serious questioning. For example, it does not appear that John Anderson was ever asked to explain the prospects for his 50 cent per gallon gasoline tax proposal in light of the "hooting and hollering" defeat by both houses of Congress of a gasoline tax only one fifth as large. Presumably in the campaign coverage's division of labor, it was not the responsibility of those covering John Anderson to ask a question related to coverage of Carter or of Congress. Instead, policy positions were put forth as part of partisan arguments, as vehicles for electioneering.

This approach was evident in coverage of the Carter campaign against Edward Kennedy. Energy differences between them were not mentioned in the TV treatment of domestic issues prior to the New Hampshire primary. After Kennedy's January 28 speech at Georgetown University, television news coverage did not emphasize the division between Kennedy and Carter in relation to gasoline rationing, except by mentioning or briefly showing the part of the speech in which Kennedy proposed rationing. Little emphasis at all was given to substantive differences between the two men. Robert Shogun, *Los Angeles Times* political reporter, stated (in Groff, Schwadel, DeWitt, Fulton, Johnson, McCormick, Randolph, & Skrzycki, 1980, p. 124) that the differences "need to be dramatic and meaningful. . . . The differences just did not lend themselves to a major piece." This perception by newspeople appears to have changed little later in the campaign.

The major difference between Carter and Kennedy on nuclear power was only noted briefly at the time of the Democratic Party platform fights. On June 23, ABC and CBS mentioned the platform "confrontation" between Kennedy and Carter supporters over nuclear power and the "claimed" (NBC) or "apparent" (CBS) victory of Kennedy forces. Both these short stories were read by the anchormen. Later, CBS and NBC mentioned the defeat of Kennedy proposals on oil taxes (8/13/80). Coverage of the Republican platform offered even less discussion of energy, other than quick mention of planks proposing to abolish the national 55 miles per hour speed limit, to lower air quality standards, and to develop more nuclear power.

Patterson (1980, p. 34) observes that "some clear-cut issues that arise during a presidential campaign are more appropriately called campaign issues than policy issues. Campaign issues are ones that develop from campaign incidents, usually errors in judgment by the candidates." But sometimes there are policy issue divisions between the candidates, even "clear-cut issues. . . that, above all, neatly divide the candidates" (Patterson, 1980, p. 31).

During September, such a seemingly clear-cut issue did emerge, an energy issue that involved one of the few "charge-response-countercharge" exchanges between candidates Carter and Reagan. ABC devoted stories to the interchange for three days, CBS for two days, and NBC for one day. The "debate" began when Carter claimed that Reagan was wrong in statements earlier that day about his energy policies and their effects (9/10/80). ABC's Donaldson only mentioned that Carter said Reagan was wrong, but CBS's Jerry Bowen and Jed Duvall spent 3½ minutes on the energy issue. Two minutes showed Reagan saying that President Carter kept the optimistic energy figures of his own energy agencies from the American people; that he increased imports from Libya ("maybe he should send his relatives there"; Billy Carter's activities were then recent news); and that Carter had conserved energy by putting "two million people out of work in a single year." Duvall then showed President Carter announcing John Sawhill's appointment as head of the Synthetic Fuels Corporation and saying that Reagan was wrong, had not checked his facts, and that coal production and crude oil production had increased.

The following night, all three network news programs included material on Reagan's response to the President's charges. ABC's Barry Serafin showed a long excerpt from Reagan: employing the line later used in the debate with John Anderson ("some people look up figures and some people make up figures"), saying oil production in the lower 48 states had declined every year the President had been in office, citing the *Monthly Energy Review* ("page 26 of your own report"), and asking rhetorically if this was why the President needed an excuse for not debating Anderson, Kennedy, and himself.

Bill Plante of CBS showed less of Reagan's statement but reported Reagan campaign officials were delighted to be on the offensive. NBC's Chris Wallace began, as had the others, with Reagan in Buffalo earlier that day where he had encountered pickets. Reagan's statement about "an excuse for not debating" was shown, though none of what he said specifically about energy was included. Instead, Wallace emphasized Reagan's attempt to appeal to blue collar workers.

Only ABC stayed with the story the third day, though it was no longer an energy story. The Secretary of Energy was shown claiming Thursday that Reagan's attacks on Carter were "factual misrepresentations." Then the ABC correspondent turned the story into a discussion of the President's campaign use of cabinet secretaries such as Neil Goldschmidt, Patricia Harris (shown making her controversial KKK statement), and Ray Marshall. Republican National Chairman Bill Brock criticized such campaigners being paid by the taxpayers. The story was not about energy but was another vehicle for showing Carter's use of incumbency. "Incompetent Carter" had become "devious J. R."

NBC did not report the "energy facts debate" at all. ABC and CBS treated it as a matter of partisan rhetoric, requiring no examination of the substance of the claims. Carter's and Reagan's positions appeared to be in direct disagreement on some key facts. An enterprising reporter might have determined who was correct or at least identified the basis for their disagreement. But no one on TV news treated it as more than a partisan disagreement.[8]

EVALUATING TELEVISION COVERAGE OF ISSUES

Very different opinions about the adequacy of coverage of campaign issues are based on very different views of their appropriate role in covering issues in campaigns. One view was expressed by David Stockman in early 1980, when he was a Republican Representative from Michigan (Foley, Britton, & Everett, 1980, pp. 87, 106):

> The way issues are used in a campaign is to convey the basic sense of the candidate's posture or attitude about government and about major constellations of issues....
>
> In that context, I think energy is being covered fairly well in this campaign, and I don't really have any sort of stirring critique about why you don't get into details....I don't thing that's a relevant part of the campaign communication process....

When back in the district, Stockman continues, you can explain issues to voters so they understand it because

---

[8] Because time constraints on television news are more limiting than space restrictions in newspapers, press accounts of the exchange were examined to determine if newspaper reporters made an effort to sort out the substance of the disagreement. The *Washington Post* reported the story briefly but did not examine the substance of the disagreement. The *New York Times* had two stories on September 11, one by Douglas Kneeland, ("Reagan Charges Carter Misleads U.S. on Threat to Energy Security") and one by Steven Weisman ("President Says Reagan Distorts Administration's Energy Record"). The Reagan story (about 34 column inches) appeared directly above the Carter story (about 30 column inches) on an inside page. Both were quite detailed in their account of the conflicting statements, but neither story attempted factual analysis of the disagreement. Two stories were located that did attempt to sort out the factual disagreements; both were Associated Press stories. Stan Benjamin (1980), Associated Press writer, examined the disagreements in a question-and-answer format story. Benjamin particularly emphasized Reagan's omission of Alaska and his choice of base years; and he also wrote, "Actually Reagan got it wrong by comparing a first half with a whole year." The story had been preceded the previous day by an unsigned AP story (1980) pointing out, as part of a larger story, that "Reagan left out the vast production of Alaska." Though one could ask for more in analysis of the energy positions of candidates, at least the two Associated Press stories did represent an attempt to sort out seemingly irreconcilable differences, to treat the differences as if they mattered.

you communicate in a kind of shorthand that tells people where you stand. And that's why I have this great trouble with the League of Women Voters' notion of campaign as an education process. . . . So I really have a hard time with the view that issues are handled very badly in campaigns because of the press, because candidates are manipulative or because somehow the whole process is deficient. I think they are handled fairly well.

This approach to issues is reinforced by the notion that voters care more about the personality, intelligence, and character of a candidate. Many journalists subscribe to this view. As Norman Miller, the *Wall Street Journal's* Washington bureau chief (Groff et al., 1980, p. 110), put it: "I think it is much more useful to try to deal with the whole person—what makes this candidate tick, what is the source and quality of the advice he receives on issues, what in his record suggests he has the savvy to deal with unpredictable, changing events."

Not only is it believed that the public deserves to hear about candidate character but the public is thought to be obsessed with the excitement of "who's ahead"—the "horse race." So give people what they want. William Greider of the *Washington Post* admitted (Groff et al., 1980, p. 96): "It's hard to resist. . . . People want to see that kind of article. We can't say we're going to ignore that kind of story because people want to see it. It's more entertaining—like a sports event."

Horse-race and candidate-character coverage leave little time for issues. One cynical view is that nothing is lost because issues are a sham. William Small, then president of NBC News, asserted that "every candidate for public office when he goes out to campaign is not interested in issues as such. What he's interested in is getting elected, and he uses issues that way" (Foley, Britton, & Everett, 1980, p. 77). Robert Scheer (p. 38) stated it more strongly: "The reason the press gets bored covering issues is the candidates are playing with the issues."

Yet even if it is conceded that more attention ought to be given to issues, some people argue that TV news has inherent limitations, in addition to the shortage of time. As one local anchorman stated (Foley, Britton, & Everett, 1980, p. 92):

> We can cover a presidential campaign fairly well, but we do not cover the issues of energy, the issues of inflation, the economy. We don't cover those stories well at all, partly because they are statistical stories that ought to be read and digested carefully, maybe even ought to be studied. And television is not studied, it's watched.

This comment leads to the frequently voiced view that there is a "low production value associated with most discussion of issues on television" and that "the medium abhors the idea of a 'talking head' or the reading of a position paper" (Bicker, 1978, p. 105). This is widely believed to reduce the possibility of examining issues not easily dramatized with visual materials.

The "old news" orientation of TV journalists compounds the problem further. It might take several days to develop a solid background story about a candidate's position, so the discussion of the background could not be made the same day as a candidate's original presentation. But a greater concern than "dated" backgrounders is the drive to avoid repetition.[9] As Lesley Stahl told Walter Cronkite on "Campaign Countdown" in response to his question about 1980 as an issueless campaign: "The candidates are discussing the issues but we aren't reporting them. They are old news. Maybe we should, but. . . ."

Whatever Stahl's misgivings, a widely shared view among broadcast journalists is that policy issues are not to be covered in depth by network news either because other campaign subjects are more appropriate and important than issues, or because the nature of the medium puts constraints on issue analysis.

A very different view of the role of the news media is suggested by Charles Peters (1976) and James David Barber (1979). The title of the article by Peters, "The Ignorant Press," refers to substantive policy ignorance and the tendency of correspondents to cover a candidate's issue positions by assessing political effects or by asking for a response from opposing candidates. Reporters are ignorant of substance so they cannot ask the right questions of the candidate concerning a policy proposal, nor can they analyze it except by reference to its political impact. In the view of Peters, their responsibility should include substantive as well as political examination of issues.[10]

Barber (1979) argued that television has an important role to play in educating its viewers, not simply during campaigns but all the time. He suggested that this is especially important because television is the main source of news for "the unmotivated and ill-informed half of the population." He listed five main problems with the way television news is now presented: (1) it is ahistorical (see also Fallows, 1979); (2) it does not follow up on the implementation of the government announcements and programs it reports; (3) it "morselizes" information into small, disconnected packages (see also Altheide, 1976); (4) it "tends to substitute opinion for

---

[9] Alter (1981, p. 16) asked, "Should the press repeat important coverage? As far as Reagan's record as governor was concerned, many reporters and editors said no. If the majority of Americans don't start paying attention to politics until after the World Series, well, that's their problem. . . . It was their fault for not paying more attention when the 'Reagan record' piece ran in May or June."

[10] Hess (1981) and Groff, Schwadel, DeWitt, Fulton, Johnson, McCormick, Randolph, and Skrzycki (1980) also suggest that the liberal arts background of most political reporters, particularly their lack of interest in and knowledge of such topics as economics, makes it difficult for them to understand and report detailed substantive issues.

fact, for example by quoting the conclusion but not the key evidence of experts or politicians"; and (5) "it tends to wrap up each story" with a beginning, middle, and end in 90 seconds.

Barber contended that TV news fails the part of the population that relies on it most because it uses a vocabulary that is too large and at too high a level; it does not involve the viewer (instead it soothes); and it is too cautious. Barber proposes simplifying the language, lengthening main stories so context and background can be presented, explaining why a story is important, adding more key facts, and removing the FCC's "balance" requirements.

In the absence of the sort of coverage Peters and Barber call for, candidates have a dilemma. Though candidates may have strong reasons for not emphasizing issues that are divisive, with the potential for losing votes, candidates are also aware that their issue positions will receive little coverage from the press. Jimmy Carter well illustrates the bind in which candidates find themselves. He is often quoted as having said that the only presidents he knew who had been specific on issues as candidates were "Presidents Dewey, Goldwater, and McGovern." But Carter also said in the famous *Playboy* interview (Scheer, 1976, p. 66):

> Issues? The local media are interested, all right, but the national news media have absolutely no interest in issues *at all*. Sometimes we freeze out the national media so we can open up press conferences to local people. At least we get questions from them—on timber management, on health care, on education. But the traveling press have zero interest in any issue unless it's a matter of making a mistake. What they're looking for is a 47-second argument between me and another candidate or something like that. There's nobody in the back of this plane who would ask an issue question unless he thought he could trick me into some crazy statement.

The entire problem is, of course, circular. Both journalists and candidates accuse each other of not being serious enough about issues. Each consequently downplays the importance of issues and each reinforces the other's perceptions. If more attention were to be devoted to issues, the circle might be broken. Both candidates and reporters (as well as the voters) might all begin to take issues more seriously if they were treated as worthy of more attention and examination.

A MORE SERIOUS TREATMENT OF ISSUES

Without minimizing the difficulties in expanding and intensifying issue coverage on television, there are various approaches to developing such coverage. Several proposals are based on the importance of context for understanding specific pieces of information and on the importance of off-year news coverage. Graber (1980, p. 135) summarized the problem as follows:

> Because individuals pick up information that is related to things they already know or in which they are interested, numerous "knowledge-gap" studies show that political elites and other well-informed people tend to absorb a great deal more mass media information than people who are poorly informed.

Thus, it is not sufficient to bombard viewers with substantive policy information during a campaign, if it has been lacking at other times. Otherwise, they may lack a context—the "things they already know." Absorbing substantive campaign information in a vacuum becomes nearly impossible.

Similarly, coverage of candidates, particularly an incumbent, during the years between election campaigns is at least as important to public perceptions as coverage of them during the campaign. Stereotypes introduced over time may persist for both news personnel and the public, so that campaign coverage really is relatively unimportant. As Graber (1980, p. 188) points out:

> President Carter's chances for reelection in 1980 therefore hinged in no small manner on the images which the media created about his presidency in the previous four years.... Newspeople shape national election outcomes by molding the images of political reality which lead to voting decisions, rather then by suggesting voting choices to an electorate that prefers to make its own choices.... Although voters pay most concentrated attention to media coverage just before elections, the crucial attitudes that determine voting choices may already be so firm that the final vote is a foregone conclusion.

The importance of off-year coverage of issues and politicians to the effective campaign coverage of issues and candidates should not be underestimated. The continual coverage of issues is crucial. Instead of the disconnected "morsels" of television news (reported as a specific narrow event, such as the passage of a bill), policy could be viewed in terms of a whole set of ongoing elements: different views of the problem a bill is intended to address, factual disagreements and uncertainties between the opponents, the significance of the differences and the issue's importance different views of the appropriate role of government, problems that ma be involved in carrying out the legislation (implementation), and so on

Patterson (1980) and others have complained about the "game" an "horse-race" coverage during campaigns. However, in relation to govern ment and to public policy generally, news media coverage treats man events as part of a game. Of course television is not the only medium tha often treats government as a game with little or no examination of th issues at stake or even whether a particular game is genuinely importan newspapers, news magazines, and members of government themselv often treat it this way. During the "budget battles" with President Reagan in the spring of 1981, Senator Christopher Dodd commented that members of Congress were themselves sometimes losing sight of the substance in pursuit of winning the game, so he said he could not be too harsh on the news media. Nonetheless, the game approach appears to be particularly pronounced on television.

When many people have only the vaguest idea of the legislative process and of the content of any particular piece of legislation, how much do they learn when told by a television anchorman that "As part of the reconciliation process today, President Reagan was victorious in the conference committee with his tax bill"? Devoid of context and relying on the assumption of considerable knowledge, such stories do little more than convey the outlines of a ball game. Instead, descriptions, such as institutional features necessary for understanding particular developments, should be a continuing part of the examination of a topic, with minimal assumptions about the background knowledge of viewers. Barber's recommendations concerning language, emphasis on facts, and so on suggest an appropriate format for programs. Though reviews of basic elements would not be part of every news story, the claim that "we did that last year" would not be accepted as a reason for not doing it again.

Various other format changes would enable TV news to treat policy issues with greater depth. One suggestion is that the day's developments be briefly summarized at the start of the program and then two or three longer segments devoted to in-depth examination of several topics—including presentation of background, significance, and so on. Or, the second half hour of an hour-long news program could follow this format.

In campaign years, journalists should surely "pursue" candidates to spell out their positions. The positions of even well-known candidates should not be taken for granted. For example, Wirthlin, Breglio, and Beal (1981, p. 44), acknowledge that "Reagan was well known, but not known well." In examining the record of an incumbent, greater care is necessary than the impressionistic one generally used. Journalists might make more of an effort to consult those who have attempted a more systematic analysis, such as political scientists, historians, and other scholars. For example, the analyses of Edwards (1980) and Fishel (1980)—and of Bonafede (1979) in drawing on their work—give a very different view of President Carter's record than the stereotypical evaluation expressed by most journalists.

Preferably this campaign coverage would be built upon continuing coverage of government and its policies—including follow-ups on how government programs are working (Nelson, 1979). With such continuing coverage, the fact that candidates and parties generally seek to keep their promises (Pomper & Lederman, 1980) and the reasons for their lack of success when they do not succeed may become clearer.

Few innovations were introduced to expand issue coverage of the 1980 presidential campaign, however. Energy issues were treated by television news either as tools for measuring candidates consistency or as devices candidates manipulated for gaining votes. Energy issues should have been presented as serious choices between alternative future directions for the United States. The differences between the candidates were not just campaign ploys; they translated into real changes in policies. For the record, it ought to be remembered that the victorious candidate did in fact proceed to, among other things, accelerate de-control of petroleum prices, minimize environmental regulations impeding energy development, and initiate the abolition of the Department of Energy.

REFERENCES

Adams, William C. and Phillip Heyl. 1981. From Cairo to Kabul with the Networks, 1972–1980. In William C. Adams, ed., *Television Coverage of the Middle East.* Norwood, N.J.: Ablex.

Alter, Jonathan. 1981. Rooting for Reagan. *The Washington Monthly* 12 (January 1981): 12–17.

Altheide, David L. 1976. *Creating Reality.* Beverly Hills, Cal.: Sage.

Barber, James David. 1979. Not *The New York Times:* What Network News Should Be. *The Washington Monthly* 11 (September 1979): 14–21.

Benjamin, Stan. 1980. Carter, Reagan Oil Figures: A Matter of Interpretation. *Lafayette* (Ind.) *Journal and Courier* (September 12, 1980): A–9.

Bicker, William E. 1978. Network Television News and the 1976 Presidential Primaries. In James D. Barber, ed., *Race for the Presidency.* Englewood Cliffs, N.J.: Prentice-Hall, 79–110.

Bonafede, Dom. 1979. Setting the Record Straight. *National Journal* 11 (November 3, 1979): 1856.

Congressional Quarterly. 1979. *Energy Policy.* Washington, D.C.: Congressional Quarterly.

———. 1980. *Energy Policy,* 2nd ed. Washington, D.C.: Congressional Quarterly.

Corrigan, Richard and Dick Kirschten. 1980. Some Results are Finally in Sight for the "Moral Equivalent of War." *National Journal* 12 (January 5, 1980): 4–10.

Cowan, Edward. 1980. Carter's Report Card on Energy. *New York Times* (October 6, 1980): 19.

Edwards, George C., III. 1980. *Presidential Influence in Congress.* San Francisco, Cal.: W.H. Freeman.

Fallows, James. 1979. The President and the Press. *The Washington Monthly* 11 (October 1979): 9–17.

Fishel, Jeff. 1980. Presidential Elections and Presidential Agendas. Washington, D.C.: American University Center for Congressional and Presidential Studies.

Foley, John: Dennis A. Britton; and Eugene B. Everett, Jr. 1980. *Nominating a President: The Process and the Press.* New York: Praeger Publishers.

Goodwin, C.D., ed. 1981. *Energy Policy in Perspective.* Washington, D.C.: Brookings Institution.

Graber, Doria A. 1980. *Mass Media and American Politics.* Washington, D.C.: Congressional Quarterly.

Groff, David D.; Francine R. Schwadel; Lynda DeWitt; William B. Fulton; Harriet C. Johnson; Linda McCormick; Chad Randolph; and Cynthia Skrzycki. 1980. *The Press and the 1980 Presidential Campaign: In the Shadow of an Economic Crisis.* Washington, D.C.: American University Center for Business and Economic Education.

Grossman, Michael B. and Martha Joynt Kumar. 1981. *Portraying the President.* Baltimore, Md.: Johns Hopkins University.

Hess, Stephen. 1981. *The Washington Reporters.* Washington, D.C.: Brookings Institution.

House, Karen Elliott. 1981. Begin Sorely Tests Reagan's View of Israel as Strategic U.S. Ally. *Wall Street Journal* (July 23, 1981): 26.

Kirschten, Dick. 1980. Coal Politics with an Eastern Tilt may boost Carter Stock in Key States. *National Journal* 12 (September 13, 1980): 1519–1522.

Nelson, Michael. 1979. What's Wrong with Policy Analysis. *The Washington Monthly* 11 (September 1979): 53–59.

Patterson, Thomas E. 1980. *The Mass Media Election.* New York: Praeger Publishers.

Pelham, Ann. 1980. Seven Years After Embargo, U.S. has an Energy Policy. *Congressional Quarterly Weekly Report* 38 (October 25, 1980): 3207–3212.

Peters, Charles. 1976. The Ignorant Press. *The Washington Monthly* 8 (May 1976): 55–57.

Pomper, Gerald M. and Susan S. Lederman. 1980. *Elections in America,* 2nd ed. New York: Longman.

Robinson, Michael J. 1981. A Statesman is a Dead Politician. In Elie Abel, ed., *What's News: The Media in American Society.* San Francisco, Cal.: Institute for Contemporary Studies, 159–186.

Robinson, Michael J. and Margaret Sheehan. 1981. Brief Encounters with the Fourth Kind: Reagan's Press Honeymoon. *Public Opinion* 3 (January 1981): 34–40.

Sahr, Robert and Tracey Gladstone. 1981. "News Media Coverage of Selected Energy Policy Proposals." (Paper presented at the Midwest Political Science Association. Cincinnati, Ohio, April.)

Scheer, Robert. 1976. Jimmy Carter Interview. *Playboy* 23 (November 1976): 63ff.

Stobaugh, Robert and Daniel Yergin. 1980. *Energy Future,* revised ed. New York: Ballantine.

Wirthlin, Richard; Vincent Breglio; and Richard Beal. 1981. Campaign Chronicle. *Public Opinion* 4 (February/March 1981): 43–49.

9

ELECTION NIGHT 1980 AND THE CONTROVERSY OVER EARLY PROJECTIONS

PAUL WILSON

The presidential election of 1980 reopened an old debate. Several presidential elections have passed since people were last concerned about or cared to know how election returns were collected, transmitted, analyzed, and broadcast so quickly on Election Night. Most people have only been interested in who won and by how much. But when Ronald Reagan was projected to be the presidential winner by NBC News at 8:15 p.m. (EST), 2 hours and 45 minutes before the polls closed on the West Coast, many people again took notice.

The early projection stunned a country which was just settling in for an "all-night" vigil; it infuriated struggling West Coast candidates, who later claimed would-be voters stayed home; and it upstaged election administration officials, who generally believe election outcomes should be sacred until the polls close. The early projection surprised most Americans, but the equally early concession speech by President Jimmy Carter confirmed a new election reality.

What has become clear in the aftermath of 1980 is that on Election Day there exists two distinct classes of people in the US: those who know the winner very early and those who are not told the name of the winner at an early time. Television election analysts and key political advisors compose the former class and the American public is the second class.

Those who had thought election winners are not known until at least a major share of the votes are counted were shocked. Congress immediately launched an investigation, summoning news chiefs to justify their actions;

many officials and public interest groups offered a variety of "remedies." However, the concerns expressed at the 1981 Congressional hearings appear unlikely to slow down the networks. Rather than postponing projections, or delaying the announcement of election returns, network practices for the 1980 balloting could foreshadow an even faster method of election reporting.

Concern over early network predictions of the presidential election was not a 1980 phenomenon. In 1964, CBS predicted Lyndon Johnson the winner over Barry Goldwater long before California polls closed, and Richard Nixon's victory over George McGovern in 1972 was called by two networks more than two hours ahead of West Coast poll-closing time. But, when the results have not shown a landslide, as with the presidential squeakers of 1968 and 1976, an early projection has been impossible. For example, NBC (the fastest predicting network in 1980) did not call the 1968 Humphrey/Nixon race until 10:00 a.m. the following morning, and their 1976 projection for Carter over Ford was not made until 3:31 a.m. (EST).

Whenever the networks have projected a presidential winner before the polls have closed, they have incurred the scrutiny of Congress. Following the 1964 presidential race, Congress began studying the matter. In a more direct attempt to stop the practice of early projections, the Senate in 1972 passed a bill that provided for 12 hours of nationwide voting, with all polls in the country to close simultaneously at 11:00 p.m. EST. A 1974 Senate move was considerably bolder with the passage of a bill prohibiting disclosure of presidential election results before midnight (EST). Neither of the two Senate bills, however, was taken up by the House.

Election coverage in 1980 again produced concern on Capitol Hill. Congressional hearings were held on the subject of whether early projections affect turnout, numerous reforms were recommended by civic organizations, and a rash of bills were introduced in the House and the Senate.[1] Yet, none of these well-meaning proposals for curtailing early projections seemed to satisfy the requirements of the First Amendment, the administrative needs of election officials, or the sophisticated methods now used by networks to project winners.

The "cures" also fail to take into account the causes. Early projections occur because of competing pressures on election night. The public has a strong desire to know who has won, major network news organizations have irrepressible incentives to be first with the news, and election administration officials are judged by how efficiently they can provide results to reporters and the public. As the desire for more speed has been

---

[1] During the 97th Congress, four bills on the subject of early projections were introduced in the Senate: S.B. 55, 56, 57, and 58. In the House there were seven bills: H.R. 85, 184, 1813, 2565, 3556, 3557, and 3559.

stoked, the pressures to rush projections have become greater in every suc-
ceeding election. As shown in the 1981 New Jersey Governor's race, two
networks rushed to project races faster, not slower.

ELECTION PROJECTION METHODS

Ask a group of people on Election Night how the results are reported
so quickly and the responses probably will fall into two categories. Some
will say that key "bellwether" precincts are used. Others will say the actual votes are counted through a high-speed computer system. Both impressions are partially correct.

On election night, the networks use two separate but related systems: one to project the winner and the other to report actual vote tallies.
The first system attempts to project a winner quickly. It is an independent
system—using exit polling and target precincts—developed by each network to serve its own competitive needs. The other system attempts to
count every vote in America, first at the precinct level and again as part of
a county total. This system is implemented by the News Election Service
(NES).

News Election Service. NES is the result of a combined effort of
major news organizations. Early in 1964, CBS, ABC, NBC, the Associated
Press (AP), and United Press International (UPI) received an antitrust ex-
emption from the Justice Department in order to pool resources for the
collection of election returns on a national basis. Pooling nationwide election tabulations was essential if the public was to be informed rapidly
about the outcome of elections. Certainly, the instantaneous needs of television dictated that a fast method of adding vote totals be developed.

Prior to Election Day, NES organizes a team of approximately 100,000
"precinct reporters" who on Election Night wait at the precinct for the
votes to be counted for President and other major offices. Each reporter
then telephones the results to one of four large centers, each with 500 telephones. From these phone centers, the results are transmitted to a central
computer in New York. Here the actual results are tabulated into race
totals by county, Congressional district, state, and nation. The output is
flashed to the networks and wire services.

In reality, this vast undertaking is something of a smoke screen for
the public. Tens of thousands of precincts can no longer be reported because they use computer voting systems which permit votes to be counted
only at the county level. Furthermore, of those precincts that are reported,
it is impossible to keep track of whether results are from a Democratic
precinct or a Republican one. Thus, the partial precinct total viewers first
see is only a random assortment of precincts with little meaning; the "total
presidential vote" count sheds no light on who might win or lose.

At the same time that miscellaneous precinct results are being reported, NES organizes a separate team of 4,600 county reporters throughout the country who report cumulative totals as they become available from the 4,600 counties and major election boards that are treated as counties. In most cases, this means reporting many times during the night. For example, a county reporter might report the results of 9 precincts, and later the same night the results with 23 precincts reporting and so on until all of the precincts have reported.

County report calls are made to a New York center. As county reports begin to flow in, the central computer compares precinct vote totals for a county with the total votes reported by the county reporters. Whenever the county total becomes larger, the computer begins to transmit only the county-generated totals, and the precinct reporting for that county is effectively ended. Precinct reporters continue to call NES, but the computer disregards new reports because county totals are larger and, by then, more complete (Eimers, 1981).

If the networks were not concerned with speed, the NES vote-counting system might suffice. However, speed is everything. When the reputation of a network's news organization depends on how fast they can "deliver" the winner—the right winner—a far faster system is required. If the race for President is close in a state, the networks may have to use this county-by-county report to determine which candidate will eventually be entitled to the electoral votes of that state. But only late on Election Night—if the race is close—will the networks actually have to rely on this method. Most of the time, ABC, CBS, and NBC depend on their own projection systems.

Network Projection Systems.   Projection systems developed by each network differ substantially from the NES system used to report actual election results. To begin with, the projection system is not limited to actual votes or even to Election Day. As the "projection time line" chart indicates, some election projections can be easily made—if not broadcast—long before the polls open. Long-time popular incumbents with weak and poorly funded opponents pose no real difficulty for the informed election prognosticator. In fact, of the 435 Congressional races every two years, only 100 or so are even strongly challenged. At the other extreme, in every election year a few contests cannot be decided until weeks after the election when the official recount is conducted.

Network projection systems depend on accurate "models" of each state's voting behavior. These models are based on a sample of a state's total precincts. In small, homogeneous states, the sample may be as small as 50 precincts; in large, heterogeneous states, the sample might include as many as 150 precincts. In view of the fact that a state like Ohio has over 13,000 precincts, the actual sample is comparatively small.

The models employ both "barometer" precincts and randomly selected precincts. The former are high in predictive value and have historically covaried with statewide results, although they may not be "typical" precincts. For example, a precinct that always votes Republican by a margin of 30 percent higher than the statewide total can be used as a bellwether precinct. A model may also use randomly selected precincts to try to tap a cross-section of state-wide voting patterns. The barometer and the random precincts may be monitored separately or incorporated into the same model.

In sophisticated models, an "estimated vote" is projected before election day. For an incumbent, estimated votes can be the incumbent's votes from a past election. When the candidate is new, a "base" vote for Republicans and Democrats is calculated. As results become available, the estimated vote is replaced by the actual result and the model adjusts the overall projection accordingly. For example, a bellwether precinct within the model might be one where the Democrat always polled 20 percent points better than the final state-wide total. If the actual returns showed that the Democratic candidate only achieved 55 percent in that precinct, the model would adjust the overall outcome to reflect that the Republican was seriously eroding traditional Democratic support.

Constructing a model to respond to the vagaries of an actual election (and including factors like turnout rates) is never easy, but the problem is compounded for the networks when actual results are not available. Many precinct results are counted too slowly to be quickly useful, so target precinct selection has to be biased toward those using faster types of voting procedures.

Currently, there are three types of voting methods in this country. Ranked by speed, they are: (1) automatic voting machines; (2) computer systems; and (3) paper ballots. Automatic voting machines are generally large machines which the voter enters; votes are cast by pulling a series of levers. A counter inside the machine counts the vote as it is cast and keeps a running total. The method is the fastest because the vote totals are available immediately when the polls close.

With computer systems, voters use a stylus, or device similar to a paper punch, to put holes in a computer card that can later be tabulated by a computer. The punched ballot cards are taken to a central location in a county for counting, so the results are not available at the precinct, nor are they available very soon after the polls close.

With traditional paper ballots, voters mark their choices on preprinted ballots and stuff them into a locked ballot box. At the end of Election Day, the ballots are removed and counted by hand. The process is extremely time-consuming. According to the Federal Election Commission

(1981), approximately 20 percent of all precincts in the country still use paper ballots.

For a projection model to be fast, data based on paper ballots or computer systems cannot be used. The problem is troublesome too because many of the computerized counties are large metropolitan areas such as Los Angeles, Houston, Dallas, and Cleveland. It is, of course, not possible to have a representative sample of precincts if major urban areas cannot be included. The result has been an increased dependence on "exit interviews."

In order to speed the projection of winners, since 1967 the networks have surveyed voters as they leave polling places. Until the 1980 election, however, no network had ever relied solely on exit polls to project winners. Typically, results from precincts using automatic voting machines would confirm exit polling results fed into the model earlier in the day. Sometimes actual precinct votes supplied information for the model from places where exit interviewing was not conducted. As the model is progressively updated, the projection should begin to approximate more closely the final results. If the race is extremely close, aggregate county totals compiled by NES may need to be entered into the model. At this late stage, the model may revert to relying primarily on actual vote totals. (See Chart 9.1.)

In recent years, reliance on exit interviews has increased because of their accuracy, speed, and the necessity of doing so. As more counties computerize their tally systems, fewer precinct results, on which the network models depend, have been available. In Ohio, for example, 66 of its 88 counties are computerized with more counties planning to change. As additional counties go to computers the network reliance on exit interviews will consequently increase.

If projection success is any indication, it can be shown that exit interviewing is effective and accurate. Including the presidential race of 1980, ABC had only two incorrect projections out of over 1,000 races, and NBC states its record as having only six wrong calls out of 1,300 contests.

Although the record is impressive, the procedure is not foolproof. In 1981, perhaps due to NBC's reliance on exit interviews to call an early Reagan victory, ABC and CBS tried to project the winner of the New Jersey governor's race solely on the basis of exit interviews. The attempt was a disaster. Both networks picked Democrat Jim Florio. Both were wrong. Almost a month after the election, the Republican Tom Kean was declared the winner by a mere 1,500 vote margin in a photo-finish recount. (See Friendly, 1981.)

Despite the New Jersey embarrassment, it is unlikely the networks will abandon the exit interviewing. The reason is that projection models

Chart 9.1
Projection Time Line

Time	Prior to Election Day	Throughout Election Day	Poll Closing + 15 Min.	Poll Closing + 1 Hr.	Poll Closing + 2 Hrs.	A.M. and Next Day	Later
Method of projecting winner	Pre-election polls and past results	Exit interviews and turnout levels	Exit interviews	Target precincts	County by county returns from NES	Statewide vote total from NES	Recount from Secretary of State

could not now work fast enough without the input from exit interviews. With over one fourth of all precincts and many large cities now computerized, and another 20 percent still using paper ballots, the networks are forced to substitute existing polling results for actual results in their vote models.

THE 1980 PRESIDENTIAL ELECTION NIGHT

Traditionally, networks report the evening news from 7 to 7:30 p.m. and begin their regular election coverage at 7:30 p.m. (EST). A review of Election Night video tapes loaned from the Vanderbilt Television News Archive shows that Election Night 1980 was different. NBC broke from the pack during their news; and before the other two networks even started their coverage, NBC had already predicted six states, including five southern states going Republican which clearly foreshadowed Jimmy Carter's defeat. (See chronological chart 9.2.) NBC almost immediately issued a projection the instant polls would close in a state. Polls in Ohio had been closed 40 seconds when NBC called this key midwestern state for Ronald Reagan. The news of who was winning, it frequently appeared, was somehow the sole province of NBC.

In reality, the only thing that had changed in 1980 was network policy, not the speed of data analysis. In the past, the race between networks had been based on projections from actual election results—even if from only a sample of precincts. For years it has been possible to predict races using data from interviews as voters leave the polls, but 1980 was the first year that a network relied on exit interviewing, rather than actual vote totals.

The result was astonishingly successful for NBC. Prior to Carter's concession speech, NBC predicted 25 states first, ABC predicted three states first and CBS was not first in calling any state. (See Chart 9.3.) In fact, CBS went for one ponderous stretch of 34 minutes without predicting any state. During the same time period, NBC projected 16 states and correctly called the presidency. Ironically, some CBS viewers first learned Reagan was projected to win when local CBS affiliates started reporting NBC's projections. Jimmy Carter officially conceded before CBS had even projected that he had lost.

In retrospect, all three networks must have had nearly identical information concerning the landslide for Reagan. Walter Cronkite said during the news, "The smell of victory is in the air for Ronald Reagan," and Frank Reynolds more guardedly said that it "appears" that Reagan was ahead.

NBC, on the other hand, chose to report what it knew from the very first seconds of its evening news. John Chancellor began by saying, "Ac-

Chart 9.2
Chronology of 1980 Presidential Projections

me (EST) rs/Min/Sec)	NBC	ABC	CBS	Poll-Closing Time**	National Vote Total
ightly News) 7:30	Ind.			6	
	Va.			7	
	Miss.			7	
	Ala.			7&9	
	Fla.			7&8	
	Ga.*			7	
egular Election Coverage Begins) 30:10		Ind. Fla.			
30:40	Oh.			7:30	
30:50			Ind.		
32:20					1,700,685 (2%)
32:40	Ky.			6&7	
35:50			Va.		
43:20		Ky.			
43:50		Va.			
45:00			Fla.		
00:40		Oh.			
01:00	Conn.			8	
01:10		W. Va.*	Oh.	7:30	
01:20	N.J.			8	
01:30	Pa.			8	
01:40	Mich.			8	
01:50	Ill.				
	N.D.			8	
02:00	S.D.			8	
02:10	Kan.			8&9	
02:20	Mo.			8	
02:30	Tenn.			8	
02:40	Okla.			8	
	Tex.			8	
04:00		D.C.*		8	
07:40		N.H.			
10:30	D.C.*				
11:20		Kan.			
13:10					
13:20		N.J.			3,382,213 (4%)
15:10	REAGAN WINS				
15:40	N.H.			Various	
	Vt.			7	
	Del.			8	
	S.C.			7	
16:30		Okla.			
21:20		Pa.			

Chart 9.2 (continued)

Time (EST) (Hrs/Min/Sec)	NBC	ABC	CBS	Poll-Closing Time**	National Vote Total
8:34:30					5,138,((6%)
8:35:00			Pa.		
8:36:40			Kan.		
8:37:00			N.J.		
8:38:30		Ala.	Conn.		
8:38:50			Okla.		
			D.C.*		
8:41:30			Ga.*		
8:42:10			N.H.		
8:47:40			Tex.		
8:48:20	W.Va.*				
8:50:40					8,507,4 (10%)
9:00:30		Ill.			
9:00:50		S.D.			
9:01:50		Conn.			
9:01:40			Ala.		
9:06:00			Neb.		
9:12:20	R.I.*				
9:18:40					13,922,2 (16%)
9:22:00		Del.			
9:23:00		Tenn.			
9:30:40	N.M.				
9:31:00			N.D.		
9:31:20			R.I.*		
9:32:00			N.M.		
9:36:20		N.M.			
		Carter Concession Speech			
Total No. of States	28	19	18		

* Indicates states carried by Jimmy Carter. All other states were won by Ronald Reagan.
** Poll-closing times are shown only for the first network to project the state. Two poll-closing tim usually means the state covers two time zones. All poll-closing times are based on EST.

cording to an NBC-AP poll, Ronald Reagan appears to be headed for a substantial victory."

Before 1980, all the networks had refused to reveal what they knew about the outcome of a race based only on exit interviewing. They used exit interviewing primarily to assist in demographic and sociological analyses of the vote. But in 1980, NBC relied on exit interviews to call the race.

One policy that was still honored in 1980 was the practice of never predicting a state before that state's polls had closed. In states with two

Chart 9.3
Earliest Network Projections of States
(7:00 p.m. EST until Carter Concession at 9:35 p.m.)

NBC (25)	ABC (3)	CBS (0)
Indiana	W. Virginia	
Virginia	Dist. of Columbia	
Mississippi	New Hampshire	
Alabama		
Florida		
Georgia		
Ohio		
Kentucky		
Connecticut		
New Jersey		
Pennsylvania		
Michigan		
Illinois		
N. Dakota		
S. Dakota		
Kansas		
Missouri		
Tennessee		
Oklahoma		
Texas		
Vermont		
Delaware		
S. Carolina		
Rhode Island		
New Mexico		

time zones (and therefore two poll closing times) the networks have customarily waited until some of the polls have closed to make projections. As the chronological chart of Election Night shows, NBC never violated that policy, although most of the projections were within minutes, and in some cases seconds, of when the polls closed.

The change in overall policy by NBC, however, and the somewhat embarrassing impression created for the other two networks was not to be taken lightly. Although the president of CBS News and the senior vice president of ABC both testified in Congress that exit interviews would not be used to predict results, the NBC preemption was quietly eating at the competive instincts of the two bested networks.

Until 1980, all three networks had possessed the nuclear bombs of election projection, but had chosen never to use them. When NBC broke this unwritten treaty, the others were forced to retaliate.

In 1981 both CBS and ABC threw aside tradition, threw aside their earlier Congressional testimony, and threw aside caution. ABC attempted to call a trend in the New Jersey Governor's race two hours before the polls closed and CBS—relying exclusively on exit polling results—incorrectly called the race at the moment polls closed in New Jersey. Both ABC and CBS were incorrect in their projections, but now that the hallowed practices of the past have been cast off, viewers may begin to see elections reported as "games in progress" rather than a completed event.

EFFECTS OF EARLY PROJECTIONS

Did the networks' early projection of Reagan as the winner and coverage of the early concession speech by Carter have any measurable impact on the 1980 turnout? This is a thorny question. It has been extremely difficult over the years to measure the true impact of early projections.

Many election officials, political scientists, and elected officials believe the likelihood of someone voting is directly related to whether the person feels their vote is meaningful. The networks respond that the impact of projections has never been demonstrated and that the issue is a "phantom problem."

William Small (1981), former president of NBC News, said that in 1980 "7 of the 10 states with the highest percentage turnout closed their polls after the NBC projection," and that "turnout increased in 9 of 13 states in the Pacific and Mountain time zones." If there were any cases of lowered turnout, the networks argue their projections should not be blamed. Instead, they say, Carter's early concession speech could be faulted, and, in any event, the landslide would have been apparent to most viewers early in the evening, even without formal projections.

Critics argue that overall turnout figures do not refute the charge that turnout was adversely affected during the three hours after the projection and before the polls closed. They point to a body of anecdotal reports of "people leaving poll lines" and election officials being innundated with calls complaining about the news. Beyond the anecdotal, there have been three studies—each flawed in certain respects—which support the claim that early projections affect turnout.

A Los Angeles County report by County Supervisor Edmund Edelman concluded that "the number of L.A. County voters who went to the polls after 6:00 p.m. (PST) declined by 3.23 percent from 1976 to 1980. There was even a more drastic decline of 4.12 percent for the period of 7 to 8:00 p.m. (PST)." Strictly speaking, however, it is not possible to attribute the decline in votes directly to nonvoters' awareness of the early projection (or Carter's concession).

In a study conducted by the Field Institute in San Francisco in January 1981, 10 percent of the respondents who were registered, but did not vote, blamed their failure to vote on the early announcement of the presidential winner. These results were hardly conclusive. Of the total 1,071 adults interviewed, only 71 registered respondents said they had not voted.

Of these 71 people, seven contended they had not voted due to the projection. With such a very small sample size, the data are subject to a large sampling error—not to mention the easy excuse the nonvoter was afforded.

The Center for Political Studies at the University of Michigan conducted the most extensive study on the question with funds from ABC News and the Markle Foundation. With the 1980 National Election Study (using data from the post-election re-interviews), John Jackson and William McGee (1982) discovered that for those who had not voted by the time election coverage began and still had time to vote, the "estimated proportion voting dropped by 20 to 25 percent." They further determined that, with the entire sample, this produced a 6 to 11 percent overall drop-off "as a result of nonvoting among those who had not voted when they heard news of the election outcome."

The study did not cleanly delineate between the separate effects of the network projection and the Carter concession speech, but did conclude that hearing about either one had the same effect on the proportion of people voting. Due to small sample sizes, it was not possible to ascertain which party was more hurt by the decline, although the candidate preference data suggested that Carter supporters may have been influenced more by the information than were Republicans and Reagan supporters.

The effect of early projections may not be as noticeable if the outcome is known long in advance. When the presidential outcome was expected in advance, as in 1964 and 1972, Jackson and McGee maintain that the impact of an early projection will not be as great. They argue that the most dramatic impact on voting participation comes when a race expected to be close is instead decided early. Turnout may be significantly altered "where the projections differ from prior expectation." Jackson and McGee (1982) understand this to be true in part because "the likelihood of voting *is* related" to people's "perception of the value of their vote in determining the election's outcome."

Prompted by the early predictions in 1980, by the impressions and tentative evidence of their impact, and by the anger of many Westerners, many proposed "reforms" were advanced after the 1980 Election Night.

PROPOSED REFORMS

Foreign observers of US presidential elections are frequently dumbfounded to learn that votes for President are first assembled and announced by private news media rather than by the government. The media have assumed near total control over Election-Night reporting in part because of the decentralized nature of the election system. With the exception of the date of the election, states have almost total autonomy in how they conduct their elections—an independence states have come to cherish.

The presidential election system is, as Gary Greenhalgh, the Director of the National Clearinghouse on Election Administration says, actually a "non-system." This decentralization is a fundamental problem in trying to negotiate or impose nationwide constraints.

The following compendium of proposed reforms must be viewed, therefore, in light of both the absence of any official national election system and the complex and redundant election reporting mechanisms that have been developed by the networks to fill the vacuum. Proposals to change the reporting of national elections fall into two broad categories: those that limit the flow of information and those that require uniform poll-closing times.

Proposals to Limit the Flow of Information

1. The Canadian System

Description. The government of Canada restricts the broadcast of election results or projections by time zone. As polls close on the East Coast, television and radio are allowed to broadcast results to East Coast viewers, and as polls close in central Canada the permissible broadcast area is extended further west.

Analysis. All the proposals which would limit the free flow of information infringe heavily on the First Amendment rights of speech and press. Limiting the dissemination of news by time zone is also complicated by the random poll-closing times of states (e.g., Indiana closes its polls before New York). Furthermore, as cable television grows and satellite distribution of "super" stations expands, monstrous technical difficulties would exist in creating time-zone blackouts. Even if such a system were feasible, there would be nothing to restrict a radio station newscaster in Sacramento from calling a friend in New York for the news. Such a system might even stimulate the dissemination of "censored" results merely because they were "censored" and thus heighten the impact of East Coast results on turnout, instead of minimizing them.

2. The News Embargo

Description. The Coro Foundation, located in California, has proposed that election results and projections of winners be embargoed "until after the election is over." The Foundation suggests that other news stories are regularly embargoed without damage to the First Amendment, and therefore a similar type of news embargo for election results would minimize the impact of early returns.

Analysis. News embargoes honored today are completely voluntary; to make them compulsory would have grave First Amendment implications. If an embargo were not compulsory, there would be no way to enforce it and there would be many incentives for breaking it. With an embargo, news organizations would know the outcome of races for hours before the public was informed. To consciously enable a nongovernmental group to be a secret repository of election results before the voters themselves can be told seems a dubious direction.

3. Voluntary Network Restraint

Description. The League of Women Voters, supported by scores of other civic organizations, have proposed that networks and wire services voluntarily refrain from projecting or broadcasting too early. As Ruth J. Hinerfeld, President of the League, explained (1981):

> On presidential Election Night, the media should report the official results of the presidential vote in each state and should not project the results when presidential polls are still open elsewhere.

Analysis. Although this proposal goes a long way in recognizing the constitutional and administrative difficulties other proposals pose, it fails to appreciate the competitive pressure networks face from each other on Election Night. Until 1980, no network had been so bold as to start predicting races solely on the basis of exit interviews, but that practice changed with NBC's lightning-quick prediction of Ronald Reagan's victory. A year later, ABC tried to upstage the other networks by calling the New Jersey Governor's race before the state's polls closed. ABC predicted wrong, but succumbed to the NBC precedent and went a step further. To ask for voluntary repression is gallant but naive. As Reese Schonfeld, then president of Cable News Network, (1981) said, ". . . the idea of being first and being right has become a touchstone in American presidential elections—it has become a touchstone of excellence. There is no way we can avoid it, the people want to know."

4. Limit Exit Interviewing Near Polls

Description. One approach[2] suggested by California State Senator Daniel Boatwright is to require Election-Day campaigners and exit interviewers to move 500 feet away from the polls. Most states only require campaigners, exit interviewers, and other election observers to be stationed at least 100 feet from the polls. Extending the limit to 500 feet might significantly reduce the success rate and selection procedures of exit interviewing. The theory is that without a high number of random exit interviews, the projection of elections would be delayed or eliminated.

Analysis. This proposal has several problems. Presumably, a 500-foot access limit would also apply to candidates, union members, and volunteers who regularly contact voters in front of the polls. Such a proposal

---

[2] This and other proposals were discussed in hearings held jointly before the Committee on House Administration and the Subcommittee on Telecommunications, Consumer Protection, and Finance of the House Committee on Energy and Commerce in 1981 and 1982.

would probably incur the wrath of groups who depend on close access to the polling place for last-minute campaigning. The proposal would also need to be implemented on a state-by-state basis, probably making it effective only on a scattered basis. Yet, even a 500-foot limit would not stop all exit interviews with voters outside the prescribed limit. (In 1980, ABC based its exit interview results on only 11,000 interviews nationwide.) Moreover, a distance limitation is not the controlling factor for exit interviewing success. Ultimately, the networks, already spending millions on their present system, could devise additional means of gaining access to the voters. For example, network poll checkers could still review poll books, determine who has voted and call them on the phone later in the day. The procedure would be more time-consuming, but still effective.

5. *Voting by Mail*

Description. One of the more unusual suggestions to suppress early projections is to have the electorate vote by mail—the ultimate method of controlling the flow of election information. Although tried for other purposes in San Diego and a few other communities, mail voting is not widespread. It is believed that voting by mail would shield voters from exit interviewers. All ballots would be mailed to a central location in a county or state and, therefore, it also would be nearly impossible to use target precinct voting models to make estimates and predictions. All balloting would end before the votes were counted or announced.

Analysis. Voting by mail comes the closest of all suggestions in undercutting the network projection systems. It is also the most radical of changes. Along with potential for fraud, double voting and other irregularities, the cost to administer such a system would be substantial. From a practical standpoint, the country seems unlikely to entirely restructure methods of voting just to avoid the unproven impact of early projections.

6. *Withhold Election Results*

Description. To prevent early predictions, election officials, under this proposal, would restrict the release of information until the polls have closed nationwide. To avoid making some states wait until midnight EST for their local results, the proposal would probably be limited only to the totals for President.

Analysis. Again, the proposal is based on the mistaken premise that the networks need actual results to project the winner. They do not. Exit interviews can and have been used to project winners. Delaying actual election results would inhibit the projection system only if the race were very close.

Uniform Poll-Closing Time Proposals

Proposals that have been given the most serious attention are those that deal with uniform poll-closing times and other aggregate solutions that do not tamper with the First Amendment freedoms of the media.

1. Uniform Poll Closing Time

Description. This proposal provides for nationwide election hours that start at a uniform time and end at a uniform time throughout the country. Under this arrangement, West Coast voters would never hear of East Coast results because all polls would close at the same time.

Analysis. The difference in time zones between the two coasts makes this proposal logistically unworkable. The Secretary of State of California (Fong Eu, 1981) said that "a reasonable opening hour on the East Coast is an unreasonable opening hour on the West Coast." The cost of keeping the polls open late in the East would be high, and yet the alternatives of closing the polls early in the West would probably cause turnout to drop even more than the estimated impact of early projections. Accommodating Alaska and Hawaii further confounds matters. Even with a uniform poll-closing time that accommodates both East and West, the networks would still be able to project elections on the basis of exit interviews, thus circumventing the process anyway.

2. Two-Day Voting

Description. To correct some of the deficiencies of the uniform poll-closing proposal, two bills were introduced into the Senate in 1981 to permit certain West Coast states to open polls the day before the national voting day, in order to accommodate voters who would otherwise not have an opportunity to vote.

Analysis. Two-day voting would substantially increase the cost of elections in the states where it would be permitted. Along with the extra wages for poll workers for both days, it would be most costly to hire security guards to protect ballots that were cast on the first day. In California alone, the cost of security, transportation, and extra precinct officials has been estimated at $2 million. Exit interviewing would still be possible under the two-day voting plan, so voters in the East would go to the polls having heard projections from first-day voting in the West.

3. Sunday Voting

Description. Another proposal before Congress is the suggestion for Sunday voting. This proposal, according to its sponsor, Representative Mario Biaggi of New York, would require a six-year trial in which all general elections would be held on Sunday and all polls across the country would open and close during the same 9-hour period of 12–9:00 p.m. (EST) in presidential election years. Currently, Italy, France, Sweden and Germany have Sunday elections—all with voter participation rates higher than the US.

Analysis. To counter the negative impact on turnout of early projections and the steady decline in voter participation, this proposal seeks to boost turnout by making it easier to vote. Like some of the other uniform poll-closing suggestions, Sunday voting would not prevent exit interviews and early projections. Objections to the proposal are logistical and religious. If turnout did increase, the entire electorate might not be able to finish voting in 9 hours. Also, thousands of conveniently located polling places are located in churches that are in use for the greater part of every Sunday. These would have to be changed.

Religious considerations would prompt opposition, so the proposal would be difficult to pass and possibly problematic if enacted. Although foreign countries that vote on Sunday do have higher participation rates, it is not clear that voter participation in the United States has fallen because of the inability of workers to get to the polls. With respect to election projections, networks would have more difficulty with a nine-hour day, but projections could still be made on the basis of exit interviews if the networks chose to do so.

Two variations on the Sunday voting concept are to have Saturday voting or to make the Tuesday Election Day a national holiday. While the chief purpose would again be to increase election turnout, such changes do not remedy the concern with early projections.

4.5. Abolish the Electoral College in Favor of Direct Election

Description. The long-standing proposal to abolish the electoral college and replace it with the direct popular election of the President has been suggested as a step that would also minimize early projections. Popular election, it is claimed, could delay the early projection of the winner because the large number of people on the West Coast could tip the balance.

Analysis. Election projections might actually become easier as a result of direct elections. Currently, the electoral college makes predictions slightly more difficult because of the state-wide "winner-take-all" format. Close races in a few states under the present system make projections harder; close races in a few states under the popular vote proposal would not be as likely to matter as much and would make projections easier. If the race were very close everywhere, then the projection would be difficult, but the same can be said for the present system.

CONCLUSION

There is some provocative evidence at least suggesting that early projections may adversely affect turnout. However, the various reforms proposed to correct the alleged problem fail to simultaneously handle the dictates of the First Amendment, election administration needs, network competitive pressures, the public's desire to know who won, and the power of exit interviewing. Current practices have so far evolved without governmental interference. To impose at this time a new or altered election system to correct a problem that has not been completely documented seems premature. Nonetheless, the subject is likely to become far more and not less controversial. There is every indication that the projection of elections will increasingly depend on exit interviews as computer voting becomes more widespread and precinct returns are no longer available at local polling places. Although their accuracy in a close race is suspect, exit-interview projections are being announced earlier and earlier. Their future use may be restrained only by the hour that the news begins.

REFERENCES

Biaggi, US Representative Mario. 1981. Testimony before the Senate Committee on Rules and Administration, May 7.

Eimers, Richard J. 1981. Executive Director of the News Election Service. Testimony before the Committee on House Administration, December 15.

Federal Election Commission. 1981. *Voting Systems Users '81: A Directory of Local Jurisdictions.* Washington, D.C.: National Clearinghouse on Election Administration, Federal Election Commission.

Field Institute. 1981. *Attitudes toward Media Coverage of the 1980 Presidential Election.* San Francisco, Cal.: Field Institute.

Fong Eu, March, 1981. California Secretary of State. Testimony before Senate Committee on Rules and Administration, May 8.

Friendly, Jonathan. 1981. Jersey Election Posed Problems for TV News Units. *New York Times* (November 5, 1981): B-7.

Hinerfeld, Ruth J. 1981. President, League of Women Voters. Testimony before the Senate Committee on Rules and Administration, May 7.

Jackson, John E. and William H. McGee, III. 1982. Election Reporting and Voter Turnout. Ann Arbor, Mich.: Center for Political Studies, University of Michigan.

Shonfeld, Reese. 1981. President, Cable News Network. Testimony before the Senate Committee on Rules and Administration, May 7.

Small, William. 1981. President, NBC News. Testimony before the Senate Committee on Rules and Administration, May 7.

10

MEDIA POWER IN PRESIDENTIAL ELECTIONS:
AN EXPLORATORY ANALYSIS, 1960–1980

WILLIAM C. ADAMS

Views on the effects of media on American politics fall into four camps—
"media impotence," "media virility," "print power," and "video power."

The "impotence" school sees all media as inert, ineffectual, and in-
consequential: So neutral and unobtrusive are the media that they never
act as an independent force in the dynamics of society. News in America is
presented objectively, and the media's mirror reflects politics with such
accuracy that no distortions or changes in the political world originate in
the media. Besides, media messages are seen as no challenge to the awe-
some forces of family, friends, party, ethnicity, class, and political elites;
and media variables rarely excel in multiple regression equations.

The "virility" school views media output as a pervasive and powerful
part of the political processes. Media selecting and shaping of stories is cast
as a crucial—unavoidably subjective and political—element in American
life. The media constantly impregnate society with the latest versions of
news. They so penetrate throughout the population that it becomes difficult to measure their precise "independent" impact. Ceiling effects are
everywhere. In this view, media messages are so saturated and diffused,
and so undifferentiated among news outlets, that media influence is like
oxygen—a critically important, integral, but invisible part of life.

A third camp concurs only in part with the notion of media power.
The locus of that political power is seen as print media, primarily newspapers. Television's news impact is dismissed as trivial and overrated.
Newspapers are more important than television, some studies suggest, in
initiating issues and setting the public's agenda (Shaw & McCombs, 1977),
in conveying factual information (Wade & Schramm, 1969), and in switch-
ing votes with editorials (J. Robinson, 1972, 1974).

161

A final perspective is that of "video power." Many would agree with David Broder (1972, p. 238) that "Television has probably changed American politics more than any other single factor in the past two decades." Reaching a massive audience, television is seen as making or breaking candidates and destroying the parties in a single bound. Neglecting newspapers, viewers see a stream of superficial, compressed stories and sink into prime-time torpor, deluded that they are informed about politics. The political process is thereby thought to be fundamentally affected by the medium of television and its nightly versions of the news.

While evidence is abundant that national campaigns have been transformed to accommodate the new medium, it is not clear how the existence of television has affected voters on election day. The growing literature on media and politics contains surprisingly few studies on media and voting preferences.

Michael Robinson and Cliff Zukin (1976) found that voters who relied on television in 1968 were more likely to vote for George Wallace. However, Thomas Patterson and Robert McClure (1976) concluded that television had little direct and independent effect on voters in the 1972 campaign. John Robinson's research has uncovered an association between voting and newspaper endorsements (1972, 1974).

To pursue the relationship between voting and the media, this study assumes five tasks:

1. To distinguish, in light of the four media "camps," between "media effects" and "medium effects";
2. To propose seven elements of media content that merit examination in media-voting research;
3. To estimate which recent presidential candidates benefited on each of the seven criteria on television in contrast to newspapers;
4. To identify the voters most likely to be influenced by variations in media content; and
5. To determine if these recent elections produced voting patterns consistent with the estimates of media content differences.

MEDIA EFFECTS AND MEDIUM EFFECTS

Research on media effects is frequently bedeviled by a confusion between (1) the joint impact of all media and (2) the relative impact of a particular medium. Many studies that ostensibly concern "media effects" actually focus on what will be termed here "medium effects," that is, the relative effects of television, newspapers, or other news sources.

The distinction is crucial for two reasons. First, as a practical matter, it is difficult to analyze the effects of combined media use versus nonuse.

Researchers are rarely able to isolate the joint effects of all American media. In voting research, for example, national surveys cannot locate any sizeable block of middle-class hermits who vote but avoid all media during the campaign. Thus, there is no control group.

Because it is so difficult to assess the cumulative impact of the media ("media virility" versus "medium impotence"), researchers focus instead on the comparative effects of particular news sources, that is, medium effects. The question shifts to the relative impact of television versus newspapers versus other news sources (i.e., "print power" versus "video power"). Substantively, this is a very different question, and ought not to be confused with studying joint media effects.

The second reason the distinction is important is that the absence of medium effects does not necessarily mean the absence of media effects. If messages are similar across all media, there may be no unique medium effects, even though the media may be jointly exerting a powerful pull on public opinion.

Confusing unique power with shared power can distort the entire subject of media impacts. If a study finds that people who rely on television do not have a significantly different outlook toward a campaign then people who rely on newspapers, the study has evidence only that unique "medium effects" are absent. Such data do not address whether both media might have together edged the electorate toward one side or the other.

An illustration of the importance of the distinction concerns the media's coverage of John Anderson's presidential campaign. One of the pivotal political decisions of 1980 was the way editors and producers opted to treat John Anderson's third-party candidacy (see Adams, 1980). The key issue was where Anderson went on the agenda, and hence the amount of status, legitimacy, and credibility to be conferred by the media. Should the media's picture of the campaign have been a triptych—elevating Anderson to create a Big Three? Or, should Anderson have been reduced to the size of Oliphant's penguin and allowed to voice only brief caustic asides?

If Anderson were denied coverage uniformly across all media, the self-fulfilling impact of that lack of visibility would not be easily discerned with survey data. The media analyst would be left to speculate about the extent to which additional media attention would have helped Anderson's efforts. If, however, television were to grant the network campaign more serious coverage than newspapers, it might be possible to demonstrate that people who relied on television viewed Anderson differently and perhaps voted differently from those who relied on newspapers. With one medium providing him prominence and another relegating him to spoiler status, researchers might find a strong "medium effect."

To the extent that American media are pervasive, it is difficult to show aggregate media effects. To the extent that American media contents are homogeneous, it is hard to show unique medium effects. Only when significant differences in campaign-relevant content occur should it be possible to find medium effects associated with those content differences.

Much scholarly and popular commentary has stressed the unique impact of television on politics. In the relative terms of "medium effects," the issue is actually how television differs from other media—how television's messages and their effects contrast with the messages and effects of other media. The question might as well be "What is the relative impact of newspapers?"

To have medium effects on presidential voting, the differences in messages would have to be substantial enough to produce different candidate evaluations and different voting choices. The discussion which follows proposes seven distinct aspects of mass media content that may be relevant to voting decisions.

SEVEN ELEMENTS OF MEDIA CONTENT

Seven elements are proposed here as factors in presidential campaigns that should be considered in any attempt to assess differences in media messages: (1) themes, (2) agenda, (3) treatment, (4) endorsements, (5) advertisements, (6) persona, and (7) entertainment.

Themes. Transcending in any particular news story or coverage of a single day's events are generalized approaches or themes that characterize television news as opposed to newspapers. Three patterns are especially noteworthy. Network television is—compared to newspapers—more devoted to news about the national government, to news about the President, and to news that is "negative." Edward Jay Epstein (1973) has shown television's fear of stories that are too local and the premium it places on national stories, along with the low level of coverage of state governments (see also Gormley, 1978; M. Robinson, 1975, pp. 116–117; Graber, 1980, p. 66).

Epstein and others (Minnow, Martin, & Mitchell, 1973) have also observed television's obsession with the White House. Activities of the President dominate television news in a way that far surpasses the relative amount of attention given the President in newspapers.

The third chief theme is that of "negative news." Television's needs for excitement, conflict, action, and compelling drama drive it toward negative news. Accounts of unresolved problems, of policies gone wrong, of politicians wrangling, of impending crises—often coupled with "worst-case" scenarios—absorb a consistently higher share of network news than newspaper news (Lowry, 1971; M. Robinson, 1975; see also Levine, 1977; Smith, 1979; Singer, 1970).

These three television themes add up to trouble for the incumbent in the Oval Office. Without necessarily explicitly blaming the party in power, the implicit linkage builds up night after night: government power and societal problems are all at the national level; the President is the pinnacle of national leadership and power; yet grave problems, foreign and domestic, persist and swell with hopelessly ineffectual responses from the citadel in Washington. The President and his epigones are everywhere on the evening news, yet every problem that wanes appears to be replaced by two that wax. The merger of these three themes suggests that the unrelenting approach of television news, relative to that of newspapers, is likely to favor the party out of power.

Agenda. One of the earliest findings of election studies was that certain issues usually help Democrats while others tend to help Republicans. Converse, Clausen, and Miller (1965, p. 331) noted that in the 1950s many Americans reacted to the parties "in terms of gross associations and moods." "Much more often than not, for these Americans the Democratic Party was the party of prosperity and good times, but also the party more likely to blunder into war. The Republican Party, conversely, was more skilled in maintaining peace, but brought with it depression and hard times." These general impressions were not entirely stable in the decade of the 1960s, however. Just how much a particular issue or cluster of issues accrued to the benefit of a party varied from election to election.

That certain issues benefit a particular party takes on added import in light of research showing the media's role in setting the issue agenda for the voting public (e.g., McCombs & Shaw, 1972; Funkhouser, 1973; Shaw & McCombs, 1977; Palmgreen & Clarke, 1977). Sustained media coverage of a particular set of issues is likely to increase the salience of those issues, and then to rebound to the advantage of the candidate and party perceived as better able to confront those issues. Similarly, an issue that has failed to surface in the media would be difficult for a candidate to convert into a campaign issue for voters who were not already primed for its significance.

Returning to the matter of medium effects, rather than media effects generally, it is the difference in the television and newspaper agendas that is important. If television news, for example, emphasizes foreign policy crises more than newspapers in a year when Republicans are widely believed to be superior for keeping peace and strength, television's news agenda is relatively more advantageous for the GOP. If newspapers stress the economy more than television news does in a year when Democrats are seen as the party of prosperity, then the newspaper agenda puts the public spotlight on a subject that helps the Democrats.

Treatment. A number of studies have sought to measure the degree to which news sources give one candidate or party more favorable coverage; much of this research is discussed in Adams (1978) and Comstock and Cobbey (1978). Some content studies make the assumption that any disparities in the coverage of candidates represent a "bias" imposed by newspeople. Causes of variations are of course important to understand (see Lichter & Rothman, 1980), but overall content differences may be significant for the public, regardless of their cause.

Whether one candidate's more favorable media slant is an outgrowth of ideological goggles worn by reporters, or a better press secretary, or more rapport with reporters, or an opponent's gaffes is not an issue here. Rather, the concern is again differences in media messages and whether a candidate is portrayed more favorably in a particular news medium, whatever the reasons.

Unfortunately, the available studies are not as helpful in making this assessment as they first appear, because almost all concentrate entirely on one medium without any cross-media comparisons. Also, many of the studies focus simply on the amount of coverage given each candidate (usually about the same amount), instead of the tone of coverage. Finally, much of the published research was conducted on the 1972 campaign—an election that must be excluded from this analysis for reasons explained later.

Some writing on the political consequences of the media has dealt almost exclusively with the factor of "treatment." This approach is based on the theory that the space or time given critics or supporters of a candidate and the comments and inferences offered by respected and presumably impartial reporters are especially powerful. Treatment of the candidates may well be an especially vital element, although it would be a mistake to assume that the public absorb without question a medium's interpretation of events or to ignore the six other content factors outlined in this chapter.

Endorsements. Discussion of the first three factors—themes, agenda, and treatment—has underscored the need to estimate which candidate was relatively benefited by what medium. With each of the four remaining elements, however, one medium has a virtual monopoly. The "relative advantage" for a candidate in each of these areas depends almost totally on one medium.

The factor of "endorsements" illustrates this point. If the nation's newspapers overwhelmingly endorse a Republican, than the Democratic candidate is relatively advantaged by television—a medium in which the Republican candidate is not dominating endorsements—because television network news never endorses a presidential candidate.

Endorsements constitute another distinct kind of mass media message —the only one besides campaign advertisements with the avowed purpose of persuading the voter to favor one candidate over another. Whatever subtle slants might be perceived from news themes, agenda, and candidate treatment, the endorsement is unambiguous.

John Robinson (1972, 1974), Michael Hooper, (1969), and Steven Coombs (1979) have found that newspaper endorsements do help candidates to a small but significant degree. While candidates might ordinarily worry more about having the working press sympathetic to their cause more than about having the editorial support of publishers, endorsements are apparently not without an impact.

Advertisements. Newspapers may have a special mechanism for influencing elections with endorsements, but television prevails as the medium for potential political influence through the factors of "advertising," "persona," and "entertainment."

Since 1960, campaign advertising budgets have gone almost entirely to broadcasting and not to print media. The ratio is usually over 10:1, and a large share of the small newspaper ad budget goes to promoting television shows about the candidates. Consequently, dominating television advertising is essentially the same as dominating advertising about the campaign. According to the logic of this analysis, if Republicans hold a 2:1 advantage in television advertising, then Republicans are helped by television—at least in terms of exposure to their commercials—and Democrats are relatively better off with the basically nonexistent advertising content of newspapers.

Assessment of this element is complicated by the matter of advertisement quality. Once a threshhold of exposure is attained, advertisement quality may be more important than quantity. One candidate's commercials, though not run as frequently, may be more persuasive and compelling. Any examination of this element should consider the effectiveness of ads, instead of assuming that quality is a constant or assuming that quantity alone determines impact.

Persona. One school of thought has long argued that television's power derives from its status as the sole audiovisual news medium. Viewers find television credible and trustworthy, Kurt and Gladys Lang suggested (1953), because of a vicarious sense that they are there and are seeing the story firsthand. In the case of watching candidates, viewers may flatter themselves that they can discern via television something about the character, intellect and personality—perhaps even the competence—of the nominees. And they may less consciously respond to the personal chemistry of a candidate as it is transmitted over the air.

John Kennedy's television image became the classic illustration of the power of persona. Richard Nixon's pallor was so damaging in contrast to Kennedy's appearance that television viewers thought him less articulate than people who heard the first debate over radio.

Candidate persona in the fullest, richest, and most vivid sense can be conveyed only through television. Mendelson and Crespi concluded that "television in particular began to focus voters' attention on personalities" (1970, p. 271). David Brown (1980) has argued that election outcomes can be predicted by the method of turning off the sound of the set and observing the comparative appeal of the images of the nominees.

Entertainment. Around 1960, "Westerns" held sway over prime-time. Half of the top 10 programs in 1959 were westerns—*Gunsmoke, Rifleman, Have Gun Will Travel, Frontier Justice* and *Wyatt Earp* (Barnouw, 1975). In that setting, it seemed fitting and stirring for the new President to call his program "The New Frontier."

George Gerbner and Nancy Signorielli (1978) argue that scholars often impose an artificial boundary between television news and entertainment programming. The worldviews of viewers, they maintain, incorporate images and information acquired from both. Gerbner and Gross (1976) have shown that heavy viewers of television are significantly more likely than light viewers to think American society is more violent, to be less trustful of other people, and to estimate that a higher proportion of the workforce is employed in law enforcement.

Recent research and speculation has begun to try to assess the nature of political messages that filter into prime-time entertainment (Stein, 1979; see also M. Robinson, 1979, and forthcoming research by Robert and Linda Lichter). In the absence of more systematic research, the political implications of television entertainment in an amalgam with the nightly news are unclear. This factor did appear to have sufficient potential as an important element in the overall package of media messages that it merited identification as an additional element in this list.

The dramatic barrage of police, detective, law-and-order, and crime shows might have accrued to the benefit of the party perceived as "tougher" on crime—the Republican party—starting with the emergence of "the social issue" in the 1964 election. (The social liberalism of situation comedies, see Robinson, 1979, and other formats will be tentatively assumed to have less immediate political impact.) Cutler and Tedesco (1974) found that the depiction of social conflict on network drama strongly favored the "forces of social control." Lieutenant Columbo probably voted Republican.

MEDIUM ADVANTAGES IN RECENT ELECTIONS

If the arguments advanced above are accurate, these seven factors constitute the most politically important elements of media messages likely to influence the outcome of a presidential campaign. To the degree that the messages received from television and newspapers diverge, there may be medium effects with one candidate having a comparative advantage among voters who rely primarily on television and the other candidate aided relatively more by newspapers.

Based on available data and the considered opinions of political analysts, it should be possible to estimate the nature of medium advantages on most of these seven criteria for presidential candidates in recent elections. Chart 10.1 summarizes these assessments in terms of the candidate relatively benefited by television in contrast to newspapers, although the chart and the discussion that follows could as easily have been put in terms of the newspaper-advantaged candidates.

Table 10.1
Candidate Estimated to Be Relatively Benefited by Television,
in Contrast to Newspapers, 1960–1976*

	1960	1964	1968	1976
Themes	JFK	BMG	RMN/GW	JEC
Agenda	JFK	LBJ	RMN/GW	—
Treatment	?	?	?	?
Endorsements	JFK	BMG	GW/HHH	JEC
Advertisements	JFK	—	RMN	—
Persona	JFK	BMG	RMN	JEC
Entertainment	?	BMG	RMN	GRF
Overall	JFK	BMG	RMN/GW	JEC

* BMG = Barry M. Goldwater   JEC = James E. Carter
 GRF = Gerald R. Ford   JFK = John F. Kennedy
 GW = George Wallace   LBJ = Lyndon B. Johnson
 HHH = Hubert H. Humphrey   RMN = Richard M. Nixon

In each of these elections, the news themes of negativism, the Presidency, and national news are adjudged to give a consistent thematic advantage on television to the party out of power. Aside from the factor of entertainment, the relative advantage of coverage on other factors seems to vary from election to election with no consistent partisan pattern.

1960. In addition to benefiting from television's out-party themes, Kennedy should have also been helped by the television news agenda. As Pool, Abelson, and Popkin (1964, p. 85) explained, "voters had little sense that Kennedy had any competence in international affairs. Insofar as they focused on foreign affairs, they were more inclined to favor Nixon." Republicans were seen as the party best for keeping the US out of war, and newspapers emphasized foreign policy somewhat more than did television. Conversely, television devoted more time to economic and other domestic news, and Americans believed Democrats were better at maintaining prosperity (Gallup, 1976).

There is no basis even to speculate as to which candidate was treated relatively better on television. Kennedy is famous for having courted reporters (White, 1961, pp. 335–338), and one study of 15 major newspapers found that the Democratic ticket received slightly more news coverage than the Republicans did (Stempel, 1961). However, there is no reason to believe television news differed from newspapers in this regard.

Newspaper endorsements went mostly to Nixon. Papers favoring Kennedy were read by only 16 percent of the population, while papers favoring Nixon had 71 percent of total circulation (Emery, 1964). Again, Kennedy was relatively advantaged by television, not newspapers.

In 1960, newspaper advertising had not yet been altogether dwarfed by television advertising. Mullen (1963) found Republicans spent twice as much on newspaper advertising as had the Democrats. Nixon forces also outspent Kennedy on television but not by as wide a margin; the television ratio was only 3:2. Many observers found the Democratic ads to be more effective than those of the GOP, both in print and especially on the air. Kennedy's commercials were adroitly constructed using findings from opinion surveys and computer simulations and were carefully targeted. Nixon's were generally considered amateurish and ineffective (e.g., White, 1961, pp. 265, 311–313; Rubin, 1967, pp. 59–62). Again, Kennedy fared better on television.

Of course, Kennedy further excelled in terms of his television persona—not just in the debates when the Kennedy tan devastated the Nixon stubble, but throughout the fall. Kennedy's cool, low-key style, and good looks easily surpassed Nixon's television image. Nixon often lamented in Six Crises (1962, pp. 337, 340–341, 422) that he did not pay enough attention to how he looked on television.

1964. Four years later, Democrats had become the party of peace and had reinforced their impression as the party of prosperity. Despite Goldwater's gaffes on atomic warfare, Republicans were still damaged slightly more by the specter of depression than by that of war. For peace, the public favored the Democrats 45 to 22 percent; but, for prosperity, the Democratic lead over the Republicans increased slightly to 51 to 19 percent. The best available information still suggests that the television news agenda gave slightly less attention to foreign affairs (e.g., Harney & Stone, 1969) and more to the economy and domestic politics than did newspapers. By this very rough assessment, Johnson should have had a slight advantage from the television agenda.

Television treatment versus newspaper treatment of Goldwater and Johnson is difficult to assess because of the absence of content analyses from that period. Stempel (1965) found that the amount of attention to each candidate in the major papers was nearly identical, but there is no measure for television. Goldwater's advisors seem to have resented television newspeople slightly more than they resented print newspeople (Shadegg, 1965, p. 271), but Goldwater himself considered his coverage by both as highly unfair (MacNeil, 1968, pp. 131–132).

For the first time in the postwar period, America's newspapers bolted the Republican ticket. Goldwater-Miller endorsements came from papers with only 21 percent of the nation's readers (Emery, 1964). On this measure, Goldwater was relatively helped more by television compared to newspapers.

Republicans outspent the Democrats in advertisements by a ratio of about 2:1, and little money was spent in newspapers (but see Mullen, 1968). Yet, Johnson's TV spots were universally considered more memorable and cogent, even without the strong and controversial ones (Kessel, 1968, pp. 237–239, "Little girls—Mushroom clouds," 1964). Goldwater's commercials were poorly placed, poorly designed, and "dreary" (White, 1965, pp. 318–330). If quality cancels out quantity, this factor should be counted as a draw.

Johnson was a less than ideal television candidate. According to Chester (1969, p. 137), Johnson projected on television an unappealing physical appearance along with a "slow drawl." McGinnis (1970, p. 23) saw him as "heavy and gross" and "syrupy" as he "stuck to the lens." The Goldwater camp believed their man would televise better to most Americans than would LBJ (Chester, 1969, p. 148). If these views are correct, Goldwater was again helped more, relatively speaking, by television than by newspapers.

1968. Democratic monopoly of the economic issue had vanished by 1968. The parties were almost at a draw—37 to 34 percent—as protectors of prosperity, with the Democrats holding a trivial lead. Republicans had regained their status as the party of peace—37 to 24 percent.

At the same time, Vietnam had become a frustrating and seemingly endless "television war." Night after night, reports from the battlefields of Southeast Asia and Capital Hill filled the screen (Bailey, 1976). Television was emphasizing foreign affairs more than newspapers did during the 1968 campaign (Graber, 1980, p. 179). This meant that television was stressing an issue that was a net plus for Republicans.

Shafer and Larson (1972) have argued that television also focused disproportionately, in contrast to newspapers, on the "social issue"—street crime, riots, busing, race problems, demonstrations, student unrest, drugs. If so, on a second cluster of issues the Democrats were damaged by the television agenda, while the candidacies of Richard Nixon and George Wallace were helped.

Estimating treatment patterns is again difficult because of the lack of comparative newspaper-television studies. Efron's controversial (1971) study found Nixon and Wallace subjected to more negative coverage on television than was Humphrey (cf. Stevenson, Eisinger, Feinberg, & Kotok, 1973). Whether or not Efron was right, newspaper coverage may not have been any different.

Nixon did receive the bulk of the endorsements from the nation's publishers and gained the support of newspapers with 70 percent of total circulation. Humphrey, with only 19 percent, and Wallace, with only 1 percent, were relatively less damaged by television on this dimension (634 for Nixon—146 for Humphrey—and 12 for Wallace, 1968).

In 1968, twice as much money was spent on television time for the GOP ticket as for the Democratic ticket, with Wallace lagging far behind (Mendelson & Crespi, 1970, p. 288). And, unlike 1960, Nixon's commercials were more calculated and clever (see McGinnis, 1970). Little money was spent on print advertisements, so the net television advantage on this factor clearly went to Nixon.

In a further departure from 1960, Nixon's television persona was cool, carefully cultivated, and colored with a tan from regular Florida and California layovers (Nimmo, 1970, p. 143). In contrast, Humphrey "became lethal in a television studio," constantly "talking too long and too fervently" (McGinnis, 1970, p. 24).

For reasons noted in a later section, the 1972 campaign will not be reviewed here.

1976. After eight years of a Republican White House, Americans saw no difference between the parties in their likelihood of keeping peace; but, by a ratio of 2:1, Democrats were seen as the party best for prosperity (Gallup, 1976). Doris Graber's research (1980, p. 179) shows little difference in the amount of attention television and newspapers devoted to economic issues in 1976. Thus, neither party was especially helped by foreign policy issues; and on the issue on which Democrats could have benefited from additional media attention—the economy—newspaper and television agendas did not vary.

There is no evidence that either medium was uniquely disposed to provide more favorable treatment to Gerald Ford or Jimmy Carter. Sparked by Patterson and McClure's (1976) findings regarding 1972 coverage, there were complaints (later verified in Patterson, 1980) that media coverage was superficial, emphasizing "hoopla and horse race" and ignoring issues. Nevertheless, there were few complaints that media coverage was persistently less fair to one side than to another.

President Ford garnered most newspaper endorsements—62 percent of total circulation (411 Dailies support Ford; 80 for Carter; 168 Uncommitted, 1976). Thus, Governor Carter, endorsed by newspapers with only 23 percent of total circulation, was hurt less by television on this factor.

Some observers thought the two candidates were almost evenly matched in television persona. Graber concluded (1980, p. 160): "In all-important visual attractiveness they were fairly well-matched. No Prince Charming here, battling against a sweaty, gray-looking opponent." Ford's camp believed that his "physical size and presence" would "come off very well" on television (Cheney, 1979, pp. 117–118), and Carter's group worried about Carter's height (Seltz & Yoakam, 1979, pp. 121–122). On balance, Carter perhaps held a slight edge from his ability to convey warmth, use pauses, speak softly, and wield a smile (Polsby, 1976; Halberstam, 1976). Ford's image was sometimes perceived as less poised (Becker, Pepper, & Wenner, 1979), and of course other critics besides Chevy Chase insisted he "came across as a vestige of primordial man" (*New Republic* editorial, 1976).

For the first time, due in part to spending limits and federal matching funds, the usual overwhelming Republican domination of television campaign advertising was minimized, with the GOP holding only a slight lead. As for quality, both Jerry Rafshoon's work for the Democrats and the Bailey Deardourff firm's work for the Republicans were praised as effective and skilled. On this factor, it is hard to assign a net television advantage to either candidate in the 1976 election.

Summing the factors. Unfortunately, there is little basis for determining how to attach weights to each of these elements. It may be that "persona" is twice as important as the issue agenda. News themes might be far more consequential than campaign advertisements. In these four recent elections, however, it is not difficult to "sum" the factors because the patterns proved to be surprisingly consistent. The absence of estimates on the element of candidate "treatment," usually presumed to be very important, may not be so harmful to the analysis, thanks to these consistent patterns.

Certainly the assessments would have been stronger and more definitive had more content analyses been conducted. In order to study media effects, more needs to be known about patterns in media content (Adams, 1978; Miller, Goldenberg, & Erbring, 1979). Nonetheless, the patterns that emerged using the best information available are interesting.

In 1960, Kennedy swept the factors as the candidate helped more by television than by newspapers. In 1964, Barry Goldwater unexpectedly became the "television candidate." Not that television coverage was more favorable to Goldwater than it was to Johnson; rather, Goldwater was relatively better off with the messages coming from television than he was with the messages from newspapers.

In 1968, Richard Nixon and George Wallace should have been relatively aided more by television than by newspapers. Hubert Humphrey, despite losing their endorsements, should have been relatively happier with newspapers. Although two factors in 1976 appeared to be a draw, of those elements that did suggest a difference, Jimmy Carter was favored by television on all but one.

MEDIUM EFFECTS IN SELECTED SEGMENTS OF THE ELECTORATE

In 1960, voters who relied on television as their primary source of news appeared to have been exposed more than newspaper readers to news themes helpful to the out-of-power Democrats. Compared to newspapers, television presented them an issue agenda with more domestic and economic news, fewer editorials endorsing Nixon, more persuasive Kennedy advertisements, the more attractive and cool Kennedy television image, and possibly even more evening drama that paralleled Kennedy's call for the frontier spirit and bold leadership. What might have been the result for Kennedy?

A uniform impact across the electorate seems highly unlikely. As political communication research repeatedly shows, media stimuli are received and selectively interpreted in a rich context of social networks, reference groups, and prior experiences. They are not necessarily absorbed and accepted at "face value." Though selectivity is not as rigid as was initially thought, mass media messages are selectively chosen, selectively perceived, and selectively retained (Sears & Freedman, 1967; Atkin, 1973; Festinger, 1957).

Two variables stand out as potentially strong influences on the reception of campaign-relevant information: party identification and educational background.

Party identification. A variety of studies have shown that party identification is often associated with a partisan perceptual screen that filters evaluations and judgments about candidates for office (Kamin, 1958; McGrath & McGrath, 1962; Sigel, 1964; Jaros & Mason 1969; Weisberg & Rusk, 1970). For example, when General Dwight Eisenhower became known as a Republican, millions of Democrats reassessed him and found him personally, as well as politically, less attractive (Converse & Depeux, 1966).

To the extent that partisanship affects perceptions of political candidates, strong partisans should be least influenced by variations in the messages between television and newspapers. Independents should be most "sensitive" to such differences, on the theory that they have the fewest psychological barriers to information more or less favorable to a particular candidate. Democrats may be the next most susceptible to medium effects, because there are many "weak Democrats" who historically defect more easily and more often than Republicans.

Republicans should be most resistant to differences in media portrayals of candidates. If their candidate looks less clean shaven, has more boring commercials, and is subjected to more criticism on television than in newspapers, Republicans should be least influenced by such differences.

Education. Along with party identification, education should be an important variable in the way voters react to medium differences. Education should operate, somewhat counter-intuitively, so that voters with more education are more influenced than those with less education.

V. O. Key observed that one effect of a presidential election was to accentuate differences in information levels between the more- and the less-educated, because the latter have less media exposure and may be less skilled in extracting information from the media (Key, 1961, pp. 348–357). Tichenor, Donohue, and Olien (1970) have also maintained that mass media information increases the "knowledge gap" between higher and lower socioeconomic status groups. They state the proposition as follows (pp. 159–160):

> As the infusion of mass media information into a social system increases, segments of the population with higher socioeconomic status tend to acquire this information at a faster rate than the lower status segments, so that the gap in knowledge between these segments tends to increase rather than decrease.

This same logic can be applied to the analysis of the impact of medium differences. It is only a short step from the knowledge gap hypothesis (which has usually been applied to newspapers) to suggest that, insofar as mass media messages have an impact in proportion to their being successfully acquired,

> segments of the electorate with more education (who thus should attend more closely and more effectively to their primary news source) will acquire more information from their primary news source than will those with less education, so the gap between the information and perceptions of television users versus those of newspaper readers will tend to be greater among more educated segments.

MEDIUM DIFFERENCES AND AMERICAN VOTING BEHAVIOR

The preceeding discussion has suggested a number of hypotheses about the relationship between media reliance and voting behavior. First, reliance on television rather than print media should have been associated with voting for Kennedy in 1960, Goldwater in 1964, Nixon and Wallace in 1968, and Carter in 1976. That association should be strongest among voters with more education, and among voters who are Independents, and, to a lesser degree, among those who are Democrats.

Adams finds media coverage predictive of voter behavior (but this is not implicit)

Merging all of these factors suggests that medium effects would have been greatest for educated Independents who relied on television and thus should have voted disproportionately for Kennedy in 1960. Their counterparts who relied more on newspapers should have voted comparatively more for Nixon.

A straightforward test of these hypotheses can be performed using Michigan Survey Research Center national election data. In the 1960, 1964, 1968, and 1976 surveys, respondents were asked on which news source they relied primarily for national campaign news. In 1972 a relative media reliance question was not asked; that election therefore has been omitted from this analysis. The basic statistical task is to crosstabulate media reliance with reported voting behavior, controlling for education and party identification. The findings, summarized in Tables 10.2 and 10.3, offer partial support for the research hypotheses, along with some inconsistencies.

In each election, a sizeable group of voters who relied on television for news voted significantly differently than their partisan and educational cohorts who relied more on print media. In every instance, the direction of the television-reliant voters was that predicted by the analysis of media differences in terms of themes, agenda, treatment, persona, advertisement, endorsements, and entertainment. In contrast to newspaper reliance, television reliance was, for at least one segment of the electorate, associated with a greater likelihood of voting for Kennedy in 1960, for Goldwater in 1964, for Nixon and Wallace in 1968, and for Carter in 1976.

In each of these elections, the significant media-voting relationship occurred among a group of better-educated voters. This supports the notion that such voters are more likely to acquire campaign-relevant information from the mass media and to have more capacity to respond to and be sensitive to differences in those media messages. In only one case was there a group of less-educated voters for whom media reliance was associated significantly with voting behavior (namely, less-educated Republicans in 1976).

The full pattern was found precisely as predicted, however, only in 1960 and 1968. In 1960, educated Independents who relied on television gave Kennedy a solid majority of their votes (53 percent), while only about one third (35 percent) of those relying on print supported him. This difference of 18 percent between media groups of educated Independents was followed by a difference of 15 percent among educated Democrats. Educated Democrats who relied on television went strongly for Kennedy (84 percent), but those who primarily used print news sources were less likely to favor him (69 percent). After the election, Kennedy referred to television and commented, "We wouldn't have had a prayer without that gadget" (Barnouw, 1975, p. 277). He was right.

Table 10.2
Media Reliance and Voting Behavior,
by Educational Level and Party Preference*

	More Educated			Less Educated		
	Demo-crats	Indepen-dents	Repub-licans	Demo-crats	Indepen-dents	Repub-licans
1960	*.001*	*.001*	NS	NS	NS	NS
1964	*.01*	NS	NS	NS	NS	NS
1968	NS	*.01*	NS	NS	NS	NS
1976	NS	NS	*.001*	NS	NS	*.001*

NS = Not significant.

* Figures express chi-square significance levels for crosstabulations of media reliance (television vs. newspapers and other media) by reported voting behavior (Democratic vs. voting other) controlling for party identification and education level (less than high school vs. high school or more).

Table 10.3
Differences in Democratic Voting Strength
Among Groups Shown in Table 10.2

1960	Independents (with high education):		
	Television-reliant	53.4%	Kennedy
	Newspaper-reliant and others	34.9%	Kennedy
	Difference	18.5%	
	Democrats (with high education):		
	Television-reliant	83.7%	Kennedy
	Newspaper-reliant and others	68.9%	Kennedy
	Difference	14.8%	
1964	Democrats (with high education):		
	Television-reliant	82.3%	Johnson
	Newspaper-reliant and others	91.3%	Johnson
	Difference	− 9.0%	
1968	Independents (with high education):		
	Television-reliant	24.5%	Humphrey
	Newspaper-reliant and others	32.5%	Humphrey
	Difference	− 8.0%	
1976	Republicans (with high education):		
	Television-reliant	17.1%	Carter
	Newspaper-reliant and others	5.8%	Carter
	Difference	11.3%	
	Republicans (with high education):		
	Television-reliant	25.3%	Carter
	Newspaper-reliant and others	4.8%	Carter
	Difference	20.5%	

NOTE: Only figures for groups with a statistically significant relationship between primary news source and reported voting behavior are reported.

Again in 1968, educated Independents stand out as the group most "vulnerable" to campaign message differences between media. Only one quarter of those who relied on television voted for Humphrey, compared to one third of those who relied on newspapers.

In two of these four elections, television's messages were estimated to have favored the Democrats and in two elections to have favored the GOP. Voting behavior and media reliance of at least one segment of the electorate duplicated those directions. That the association alternately helped both the Democrats and their opponents strongly indicates that the findings are not an artifact of television-reliant voters inherently being more pro-Democratic for socioeconomic or psychological reasons not entirely controlled for by party and education.

The findings also confirm that media message differences do not have an impact evenly across the electorate. Message differences appear to have been sufficiently subtle, and perceptual screens sufficiently powerful, that message differences have not been associated with differing voting behavior for most segments of the electorate. This is not to say that newspapers and television did not *together* pull the electorate in a certain direction; that, as argued earlier, is a separate subject. Rather, the findings show that differences in media messages are likely to hit certain groups of voters more than others.

Just which groups of voters are most likely to be influenced must be qualified in light of the results of 1976 and 1964. In 1964, educated Democrats rather than educated Independents had the more significant relationship between media reliance and reported voting behavior. The 1976 results were also unexpected. First, 1976 was the only year in which there was a statistically significant difference among a less-educated group. Second, the media-voting associations showed up among Republicans and not at all among Independents and Democrats. Republicans were supposed to have been most resistant to distinctions in media messages.

A revised interpretation can be offered. Particular appeals of candidates and media coverage seem to interact so that in some instances partisans are more influenced by differences in media information than are Independents. The precise pattern seems to be election-specific. The impact does appear more likely to surface among voters with more education, although 1976 suggests that those with less education are not immune to varying their voting in line with media input.

In each of these elections, television reliance was associated with support for the party out of power. One factor was that television's news themes favor the "outs," but that slant also happen to coincide with the relative advantage television was usually giving the "outs" in terms of agenda, persona, advertising, endorsements, and entertainment. Together the cumulative impact parallels Michael Robinson's findings (1976) of associations between television viewing and dissatisfaction with the status quo, mistrust of government, and cynicism—all reactions likely to help the "outs."

Both in 1964 and 1976, partisans who relied on television defected from the incumbent President of their own party more often than partisans who primarily used other news sources. In 1964, television-reliant, educated Democrats were more likely to be unhappy with Lyndon Johnson and to prefer the challenger. In 1976, television-reliant Republicans (whatever their education) were more likely to be displeased with Gerald Ford and to defect to his challenger. In both elections, only among the incumbent's own party was television reliance associated with disaffection toward the incumbent. One inference to be drawn is that television provided a vehicle for the appeals of the challenger to reach successfully some partisans who were amenable to those appeals. A second inference is that television news may have intensified partisans' dissatisfaction with the incumbent in a way that selective reading of newspapers did not.

SUMMARY AND THE ELECTION OF 1980

The arguments, proposals, hypotheses, and findings of this chapter may be summarized as follows:

1. Four perspectives characterize thinking on the effects of the media on American politics: "media impotence," "media virility," "print power," and "video power."
2. A distinction between "media effects" and "medium effects" is important because the absence of unique effects from newspaper-television differences is not the same as the absence of overall joint media effects.
3. If the campaign-relevant content of newspapers and television has differed systematically, there may be medium effects associated with those content differences.
4. Campaign-relevant content of mass media messages includes at least the following seven elements: themes, agenda, treatment, endorsements, advertisements, persona, and entertainment.
5. Based on the best available information, the sum of television content—relative to newspaper content—on these seven factors favored Kennedy in 1960, Goldwater in 1964, Nixon and Wallace in 1968, and Carter in 1976.
6. The "knowledge gap hypothesis" can be extended to suggest that differences in television and newspaper content are likely to be more consequential for better-educated voters.

7. In each recent election, there was a sizeable group of voters who relied on television and voted significantly different from their partisan and educational cohorts who relied primarily on print media. The associations between television reliance and voting by susceptible groups conformed to the expectations flowing from the assessments of content.

8. The partisan group for which media message differences was most critical varied according to the election: in 1960, educated Independents and educated Democrats who relied on television were more favorable to Kennedy; in 1964, educated Democrats who relied on television were more favorable to Goldwater; in 1968, educated Independents who relied on television were more favorable to Nixon and Wallace; in 1976, Republicans who relied on television were more favorable to Carter. In each election, the candidate of the party out of power was relatively advantaged by television. When incumbents ran for reelection, educated partisans of the President's party who relied on television were especially likely to defect to the challenger. Did this pattern recur in the 1980 presidential election?

Who was likely to have profited more from television than from newspapers—Jimmy Carter or Ronald Reagan? In terms of "themes," Reagan acquired television's usual out-party advantage which Carter had enjoyed four years earlier. But, the rest of the key elements reveals a mixed list.

On the "agenda" variable, the result was a draw. Neither candidate could be said to have profited from the news agenda of television over that of newspapers, because the public saw the candidates as about equally strong (or weak) across most issues. As one Gallup report stated (1980, p. 56):

> A mid-September survey showed only 33 percent of respondents surveyed expressing approval of Carter's handling of domestic policy. The same low percentage approved of his handling of the nation's foreign policy, making it impossible to say that either was definitely the President's Achilles heel.

Similarly, after Reagan dispelled fears about his foreign policy belligerency, perceptions of Reagan on foreign and domestic policies began to even out. Thus, neither candidate seemed positioned to benefit from any agenda differences between the media.

The factor of "treatment" goes slightly to Reagan's favor on television. Michael Robinson and Margaret Sheehan's (1982) detailed comparison of CBS and UPI coverage of the campaign suggests that—although Reagan received less negative coverage than Carter on both CBS and UPI

—Reagan's net advantage over Carter was greater on CBS. To the extent that this finding can be generalized to other networks and newspapers, it gives Reagan a TV plus.

"Endorsements," however, confuse the pattern. On this dimension, Carter was advantaged by television because Reagan was endorsed by newspapers having circulations more than twice as great as that of those endorsing Carter (Consoli, 1980).

"Advertisements" were closely matched. Reagan held only a slim lead in the quantity of television commercials, and there was considerable concern among many Reagan sympathizers who believed the ads were much too repetitious, sometimes dull, and insufficiently aggressive. In retrospect, a winner's advertising campaign usually seems brilliant. At the time, however, there was no evidence to indicate that Reagan's spots were more powerful than Carter's. (Of course, Reagan's ads may have been "effective" simply by showing that he was not a Neanderthal and was not Jimmy Carter.)

"Persona" did give another television advantage to Reagan, who won the critic's award for the outstanding performance by a leading actor in a dramatic series. After two decades of politicians who had embarrassed media analysts by their failure to master the tactics of the media age, the times finally obliged with a candidate almost literally from "central casting." Reagan's ease, poise, and warmth before the camera may have been most devastating to Carter at the time of their debate, but it was a Reagan asset throughout most of the campaign.

The final element of "entertainment" was speculated to have given Republicans a television advantage derived from the 1964–76 approach of police, detective, law-and-order shows. By 1980, however, entertainment television had taken a sharp turn in another direction. The major villain on prime-time television became the businessman, especially the corporate executive. (See, e.g., *Crooks, Conmen, and Clowns: Businessmen in TV Entertainment*, 1981.) Business people were consistently shown to have no concern for the public's welfare. Consequently, such a parade of shows crying out for antitrust, OSHA, and consumer protection removes the GOP's TV entertainment advantage and hands it to the Democrats. Dr. Quincy would never vote for Reagan.

Summing the separate factors for the earlier campaigns was easy because in each campaign the estimates indicated one particular candidate benefited from television (compared to newspapers) on almost all of the factors. In this instance, the pattern is more complicated. It gives Reagan a television advantage on three of the seven factors—themes, treatment, and persona. Carter appeared to have the TV advantage on two elements —endorsements and entertainment. Two variables, agenda and advertisements, seemed to be a draw.

Without a system for weighting the relative importance of these factors, the simple 3:2:2 score suggests that, unlike the previous elections, in 1980 neither candidate had a marked net advantage from television as opposed to newspaper messages. If, on balance, the messages from each medium were relatively indistinguishable, there is no reason to expect that voters who relied primarily on one medium would be influenced to vote any differently from voters relying largely on the other medium.

Reagan's slight 3:2 television lead over Carter might mean that educated viewers who relied on television would be more inclined to vote for Reagan than their counterparts who relied on newspapers. In the previous elections, it was observed that educated partisans who relied on television were more likely to bolt the incumbent President of their party in order to vote for the challenger. Television-reliant Republicans voted more for Carter in 1976 and educated television-reliant Democrats voted more for Goldwater in 1964. If this pattern were followed, educated Democrats who relied on television would have been more likely to vote for Reagan than their print-oriented counterparts.

The results obtained from the national poll by Michigan's Survey Research Center were interesting. Controlling for education, there was no significant relationship between media reliance and voting for Democrats, Independents, or Republicans. While not statistically significant, the group that showed the largest percentage differences consisted of educated Democrats, precisely the group predicted by the past pattern. Educated Democrats who relied on television voted 23 percent for Reagan, while those favoring print sources voted only 14 percent for Reagan. With controls, this subsample was small (n = 148) and the 9 percent point difference failed to attain statistical significance. Nonetheless, the tendency coincides well with the previous findings. That the tendency is weaker than those in earlier elections is consistent with the finding that the messages of the two media were less distinct than in past years.

Television is unlikely to have a unique election impact if the sum of its messages differ little from those of newspapers. Yet, when television's outputs are consistently more favorable than newspapers toward one of the candidates, then, among susceptible segments of the audience, those distinct messages do appear to be capable of influencing voting.

REFERENCES

Adams, William C. 1980. Make-or-break Coverage of John Anderson. *Washington Star* (August 24, 1980): G-1-4.

———. 1978. Network News in Perspective: A Bibliographic Essay. In William Adams and Fay Schreibman, eds., *Television Network News: Issues in Content Research.* Washington, D.C.: George Washington University, 11-46.

Atkin, Charles. 1973. Instrumental Utilities and Information Seeking. In Peter Clarke, ed., *New Models for Mass Communication Research.* Beverly Hills, Cal.: Sage, 205-242.

Bailey, George. 1976. Television War: Trends in Network Coverage of Vietnam, 1965-1970. *Journal of Broadcasting* 20 (Spring 1976): 147-158.

Barnouw, Eric. 1975. *Tube of Plenty.* New York: Oxford University Press.

Becker, Samuel L.; Robert Pepper; and Lawrence A. Wenner. 1979. Information Flow and the Shaping of Meanings. In Sidney Kraus, ed., *The Great Debates: Carter vs. Ford, 1976.* Bloomington, Ind.: Indiana University Press, 384-397.

Broder, David. 1972. *The Party's Over.* New York: Harper and Row.

Brown, David S. 1980. How to Predict Presidential Elections. *Washington Post* (July 6, 1980): D-2.

Cheney, Richard B. 1979. The 1976 Debates: A Republican Perspective. In Austin Ranney, ed., *The Past and Future of Presidential Debates.* Washington, D.C.: American Enterprise Institute, 107-136.

Chester, Edward W. 1969. *Radio, Television and American Politics.* New York: Sheed and Ward.

Comstock, George and Robin Cobbey. 1978. Watching the Watchdogs: Trends and Problems in Monitoring Network News. In William Adams and Fay Schreibman, eds., *Television Network News: Issues and Content Research.* Washington, D.C.: George Washington University, 47-64.

Consoli, John. 1980. E & P Poll. *Editor and Publisher* (November 1, 1980): 9-13.

Converse, Phillip E.; Aage R. Clausen; and Warren E. Miller. 1965. Electoral Myth and Reality: The 1964 Election. *American Political Science Review* 59 (June 1965): 321-336.

Converse, Phillip E. and Georges Depeux. 1966. DeGaulle and Eisenhower: The Public Image of the Victorious General. In Angus Campbell, Philip Converse, Warren Miller, and Donald Stokes, eds., *Elections and the Political Order.* New York: John Wiley & Sons, Inc., 292-345.

Coombs, Steven L. 1979. "The Electoral Impact of Newspaper Editorials." (Paper presented to the Midwest Political Science Association. Chicago, Illinois, April 21, 1979.)

Crooks, Conmen, and Clowns: Businessmen in TV Entertainment. 1981. Washington, D.C.: The Media Institute.

Cutler, N. E. and A. S. Tedesco. 1974. "Differentiation in television message systems: A Comparison of network television news and drama." (Paper presented to the International Communication Association, New Orleans, Louisiana, April 10, 1974.)

Efron, Edith. 1971. *The News Twisters*. Los Angeles, Cal.: Nash Publishing Corp.

Emery, Edwin. 1964. Press Suppoort for Johnson and Goldwater. *Journalism Quarterly* 41 (Autumn 1964): 485–488.

Epstein, Edward Jay. 1973. *News From Nowhere: Television and the News*. New York: Vintage Books.

Festinger, Leon. 1957. *A Theory of Cognitive Dissonance*. Evanston, Ill.: Row, Peterson.

411 Dailies support Ford; 80 for Carter; 168 Uncommitted. 1976. *Editor and Publisher* (October 30, 1976): 5.

Funkhouser, Ray. 1973. The Issues of the Sixties: An Exploratory Study of the Dynamics of Public Opinion. *Public Opinion Quarterly* 37 (Spring 1973): 62–75.

Gallup Opinion Index. 1976. October (No. 135): 5–6.

———. 1980. December (No. 183): 56.

Gerbner, George and Larry Gross. 1976. Living with Television: The Violence Profile. *Journal of Communication* 26 (Spring 1976): 173–199.

Gerbner, George and Nancy Signorielli. 1978. The World of Television News. In William Adams and Fay Schreibman, eds., *Television Network News: Issues in Content Research*. Washington, D.C.: George Washington University, 189–196.

Gormley, William T., Jr. 1978. Television Coverage of State Government. *Public Opinion Quarterly* 42 (Fall 1978): 354–359.

Graber, Doris A. 1976. Effects of Incumbency on Coverage Patterns in 1972 Presidential Campaign. *Journalism Quarterly* 53 (Autumn 1976): 499–508.

———. 1980. *Mass Media and American Politics*. Washington, D.C.: Congressional Quarterly Press.

Halberstam, David. 1976. The Coming of Carter. *Newsweek (July 19, 1976): 11*.

Harney, Russell F. and Vernon A. Stone. 1969. Television and Newspaper Front Page Coverage of a Major News Story. *Journal of Broadcasting* 8 (Spring 1969): 181–189.

Hooper, Michael. 1969. "Party and Newspaper Endorsements as Predictors of Voter Choice." *Journalism Quarterly* 46 (Summer 1969): 302–305.

Jaros, Dean and Gene Mason. 1969. Party Choice and Support for Demagogues: An Experimental Examination. *American Political Science Review* 63 (March 1969): 100–110.

Kamin, Leon J. 1958. Ethnic and Party Affiliations of Canadians as Determinants of Voting. *Canadian Journal of Psychology* 12 (1958): 205–212.

Kessel, John H. 1968. *The Goldwater Coalition*. Indianapolis, Ind.: Bobbs-Merrill.

Key, V. O. 1961. *Public Opinion and American Democracy*. New York: Alfred A. Knopf, Inc.

Lang, Kurt and Gladys Engel Lang. 1953. The Unique Perspective of Television and Its Effect. *American Sociological Review* 18 (February 1953): 2–13.

Levine, Grace Ferrari. 1977. Learned Helplessness and the Evening News. *Journal of Communication* 27 (Autumn 1977): 100–105.

Lichter, S. Robert and Stanley Rothman. 1981. Media and Business Elites. *Public Opinion* 4 (October/November 1981): 42–46, 59–60.

Little girls—mushroom clouds. 1964. *Broadcasting* (September 21, 1964): 30.

Lowry, Dennis T. 1971. Gresham's Law and Network TV News Selection. *Journal of Broadcasting* 15 (Fall 1971): 397–408.

MacNeil, Robert. 1968. *The People Machine*. New York: Harper and Row.

McCombs, Maxwell E. and Donald L. Shaw. 1972. The Agenda-Setting Function of Mass Media. *Public Opinion Quarterly* 36 (Summer 1972): 176–187.

McGinnis, Joe. 1970. *The Selling of the President, 1968*. New York: Pocket Books.

McGrath, Joseph E. and Marion F. McGrath. 1962. Effects of Partisanship on Perceptions of Political Figures. *Public Opinion Quarterly* 11 (Summer 1962): 236–248.

Mendelson, Harold and Irving Crespi. 1970. *Poll, Television, and the New Politics*. Scranton, Pa.: Chandler Publishing.

Miller, Arthur H.; Edie N. Goldenberg; and Lutz Erbring. 1979. Type-Set Politics: Impact of Newspaper on Public Confidence. *American Political Science Review* 73 (March 1979): 67–84.

Minnow, Newton.; John Martin; and Lee Mitchell. 1973. *Presidential Television*. New York: Basic Books.

Mullen, James J. 1963. Newspaper Advertising in the Kennedy-Nixon Campaign. *Journalism Quarterly* 40 (Winter 1963): 3–11.

———. 1968. Newspaper Advertising in the Johnson-Goldwater Campaign. *Journalism Quarterly* 45 (Summer 1968): 219–225.

New Republic editorial. For Carter, with Reservations. 1976. *New Republic* 17 (October 23, 1976): 3–5.

Nimmo, Dan. 1970. *The Political Persuaders*. Englewood Cliffs, N.J.: Prentice-Hall.

Nixon, Richard M. 1962. *Six Crises*. Garden City, N.Y.: Doubleday & Co., Inc.

Palmgreen, Phillip and Peter Clarke. 1977. Agenda-setting with Local and National Issues. *Communication Research* 4 (October 1977): 435–452.

Patterson, Thomas E. 1979. Assessing Television Newscasts: Future Directions in Content Analysis. In William Adams and Fay Schreibman, eds., *Television Network News: Issues in Content Research*. Washington, D.C.: George Washington University, 177–187.

———. 1980. *The Mass Media Election: How Americans Choose Their President*. New York: Praeger Publishers.

Patterson, Thomas E. and Robert D. McClure. 1976. *The Unseeing Eye*. New York: G. P. Putnam's Sons.

Polsby, Nelson. 1976. On Ford. *U.S. News & World Report* (September 20, 1976).

Pool, Ithiel de Sola; Robert P. Abelson; and Samuel L. Popkin. 1964. *Candidates, Issues and Strategies*. Cambridge, Mass.: M.I.T. Press.

Robinson, John P. 1972. Perceived Media Bias and the 1968 Vote: Can the Media Affect Behavior After All? *Journalism Quarterly* 49 (Summer 1972): 239–246.

————. 1974. The Press as King-Maker. *Journalism Quarterly* 51 (Winter 1974): 587–594.

Robinson, Michael J. 1975. American Political Legitimacy in an Era of Electronic Journalism. In Douglas Cater, ed., *Television As A Social Force*. New York: Praeger Publishers, 97–139.

————. 1976. Public Affairs Television and the Growth of Political Malaise. *American Political Science Review* 70 (June 1976): 409–432.

————. 1979. Prime-Time Chic: Between Newsbreaks and Commercials the Values are L.A. Liberal. *Public Opinion* 2 (March–May 1079): 42–48.

Robinson, Michael J. and Clifford Zukin. 1976. Television and the Wallace Vote. *Journal of Communication* 26 (Spring 1976): 79–83.

Robinson, Michael J. and Margaret Sheehan. 1972. *Over the Wire and on TV: CBS and UPI in Campaign '80*. New York: Basic Books.

Rubin, Bernard. 1967. *Political Television*. Belmont, Cal.: Wadsworth Publishing.

Sears, David O. and Jonathan L. Freedman. 1967. Selective Exposure to Information: A Critical Review. *Public Opinion Quarterly* 31 (Summer 1967): 194–213.

Seltz, Herbert A. and Richard D. Yoakam. 1979. Production Diary of the Debates. In Sidney Kraus, ed., *The Great Debates: Carter vs. Ford, 1976*. Bloomington, Ind.: Indiana University Press, 110–157.

Shadegg, Stephen. 1965. *What Happened to Goldwater?* New York: Holt, Rinehart & Winston.

Shafer, Byron and Richard Larson. 1972. Did TV Create the "Social Issue?" *Columbia Journalism Review* (September/October 1972): 10–17.

Shaw, Donald L. and Maxwell E. McCombs. 1977. *The Emergence of American Political Issues: The Agenda-Setting Function of the Press*. St. Paul, Minn.: West Publishing.

Sigel, Roberta S. 1964. Effects of Partisanship on Perceptions of Political Candidates. *Public Opinion Quarterly* 26 (Fall 1964): 483–497.

Singer, Benjamin D. 1970. Violence, Protest, and War in Television News. *Public Opinion Quarterly* 34 (Winter 1970): 611–616.

634 for Nixon—146 for Humphrey—and 12 for Wallace. 1968. *Editor and Publisher* (November 2, 1968): 533.

Stein, Ben. 1979. *The View From Sunset Boulevard*. New York: Basic Books.

Stempel, Guido H., III. 1961. The Prestige Press Covers the 1960 Presidential Campaign. *Journalism Quarterlly* 38 (Spring 1961): 157–163.

————. 1965. The Prestige Press in Two Presidential Elections. *Journalism Quarterly* 42 (Winter 1965): 15–21.

Stevenson, Robert L.; Richard A. Eisinger; Barry M. Feinberg; and Alan B. Kotok. 1973. Untwisting *The News Twisters*. *Journalism Quarterly* 50 (Summer 1973): 211–219.

Tichenor, P. J.; G. A. Donohue; and C. N. Olien. 1970. Mass Media Flow and Differential Growth in Knowledge. *Public Opinion Quarterly* 34 (Summer 1970): 159–170.

Wade, Serena and Wilbur Schramm. 1969. The Mass Media as Sources of Public Affairs, Science and Health Knowledge. *Public Opinion Quarterly* 33 (Summer 1969): 197–209.

Weisberg, Herbert F. and Jerrold G. Rusk. 1970. Dimensions of Candidate Evaluations. *American Political Science Review* 64 (December 1970): 1167–1185.

White, Theodore. 1961. *The Making of the President, 1960*. New York: Atheneum Publishers.

———. 1965. *The Making of the President, 1964*. New York: Atheneum Publishers.

NAME INDEX

Page numbers in *italic* indicate where a complete reference can be found; *n* indicates footnote.

SUBJECT INDEX